D0982765

PQ 2625 .A755 Z7 1987
Hanley, Katharine Rose.
Dramatic approaches to creative
fidelity : a study in the theater and
philosophy of Gabriel Marcel

DRAMATIC APPROACHES TO CREATIVE FIDELITY

A Study in the Theater
and Philosophy of
Gabriel Marcel (1889-1973)

By
Katharine Rose Hanley
Introduction by
Paul Ricoeur

UNIVERSITY
PRESS OF
AMERICA

Lanham • New York • London

PQ
2625
.A755
Z7
1987

Copyright © 1987 by

University Press of America,® Inc.

4720 Boston Way
Lanham, MD 20706

3 Henrietta Street
London WC2E 8LU England

All rights reserved

Printed in the United States of America

British Cataloging in Publication Information Available

Library of Congress Cataloging-in-Publication Data

Hanley, Katharine Rose.
Dramatic approaches to creative fidelity.

"Works by Gabriel Marcel in chronological order of
composition": p.
Bibliography: p.
Includes index.
1. Marcel, Gabriel, 1889–1973—Dramatic works.
2. Marcel, Gabriel, 1889–1973—Philosophy. 3. Philosophy
in literature. I. Title.
PQ2625.A755Z7   1987   842'.912   87–13709
ISBN 0–8191–6533–6 (alk. paper)

All University Press of America books are produced on acid-free
paper which exceeds the minimum standards set by the National
Historical Publication and Records Commission.

To Eleanor and Bud Tietje

whose prime value

is family

the way of sharing

all the others

Acknowledgement of kind help and encouragement:

To the Officers of the international association Présence de Gabriel Marcel,

To Monsieur and Madame Jean-Marie Marcel for their cordial friendship and most helpful patronage,

To Madame Jeanne Parain-Vial for her special friendship and her encouraging support of my projects,

To Professor Paul Ricoeur for his longstanding friendship and his gracious kindness in providing an introduction for this work,

To Madame Bernadette Gradis and Monsieur Joël Bouëssée, officers of the Fondation Européene de la Culture, for their gracious recognition and promotion of my work,

To Le Moyne College Committee on Faculty Research for several important financial grants in support of this study,

To Dr. Taisto Niemi, Le Moyne College Librarian (1963-81), whose vision and kindness lent support to my research efforts and projects of the Gabriel Marcel Institute for Existential Drama,

To Ms. Theresa Santillo, Administrative Assistant, Le Moyne College Library for her help in procuring texts by Gabriel Marcel,

Acknowledgement of kind help and encouragement continued:

To the Director and Personnel of Le Moyne College Audio Visual Department, Professor Thomas Hogan and his staff for their excellent technical services and generous cooperation,

To the officers and members of the Gabriel Marcel Institute for Existential Drama for their excellent spirit and theatrical productions,

To Mireille Goodisman and Christiane Moloney for their helpful suggestions and assurance that I could communicate in French--with a little help from my friends,

To Professor and Mrs. G. Charles Paikert who so graciously encourage my intellectual and international adventures,

To Andrea Adams-Pierce, whose energies and businesslike efficiency helped immeasureably in materializing this text,

To Alan Clark for the service of his editorial skills,

To Stephen Healy for his artful illustrations depicting the commemorative medal struck for the International Society Préssence de Gabriel Marcel.

To my family and all my dear friends who loved me and prayed for me, thereby helping this project to come to fruition.

Acknowledgement of permission to print:

Revue Philosophique de Louvain, permission to print an English version, Chapter II. The Unfathomable : A Search for Presence, of an article originally published in French "Réflexions sur la présence comme signe d´immortalité d´après la pensée de Gabriel Marcel," Revue Philosophique de Louvain, tome 74, mai 1976, pp. 211-34.

Société Française de Philosophie, permission to print an English version, Chapter III. "The Lantern: and The Light of Truth," an article originally entitled "Le Fanal et la fidélité creatrice," published in the Bulletin de la Société fraçaise de Philosophie, avril-juin 1984, 78 annee, No. 2, pp. 50-53.

World Congress of Philosophy, for permission to reprint Chapter IV. "Dot the I : An Existential Witness of the Light of Truth." Originally printed in the Acts of the XVIIth World Congress of Philosophy: Culture and Nature Montreal, Canada, August 21-27, 1983.

Association des sociétés de philosophie de langue française for permission to print an English version, Chapter VI. The Rebellious Heart: and Human Creation, originally published in French as "Le Coeur des autres et la création humaine" in La Création, Actes du XXe congrés de l´Association des sociétés de philosophie de langue francaise, Quebec, Canada, 20-23 aout 1984, L´ Université de Quebéc à Trois-Rivières; and an English version, Chapter IX. Rome is no longer in Rome: the Challenge for Creative Incarnations of Fidelity," of Rome n´est plus dans Rome et l´avenir des valeurs" presented in French and printed in L´Avenir, Actes du XXIe congrès de l´Association des sociétés philosophiques de langue francaise, August 21-24, 1986, Athens, Greece.

American Catholic Philosophical Association for permission to reprint the text of Chapter VII. "Colombyre or the Torch of Peace: the Role of Person-Communities in Living Creative Fidelity to Values, originally published under the title: "Dramatic Approaches to Creative Fidelity" in Ethical Wisdom East and/or West: Proceedings of The American Catholic Philosophic Association, Vol LI, Washington, D.C., 1977, pp. 193 - 99; and to reprint the text of Chapter VIII. "The Sting: Threatening the Foundations of Fidelity" of which an earlier version appeared in the Proceedings of the American Catholic Philosophical Association, Vol. LX, Washington, D.C., 1986, pp. 166-177.

TABLE OF CONTENTS

xii

"Being is an affirmation

of which

I am the stage

rather than the subject."

G. Marcel, The Philosophy of Existentialism, p. 18

Introduction

Katharine Rose Hanley has given herself the double task of introducing English-speaking audiences to Gabriel Marcel´s theater and of showing how theater and philosophy complement one another in Marcel´s work. I can attest that this book by Professor Hanley fulfills that double promise.

As to the first task that the author assigned herself, it is quite remarkable that she did not limit herself to merely stating in general terms that the dramatic work of Gabriel Marcel introduces questioning that the philosophic work continues, using conceptual analysis. She shows in detail, through a judicious choice of several highly representative plays, how the intrigue and development of the characters propose in each instance a clearly defined enigma that calls for an effort of thought that members of the audience can, if they wish, pursue under the guidance of a philosophic essay easily identifiable in the master´s work. Thus the preoccupation with the presence of a loved one among the living after his or her death--in The Unfathomable and in The Lantern --is followed up by a philosophic reflection in "Presence and Imortality." Likewise, the question posed by Dot the I is to know the meaning of living in the light of truth: is it according to childlike simplicity or with adult sophistication? The Rebellious Heart opens up the question of authentic creation, principally in art. The Double Expertise introduces the question of fidelity in interpersonal relationships, and so forth. On this topic, one point struck me particularly in the detailed analyses of the plays selected, namely what one might call the heuristic function of the final scene, and even at times the last exchange between the characters. The last scene most often serves the dual function of terminating the dramatic action and beginning the philosophic reflection. More precisely, this nexus between the dramatic closure and the opening of speculation differs from one play to the next. In order to chart a course amid the profusion of dramatic "conclusions," one can very easily follow the lead idea adopted by Professor Hanley to explore the relation between theater and philosophy, namely the theme of creative fidelity. One could also try situating the various dramatic endings on a single scale, as Victor Goldsmith has done in the past for the Dialogues of Plato, according to whether "the conclusion" of the dialogue was nearer to the pole of unresolved enigma, of aporia, or the pole of episteme, of certain truth. The case could be the same for the dramatic endings of Gabriel Marcel´s plays. On an axis defined by the title in French of a collection of essays that is referred to most frequently in this study-- Du Refus à l'Invocation (From Refusal to Invocation), translated with the English title of Creative Fidelity, certain endings only witness negatively and as if by default, in favor of a "creative presence"; then it is the impasse in which the characters are trapped that invites spectators to follow at their own risk and peril the investigation of the ways that the characters in the play did not know, could not, or would not explore. Such is the situation of The Rebellious Heart and its final note of mute despair. At the other end of the spectrum, we find plays where the liberating word is clearly spoken; these are the plays of which Gabriel Marcel could say that they anticipated his reflection, even at times his conversion, or in any event the formulation of a "problem" on the point of turning itself into a "mystery." Such is the case with The Unfathomable and, up to a point, The Lantern with its ending that is both surprising and ambiguous. It is a scale of creativity that one would have to speak of in the case of Gabriel Marcel. But that scale is not, as for the Dialogues of Plato, a scale of knowledge, but a scale of mystery. Between the two poles of "refusal" and "invocation" are situated plays in which the accent is placed on threat and challenge; such is the case of The Sting and Rome is No Longer in Rome, plays with a decidedly pessimistic turn.

In fact, all the plays draw their dramatic quality, not only from the opposition between the characters but from the ambivalence of the responses that one or another character gives to the threat or the challenge that distinguishes each of the Marcel plays. In that sense, the "refusal" or the "invocation" designate not so much extreme poles as spiritual directions that are opposite but equally operative. This is why our image of a scale along which the plays of Gabriel Marcel would distribute themselves in a hierarchical order is finally deceptive and must be abandoned after it has rendered the didactic service we sought from it. We should speak rather of a dramatic constellation, even an archipelagic formation (to approximate the magnificent title: "the secret is in the isles"). The remark applies especially to the plays that we have situated midway, and in which neither pure despair nor total light prevails starkly, but an ambiguous, even elusive or ironic, end, if not a satirical one as in The Double Expertise, or one with a nostalgic note as in Colombyre or the Torch of Peace. It is here that the uniqueness of the dramas requires an image less linear, if one may say so, more arborescent, of the plays in half-tones. By the same fact, the reflection that the dramatic conclusion calls for is different in each case; the very words of "creative fidelity," of "light of truth," of "presence" should lose their air of vague generality to designate in each case a singular response to a singular challenge.

This last remark leads me to the philosophic side of Professor Hanley's book. If it is true, as she demonstrates, that the principal themes of Gabriel Marcel's philosophy maintain an organic relationship with the dramatic situation, one cannot characterize "second reflection" without an explicit reference to the theater, if one understands by "second reflection" a recollection on the conceptual level of the fundamental experiences of "presence," of "fidelity," of "invocation," etc., beyond the objectivations that a first reflection brings to them, whether the latter be of Cartesian, Kantian, or Husserlian origin. It is not sufficient to say that philosophy prolongs a reflection that a member of the audience may have begun once the curtain has fallen on the play. One must go as far as to say that second reflection conserves, on its own proper level, something of the dramatic structure of the plays. My earlier allusion to the Dialogues of Plato is pertinent here in another sense, one highlighted by the designation of "neo-Socratic" that Gabriel Marcel himself accepted for his work. Second reflection, I will say in following the insistent suggestion of Professor Hanley, is itself of a structure that is radically dialogal, or better dialogical (conflict included). If the philosophical essays of Gabriel Marcel appear often disconcerting, that is because the reader wants to go directly to the theses that could constitute a great Marcelian monologue. The reader simply finds the comings and goings of a thought that advances only at the cost of incessant corrections. These rectifications are nothing but the reflective transposition of an interplay of questions and answers among virtual protagonists in a discussion. It is the first objectifying reflection that is monological. The second reflection is dialogical, not for any pedagogical concern, but by its essence. Gabriel Marcel reflecting becomes himself the living theater where multiple voices respond to one another within a discourse that appears to be spoken by one voice only. In this sense, Professor Hanley was truly inspired in placing as introductory quotation this statement by Gabriel Marcel: "Being is an affirmation of which I am the stage rather than the subject." This stage is indeed the scene for the theater of thought. Reflection remains a continuation of theater to the extent that it assumes the logic of the question and answer, such as Gadamer, following Collingwood, articulates it. The interpersonal dialogue becomes the dialogue of the soul with itself, according to the beautiful definition of thought given in the Theatetus. That's why it is not astonishing that dialogical reflection obeys as does dramatic dialogue, the double gravitation of despair and of invocation. It is in this manner that philosophy develops a "concrete approach to the ontological mystery."

It is in this exchange between the <u>explorative</u> character of the theater and the <u>dialogical</u> character of the philosophy that is founded, in Gabriel Marcel's work, the complementarity between the theater and philosophy. That complementarity Professor Hanley goes well beyond affirming in general terms, she establishes it in full detail in her excellent analyses of several of the best plays of our common master-teacher, Gabriel Marcel.

Paul Ricoeur

FOREWORD

This work stands as a tribute to Gabriel Marcel. Its purpose is to share with readers some idea of the interest that can accrue from the interaction of an individual's thinking with Marcel's writings in theater and in philosophy.

Three encounters with Gabriel Marcel have greatly influenced my personal and philosophic life. After a lecture given at Louvain University in Belgium in 1958, Marcel autographed a copy of The Decline of Wisdom for me.(1) Although the question he asked me on that occasion was a quite practical one "Who are you?" its cogency, along with the personally engaging look in his eyes, makes it a vivid question for me every time I recall that incident.

During his lecture tour around the United States in 1965, Marcel visited Le Moyne College and received an honorary doctoral degree. At the end of his five-day visit to Syracuse, he inscribed a copy of Creative Fidelity for me, "in remembrance of an encounter which I hope will one day be renewed."(2)

Just three weeks before his death on October 8, 1973, at the conclusion of a conversation after luncheon in his home in Paris, Gabriel Marcel inscribed Five Major Plays for me, affirming "a bond of spiritual kinship that once renewed would not be broken."(3)

Many other people can relate similar happenings, for Marcel had a gift of powerful personal presence that touched friends and readers alike. It is my hope for those who read this book, that Marcel will become a friend, one with whom a bond of spiritual kinship develops, one who leaves a deep and lasting influence upon their lives.

Several months after Marcel's death, I was among those invited to speak at De Paul University's Day of Commemorative Tribute, February 4, 1974. I wanted to communicate some perspectives from my last conversation with Gabriel Marcel. But the challenge for me was to make these recollections alive and meaningful to people who were not present at that particular and very moving moment when Marcel talked of presence from beyond death. Quite fortunately I thought of his book, Presence and Immortality. (4) Not only its subject, but also its format were just what was needed. This book combines, in one volume, the first act of an unfinished play, journal entries from the years 1938-1943, and philosophic essays, all focusing on one common topic.

In preparing that talk, I realized that theater enables

spectators to enter into a concrete life situation wherein a mystery reveals itself to those whose lives are touched by its impact. Thus each person can be caught up in a situation where certain questions are explored and certain perspectives of insight come to light. In the case of The Unfathomable (5), the fact that Maurice Lechevalier is officially reported as missing in action significantly affects the lives of various members of his family. Their reactions and interpretations differ according to the relationship each had had with Maurice before his disappearance.

The dramatic presentation enables audiences to enter into the situation where a loved one, a family member, a friend, or a mere acquaintance dies or otherwise disappears from the daily scene and the familiar ways of interacting. The dramatization of this event raises questions clearly and poignantly. What has become of the loved one who has passed on? What will become of the bereaved, the loved ones left behind? Is survival of loved ones beyond death possible? Can the bereaved continue to live on without the idea that the loved one still actively intervenes in their lives even from beyond death and that the gifts of the loved one's presence are still received? These questions occur, not merely theoretically but as real alternatives, dramatic heart-rending speculations that can touch and radically alter our lives.

Inquiry about these questions, and research about the various possible answers that will drastically affect our lives, are pursued as these issues engage our own personal being. What is at stake is a determination of the emptiness or fullness of our own lives. The questions and the way they are treated are truly existential. The dramatic action brings into clear focus questions arousing the interest and speculation of members of the audience about their own relationships, as well as those of characters in the play.

This discovery of how Marcel's theater lets many people come into personal and experiential contact with a reality that calls for reflection and clarification in their own lives, as well as in the lives depicted on the stage, was not only significant for that particular day of commemorative tribute. It revealed to me an approach for entering into dialogue with Marcel's thought, an approach that has remained significant for whatever subsequent study I have undertaken.

After that event, I began collecting and studying Marcel's thirty plays. I also collected the numerous articles he wrote as a drama critic, as well as essays and lectures wherein he comments on the nature of his existential theater and at times clarifies its relationship to his philosophic reflections.

In conjunction with metaphysics classes and seminars on the theater of Gabriel Marcel, The Gabriel Marcel Institute for Existential Drama at Le Moyne College has produced seven plays on stage, for television, and as readers´ theater adaptations: The Rebellious Heart, 1975; The Lantern, 1976; The Double Expertise, 1977; Dot the I, 1978; A Man of God, 1978; The Broken World, 1979; and Colombyre or the Torch of Peace, 1980.(6) Similar productions have occurred at other colleges and universities, and always with noteworthy benefits.

This hands-on experience of producing Gabriel Marcel´s plays, plus the opportunity for seminars studying his theater as a way of access to his philosophic thought, provided more than ample evidence that the approach of studying dramatic works as a gateway to philosophic reflection was as exciting and perhaps more illuminating even than Marcel´s commentaries had suggested.

In 1983-1984 a series of invitations to lecture before various prestigious audiences afforded me the opportunity to articulate the thesis that Marcel´s theater and philosophy should be studied together. This series of lectures also enabled me to flesh out an illustration of how this method of study allows us to clarify some essential features of creative fidelity, a key theme in Marcel´s life and work.

This book is the fruit of these various moments of encounter, theater production, philosophic reflection, and dialogue. The work includes three parts: an introduction to Gabriel Marcel´s theater, a study of eight pairings of plays and essays that clarify various aspects and dimensions of creative fidelity, and a section of information helpful for those interested in knowing more about Gabriel Marcel´s life and work.

The tone of this book is largely conversational, perhaps emulating somewhat the style of Marcel´s writing and thought. Chapters Two through Nine are derived from lectures delivered on various occasions. Some of these presentations have already been published elsewhere either in English or in French.

It is my hope that this work will concretely suggest some of the advantages to be gleaned from studying Marcel´s theater on its own as theater, and also as a privileged gateway into the realm of his philosophic reflections.

It is also my hope that this book and the approach it suggests will appeal to students and teachers in interdisciplinary and humanities courses. I am sure the book will help all who desire a concrete approach to and a personal involvement in philosophic investigations. It may also prove to be of interest and benefit to theater people who will find

Marcel´s existential theater profound in impact and accessible not merely to a restricted intellectual elite, but rather to all who have a sensitivity of spirit to compassionately live the heights and the depths of human experience as these are being portrayed in the lives of members of the human family.

Finally it is my hope that this book of meditations on various aspects of creative fidelity will entice readers to seek directly and personally fresh insights into the rich values of human life that Marcel´s works bring to light.

This work will have succeeded and fulfilled my expectations for it if it sends readers directly to the writings of Gabriel Marcel, and lets the concrete approach of theater open up the way of access to philosophic reflection and insight whose motherlode is deep and rich.

Katharine Rose Hanley

Notes to the Author´s Foreword.

Books by Gabriel Marcel mentioned in the Foreword:

1. The Decline of Wisdom, London, Harvill Press, 1954; New
    York, Philosophical Library, 1955.

2. Creative Fidelity, New York, Farrar, Straus and Giroux,
    1964; New York, Crossroad Press, 1982.

3. (Five Major Plays), Cinq Pièces Majeures, Paris, Plon,
    1973.

4. Presence and Immortality, Pittsburgh, PA., Duquesne
    University Press, 1967.

5. The Unfathomable, pp. 254-84 in Presence and Immortality,
    cited above.

6. The Rebellious Heart and The Broken World with an
    Introduction by the author appeared in The Existential Drama
    of Gabriel Marcel, West Hartford, CT., McAuley Institute,
    1974.

    The Lantern appeared in Cross Currents, Spring 1958.

    A Man of God appeared in Three Plays by Gabriel Marcel, New
    York, Hill and Wang, 1965.

    Two One Act Plays by Gabriel Marcel: Dot the I and The
    Double Expertise, Lanham, MD., University Press of America,
    1986.

    Colombyre or the Torch of Peace, translated by Joseph
    Cunneen, is an English version of the original French
    Colombyre ou le brasier de la paix, published with Le
    Divertissement posthume, La Double Expertise et Les points
    sur les I, in Théâtre comique, Paris, Albin Michel,
    1947.

    The Lantern and Colombyre or the Torch of Peace are being
    reedited for publication in Two Plays by Gabriel Marcel: The
    Lantern and The Torch of Peace, Lanham, MD., University
    Press of America, forthcoming.

* English titles for works by Gabriel Marcel that have not yet
  been published in English are not underlined.

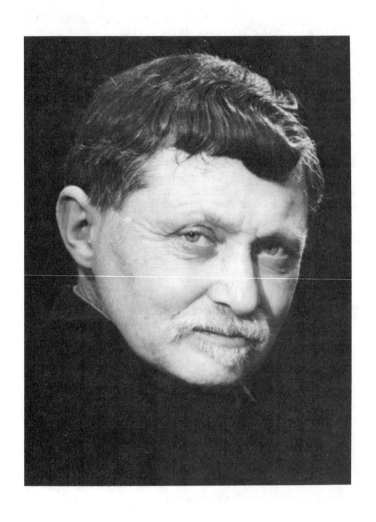

PART ONE:

GABRIEL MARCEL

PHILOSOPHER-DRAMATIST-MUSICIAN

Chapter I. An Introduction to Gabriel Marcel's Philosophic
Quest

Gabriel Marcel is principally known to an English-speaking
audience as a philosopher, an existential thinker of
international renown. He was also a playwright whose dramas
were staged in major theaters in Paris, and also in Belgium,
Germany, the United States, and elsewhere. When Marcel gave the
William James Lectures at Harvard University in 1961, some
twelve years after presenting the Gifford Lectures in Aberdeen,
Scotland, he expressed the hope that an English-speaking
audience would soon no longer know his theater only in an
abstract way but would have a direct and concrete experience of
its performance.(1) Marcel was also an accomplished musician,
improvising and writing piano compositions, often bringing
favorite poems to full expression as songs.(2)

In a talk sponsored by the Alliance Française, Marcel
noted that for him music, theater, and philosophy were like
three concentric rings, or concentric levels of communication.
Music is the innermost and deepest center; theater is next, with
its dialogue among incarnate persons; and philosophy is the
outermost and last, with its discussion in general terms of
questions and challenges affecting the meaning of human life.(3)
He also wrote in 1962 that unlike past readers who first
approached his philosophy, in the future those who wish to
fathom his thought would have to conceive the theater in
relation to the music, and the philosophy in relation to the
theater. He even added that those with a sensitivity to music
will have a special advantage.(4)

These remarks suggest that the interrelationship of music,
theater, and philosophy may provide a significant clue as to how
to approach Gabriel Marcel's thought. These comments, while
clear, remain quite succinct. Marcel does not explain their
sense; rather he leaves to us the task of reflecting to clarify
their meaning.

The deploying of this image will be the leitmotif of this
essay, which will also highlight some of the distinctive
features of Marcel's work and suggest the importance of letting
his theater serve as channel to his philosophic reflection.

MUSIC

Music played a dominant role in Marcel's life and for a
time he considered a career as a concert pianist. He often

3

wrote about music, and even improvised musical compositions, most often to give some of his favorite poems their full expression in song. A commemorative medal struck after his death shows his likeness with his dates of birth and death (1889-1973) on one side; on the other side is a figure of Orpheus with the caption, "Availability, fidelity, hope."(5) Marcel once wrote that if he had to select a character from mythology to typify his own life, he would have to choose Orpheus, so central was the role of music in his life. He even spoke of his marriage, about which he was always discrete, as being under the sign of music, pure joy. His wife was an accomplished musician who worked with him, transcribing his musical compositions. Marcel also wrote that in his early years it was music that provided for him the presence and assurance of the sacred in human life.(6)

Music not only played an important role in Marcel's life, it also remains a significant metaphor revealing the kind of knowledge and communication he hoped for. Music is present to us personally, affecting each individual according to his or her sensitivity to hear. Music moves us integrally, touching us bodily and spiritually and influencing our feelings and consciousnesses. Marcel wanted ideas to be realistically founded, rooted in encounters with realities as personally experienced in concrete incarnate situations involving our feelings, our attitudes, and our persons as well as our rational consciousnesses.

Music reveals in a privileged way the dimension of life that Marcel's searchings bring to light, a spiritual dimension without which our lives would lack a level of humanness, dignity, and depth.(7) Marcel was concerned with the sacred in human life and he found witnesses to it in the works of Bach, Beethoven, Mozart, and others. He was curious to conceive of how these sacred realities can be encountered by us. In his "Essay in Autobiography" he wrote that it was a central preoccupation of his thought to explore how a transcendent dimension of life can be present to an individual.(8) Music illustrates a response to that question. Music, like many realities we experience bodily and spiritually, is present to us in our individual subjectivity by way of inwardness and depth.(9) Music is a reality that can be present to many individuals and to each one by way of interiority and depth. Finally, music, by its presence, effects a certain assurance of the message it conveys.

For Marcel, music is significant in its own right as a mode of communication; it is also present in his dramatic and philosophic works both directly by explicit reference and indirectly by its influence on his style of composition.

4

References to Strauss waltzes, music of Solesmes, and Beethoven sonatas and symphonies have their own peculiar resonance in the context of the plays in which they occur. Music appears as a central theme in several plays, (Quartet in F#), (My Time is not Your Time), and (The Sting). Music figures as a secondary theme in others, for example, Ariadne and (Increase and Multiply). Music is also present directly or by allusion in The Unfathomable, The Broken World, (Grace), Colombyre or the Torch of Peace, in fact, in almost all of his plays.(10) Marcel´s dramatic works reveal an architectonic structure similar to that of musical compositions. His dramas show the influence of a musical style of composition in the development of dramatic situations, and in the denouement that often ends on a note of dissonance.(11) One can also recognize the style of one who improvises and composes musically in the way his thought progresses in his philosophic writings.

These reflections on music as the first and innermost of three concentric layers of communication should alert us to the fact that Marcel expects each person who philosophizes about the human condition to root his or her reflections in an experential awareness of those realities as they can be encountered by way of inwardness and depth. Marcel offers the encouragement that those initiated to the deep secrets of the art of music may be more apt to follow the transposition to other modes of consciousness that theater and philosophy effect. If we heed Marcel´s important remarks in the preface to Kenneth Gallagher´s very fine book, The Philosophy of Gabriel Marcel, "that whoever approaches my work will have to conceive the drama in function of music, and the philosophy in function of drama . . .,"(12) we may indeed expect to see the drama as a way of leading us into a world of darkness and light wherein we encounter important existential questions, not only on stage but within the theater of our own inwardness and depth.

While Marcel wrote only a few succinct, though cogent, statements about the role of music in his life and work, he wrote numerous commentaries about the significance of his theater in itself and as a gateway to his philosophic writings.(13)

THEATER

Marcel writes about his reaction to the theater, which was his first vocation and for a while, he thought, his only one. His way of conceiving questions is through a dramatic imagination that envisages people caught up in a situation of conflict. From the time he was a child he was at home in the world of theater. He reveled in creating imaginary characters who peopled the otherwise lonely landscape of his universe as an only child. A play he wrote at age twelve was favorably evaluated by a critic and was later produced in a modified version as A Man of God. (14) Marcel had a real gift for dramatic composition and a predilection for theater. He enjoyed hearing his father read plays aloud to him and in later years they delighted in attending theater performances together. He noted that theater seemed to gratify the exigency they shared for the aesthetically pleasing coupled with an intellectual rigor.

Marcel worked for more than forty years as a drama critic, writing for prestigious reviews. In 1923 he was named drama critic for L'Europe Nouvelle. He also wrote for Sept, Temps Present, La Vie intellectuelle, and others. In 1944 he was named drama critic for Nouvelles Litteraires. He wrote numerous articles and essays and three full-length books of drama criticism.(15) All this he did in addition to being a playwright who created some thirty plays that appeared from 1911 to 1961. One of his plays, The Lantern, remains in the permanent repertory of the Comédie Française and his work received numerous French and international awards.(16)

Marcel acknowledged that theater enabled him to break a path for freedom in his own life, a life that, though gifted and privileged in many ways, was also marked by tragedy and loss. Furthermore, through the immediate milieu of his family he became aware of the suffering wrought by fundamental conflicts. Dramatic imagination let Marcel see these antinomies played out in the light of the theater and deal with them in his own life, thus gaining greater lucidity and freedom. We can understand that Marcel creates his theater with the hope that it may help others to recognize and deal with some of the fundamental questions and conflicts in their lives, and thus attain greater freedom for themselves.

Marcel saw that his was a theater of consciousness, one of dawning light that opens up paths for freedom to explore. For him, theater is the second, more exteriorized circle of communication. His theater, like his music, deals with tensions and conflicts around various themes. While his dramas depict the playing out of life's conflicts and antinomies as these can lead to despair, they also convey the possibility of moving beyond them in hope. If we heed Marcel's dictum that his theater is to be conceived as a function of music, we will not be surprised to discover that his theater in its own proper way also leads audiences to a depth of their hearts where they experience a certain call to be. Both music and drama work through the tension of opposition that conflict brings, and Marcel's theater, like his music, moves toward some kind of resolution, even one that may end on a note of dissonance. Music moves us through this experience on a level of inward listening that is beyond eris (verbal argumentation). Theater lets the theme play itself out in the more externally manifest expression of incarnate subjectivities and their more verbal form of interpersonal dialogue. Yet theater, like music, enables us to open onto perspectives of light and hope that reveal themselves to us as we live through the tragic, transcending it by way of a path of interiority that leads to the deepest center in our selves.

Theater presents a living world concretely: lights, music, decor are set on stage with live actors and actresses. As Marcel wrote in (The Secret is in the Isles), the medium of theater lets spectators jump right into the life world the drama portrays. Theatrical presentation permits audiences to be caught up in the dramatic action occurring on stage and to live it not only as affecting the characters of the play but also as engaging the very being of the spectator. Theater is such a complete mode of communication that it allows for this kind of total participation, even inviting personal identification with what is being enacted on stage.(17)

Marcel's plays are imaginatively conceived, well crafted, and artfully structured. They are also dramatically powerful. They usually depict domestic situations, with settings and themes familiar to all of us. He presents a drama with which we can easily identify. In this, as well as in a certain characteristic style involving suspense, surprise turns of events, and unexpected shocking developments, Marcel's plays are not unlike some of the "soaps" popular on television today. Marcel's plays depict situations wherein there are issues about identity and desire for communication and love. They show challenges to fidelity and situations involving infidelity. Some explore the tensions of political differences and examine the struggle of individual conscience. Others portray the generation gap, concern for soldiers missing in action, and fears before the menace of war. Still other dramas explore individuals' struggles for success and authenticity, or deal with questions about faith, music, artistic integrity, survival, and life after death. Marcel's plays focus on aspects of human life that are of common concern. (18)

As these plays present domestic settings, with family and friends trying to come to grips with crises over fundamental issues plaguing their relationships, they bring to light

7

questions that confront individuals who are curious about
whether or not there is a sense to their lives. Several
features of Marcel´s dramatic art enable audiences to come to a
vivid and personal awareness of some of these basic issues.

The characters of Marcel´s plays and their personal
relationships seem to be the focus of the dramatic action.
Marcel has a real forte for creating characters who are
lifelike, whom we feel we´ve met or whom we´d certainly
recognize if we did meet them in real life. As these characters
develop and reveal themselves during the course of the play,
the audience begins to sense something of who these characters
are and what they live by. (19)

Theater of Interiority

Marcel´s theater has been called "a theater of
interiority." Marcel himself once wrote that he knows and
creates the characters of his plays, as it were, "from within."
Spectators then participating in what dramatis personae are
living on stage are moved to a deep level of compassionate
sensitivity within themselves as they identify with the dawning
of consciousness that occurs "within" characters in the play.

As the play progresses and spectators become aware, not
only of the external events that are happening, but also of the
interior drama that the characters are living, there dawns a
consciousness of the tragic that is emerging in these peoples´
lives. There is usually at least one person of striking
lucidity or remarkable sensitivity in Marcel´s plays. These
people project a sense of the tragic in their situation.
Sometimes this consciousness is communicated directly, as in the
case of the exceptionally lucid and articulate Raymond Chaviere
in The Lantern. (20) In other cases the characters themselves
are not so translucent, but the consciousness of the tragic in
their life situation is reflected to the audience by characters
who themselves remain somewhat opaque as in the case of
Françoise in "Grace." (21)

This tragic consciousness is not so much a theoretical or
an intellectual awareness as it is an awareness that is enmeshed
in a concrete situation, one that is lived bodily and felt in
terms of sensitivity before it emerges on a level that can be
articulated and then reflected upon. Marcel observed that his
was the paradoxical situation of one who is a
philosopher-dramatist. His theater is not a theater of ideas as
theoretic notions to be expounded and argued. Neither is it a
theater that proselytizes an ideology, or a showcase for puppets

8

who merely mouth an author's convictions. Marcel observed that any serious drama brings about a heightening of consciousness.(22) His theater, however, assists at the birth of consciousness in a distinctive way. In (The Invisible Threshold), Le Seuil Invisible, in the preface he wrote for his first published plays, Marcel spoke of the dawning of a tragic consciousness.(23) His dramas present real people coming with almost palpable birthpangs to a lived awareness of the tragic dimension in their life situation. In Marcel's dramas his tragic awareness relates to the fundamental issues and drama of human life.

Marcel's plays communicate not only ideas but also an awakening of consciousness. Actors present the anguish they live. With lucidity and compassion spectators can identify with the consciousness and drama of interiority that characters on the stage are living. The action, with its heightening of consciousness, is played out not only on the stage before us but also on a stage within us, the intimate theater of each individual's personal and deepening awareness.

Theater, like music, brings audiences to a deep personal center within themselves. Theater and music also effect a searching concern for a significant spiritual dimension in their lives. Both media affect the person bodily as well as spiritually and in that manner permit an awareness that is incarnate, holistic, and integral while being intensely personal. In contrast to music, theater is more verbal. The argument of conflict is more explicit, and the focus on a particular tragic dimension in human life is sharpened. Incarnate portrayal facilitates audience identification with the lead characters in the play, and dramatic action heightens an increasingly explicit and articulated consciousness of the precise tragic dimension in this particular life situation.

Marcel's dramas portray the shadowed side of life. Compared to his music or his philosophy, his plays have a more somber tone, often conveying the pathos that is part of life's tragic aspect. Still, even these plays enable us to perceive a glimmer of light that invites us to explore pathways to freedom. This occurs through a peculiar kind of breakthrough or transcendence beyond the tragic.(24)

Theater for a Broken World

Marcel refers to his theater as a theater of a broken world. The sentiment first found expression on the lips of Christiane Chesnay in her conversation with Denise Furstlin in

9

first act of the play The Broken World. "Don´t you feel...that
we are living...if you can call it living...in a broken world?
Yes, broken like a broken watch. The mainspring has stopped
working. Just look at it, nothing has changed. Everything is in
place. But put the watch to your ear, and you don´t hear any
ticking. You know what I´m talking about, the world, what we
call the world, the world of human creatures. . .it seems to me
it must have had a heart at one time, but today you would say the
heart had stopped beating..."(25)

In an introduction written for the publication of two plays,
The Rebellious Heart and The Broken World, Marcel observes that
the consciousness of a broken world takes a different form in
each of these plays. For Christiane in The Broken World, it is
the world around her that disintegrates and breaks apart. This
was a world she´d constructed from a disillusioned level of
herself. For Rose in The Rebellious Heart, the breaking up of
her world is manifest through a gradual awareness of that
breaking deepening in her heart.(26)

Marcel also acknowledges that "theater of a broken world"
can aptly be applied to the entire corpus of his dramatic works.
In each of his plays, as the lead characters become conscious of
the fact that their world has fallen apart, a certain light also
dawns for them. This light is not an intellectual explanation,
it is not necessarily even a conscious awareness, but there
occurs an illumination of a mysterious dimension of their lives
that transcends the tragic. In some instances the light is
somber, in others it is brighter--almost a light of hope in the
darkness, and in one or another exceptional case the light
appears as a flash of awareness that illuminates the entire
landscape of their lives.(27)

In The Rebellious Heart Rose cried plaintively, "There is
but one suffering and that is to be alone."(28) Yet as the play
comes to its climax it becomes clear that the intense suffering
in her life is not caused by her aloneness but by the quality of
the relationships she has with others around her: a husband,
Daniel, who uses her but who does not appreciate her or really
relate to her as a person; and a stepson, John, taken from her by
the selfishness of a father whose ways the son will probably
follow, for he has abdicated any real hope for happiness in this
life. As the play ends, heavy with the sadness of despair, there
is an aura of questioning. Perhaps the questions are quickened
more in the rebellious hearts of the audience than in the
explicit consciousness of the characters of the play. Couldn´t
something have been done to provide for an understanding and
communion of love between Rose and Daniel? Couldn´t John have
been saved?

The Broken World ends with a light of hope flooding onto the final scene of the broken world, when Christiane, who thought herself rejected and incapable of ever finding true love or real happiness in this life, by a strange change of circumstances finds that, contrary to what she felt and believed, she has been and is really loved and not forsaken. On the strength of this discovery, the realization awakens within her that there is hope for love in her life. In humbly communicating this experience to her husband, she invites him to live out with her the realization of that hope.(29)

In "The Iconoclast," a play written in 1921, which Marcel also mentions in this same introduction, the world is off-center because of the death of Vivian, Jacques´ first wife. The world becomes more out of tune when their friend, Abel, who had not expressed his passionate love for Vivian out of respect for his good friend Jacques, learns that Jacques has remarried. Fired by resentment, Abel feels that Jacques is unworthy of a pure memory of his first marriage to Vivian, and so he contrives to arouse Jacques´ suspicion about Vivian´s fidelity. Abel, for his part, is crushed when he later learns that it was Vivian´s urging and her express request that moved Jacques to remarry and to carry on living after her death. Abel would now like to restore Jacques´ confidence in Vivian´s fidelity. The following quote from a commentary written twenty-four years after the play speaks well of the opening onto mystery Marcel´s plays effected even before the author was consciously aware of this.

Abel, who has realized his own mistake, suddenly sees the whole tragedy in its true light. He becomes aware that, in a sense infinitely surpassing the still too physical and crude image of her in Jacques´ mind, Vivian´s presence remains with them. She is still there to draw them together once more, but only by recognizing this mystery can they create the harmony in which the soul can at last possess itself. "You could never," says Abel to Jacques, "be satisfied for long in a world deserted by mystery...Life without mystery, would be stifling." But the mystery must be approached with humility. As Abel says again: "Life itself will confound the iconoclasts and the self-appointed judges...Life, or He who is beyond words." And now at last Jacques too--though as yet confusedly--feels awakening like music in his soul the consciousness of this fruitful peace.(30)

11

In "The Drama of the Soul in Exile," the essay from which this last quote was taken, as well as in other critical essays, Marcel stresses the importance of the final act, and especially the last scene of a play, both for the unity they bring to the entire work and for the questions they raise.(31)

Marcel's plays often end on a disquieting, dissonant note, with surprises that leave audiences stunned. Yet the end of a Marcel play is disquieting also for the kind of questions it raises, and for the way these questions affect audiences.

One theater-goer commented that Marcel's dramas have a haunting quality.(32) The characters and key moments of the drama remain with the spectator long after the final curtain has fallen on stage. Gradually the questions come to light, in terms of the situation and interaction of the characters in the play, and also in reference to one's own life situation. Furthermore, the questions now come to light in one's own consciousness as one seeks to fathom their meaning and then find an acceptable sense that can illuminate a path toward freedom in one's own life.

The end of a Marcel play can indeed be very unsettling. These plays do not have "and they lived happily ever after" endings. The conflicts and the tensions of fundamental antinomies remain, though they also are somehow transcended. The dramatic situation is not neatly resolved like a problem that is solved when all the pieces of the puzzle fall into place. The tragic remains but there also appears the light of a pathway to one's freedom. Marcel's plays do not seek to explain, or answer questions. They do not settle problems or resolve conflicts. The role of the theater, the playwright states, is not to explain, it is to show.

What a Marcel play shows raises questions and opens pathways for reflection to clarify them. These questions can be formulated clearly and concretely in terms of the life situation of the characters in the play. With this articulation of these questions the process of reflective clarification already begins. Marcel Belay, an exceptionally fine critic of Gabriel Marcel's theater, remarked that drama is already a first reflection.(33) This first reflection can be followed up with the further reflection of drama criticism, reconstructing the play in reverse by starting with the questions raised after the curtain falls. Marcel's plays also invite another form of ongoing reflection, a personal one that can eventually become technically philosophical.

Theater of Inquiry

Marcel acknowledges that his theater is indeed a theater of inquiry.(34) His dramatic imagination envisions situations wherein characters are working through questions and challenges that flow from the tension of fundamental conflicts. This dramatic development is shown throughout the plays. His dramas conclude, having raised certain questions that neither the play nor the playwright attempts to explain.

These questions are latent throughout the play, but are brought sharply into focus in the final moments of the last scene or the last act. The audience is left with questions about the characters. What becomes of them after the denouement of the drama? What do they do next? Why didn´t they act or react differently during the course of the play? For example, apropos of The Rebellious Heart, does John become a dandy ne´er do well? Can´t Rose convince Daniel to bring the boy home and help him? Why doesn´t Rose leave Daniel and make a home for John? Why doesn´t Rose refuse to be used merely as a provider of tenderness, a subject for plays? Why doesn´t she insist on being loved for her true worth? Why doesn´t Daniel understand, why can´t he see? Why doesn´t she make him see? The tragedy is that these people in this situation can´t make it work. That tragic awareness is stunning, and it leads to a deeper and broader level of questioning. Is a genuine communion of love possible between Rose and any of her intimates such as Daniel, her husband, or John, her stepson? If a communion of love is not possible, why not? This level of questioning gives rise to another where the perspective broadens. Is a genuine communion of love possible in my life or in any human life? What attitudes and circumstances seem to prevent or destroy true love? What attitudes and circumstances would be requisite for true love to occur or endure? What is the nature of genuine human love? Can its traits be recognized and its essential dimensions lived out effectively? What is a human life worth, if love is possible or if it is not possible? What is the worth of life if true love does not occur, if tragedy prevails? What is the worth and sense of life if true love does grace people´s lives?

All of Marcel´s plays, his comic as well as his tragic works, end by raising questions in the hearts and minds of those who see them performed and are touched by their drama. Each raises questions about the characters, the situation, the play´s motif and themes. Each raises and leaves open with the spectators questions about a paradoxical situation that affects fundamental aspects of their own lives as well as the lives of the characters on stage. The questions Marcel´s theater brings to light are experienced as a fundamental call to be that invites

13

our free response and engages us personally, for they affect our very lives and being.

Theater and Mystery

The conclusions of Marcel´s plays open onto mystery. Gaston Fessard, one of Marcel´s finest critics, rightly affirmed that the hallmark of Marcel´s theater is its communication of mystery.(35)

This communication occurs in a distinctive manner. One of Marcel´s fortes is the creation of characters who live and move and speak as "I´s," as unique conscious subjectivities, characters whom the author has created from within. Then, because the action of the play allows these characters to reveal their growing consciousnesses, the spectator has the opportunity to participate in the realities occurring in their lives in a person-to-person encounter. Through dialogue and action, and especially through the incarnate magic and art of the theater that actors and actresses effect, the character reveals him or herself as a person. The actor or actress manifests that person from within, effecting what Marcel later and in another context called an "existential witness." The person in the play becomes "present" for the audience, communicating not only the words said but the very reality that he or she is living. As the actors and actresses "presentify" what they are living and even at times what they live by, the audience can be touched by the reality that is manifesting itself through the lives of the people in the play. Thus in an effective way Marcel´s drama communicates an experience of mystery that touches people in the play and in the audience alike.(36)

When a Marcel play comes to an end, the spectator has been drawn into a conscious experience of the tragic and has also encountered the presence of a mysterious dimension in the lives of the people in the play. He or she has been drawn into the dramatic climax that gives rise to questions, yet provides the wherewithall for ongoing reflection, for it opens onto a dimension of mystery that invites inquiry and offers a pathway of light. Thus freedom can begin to find a way as people struggle to transcend the tragic in their lives.

Drama, like music, can lead audiences to an experiential knowledge of some of the fundamental mysteries of life. Both music and drama enable audiences to encounter these realities inwardly and deeply. Still, drama communicates this awareness in a different manner than music does. Drama´s mode of communication is incarnate interpersonal dialogue. Drama

14

heightens our consciousness of the tragic that can emerge from
some of the fundamental antinomies in human life. Drama brings
audiences to the point of beginning to deal with these issues in
a consciously reflective, interrogative, and reasoned fashion.
Yet Marcel´s dramas, like poetry and song, would have audiences
deal with these issues, not in an abstractly reasoned fashion,
but in a reasoned reflection that clarifies the concrete
situation of unique human beings. Marcel´s dramas allow
audiences to experience the situations of others, to recognize
the reality of these situations as also their own, and to
understand them with that blend of sympathy and intelligence that
tragic pity evokes. Tragic pity enables us to identify with the
suffering of others and to compassionately understand it from a
central focal point deep within our own conscious being.(37)

Theater Introduces Philosophy

Philosophy, as rational discourse expressed in general
terms, is the third and outermost ring among Marcel´s three
concentric circles of communication. Yet if we heed Marcel´s
dictum that his philosophy should be construed in relation to his
theater, we shall see how Marcel´s theater provides a uniquely
appropriate, if not indispensable, gateway to his philosophic
reflection.

Marcel´s plays raise the questions upon which his
philosophic writings reflect. These questions are posed
concretely as they arise in the lives of real, individual
persons. As the characters in a play are brought to deal with
these questions in their everyday lives, their consciousness of
them is heightened. This consciousness of the questions is
communicated dramatically to the audience, who can also feel the
weight of these issues affecting their own lives.

Marcel´s theater poses these questions in a fortunate manner
by conscious subjects, who speak in the first person and ask
about the sense of their lives in view of the crises and
conflicts that the dramatic action brings to light. It is easy
then for audiences to pose these questions on their own account
too, because they see their impact spelled out concretely in the
lives of persons whose situation is not ultimately that different
from their own. The fundamental issues that give rise to the
dramatic tensions and the consciousness of the tragic that emerge
in the play pertain to questions about the quality of
interpersonal relationships that these people have or fail to
have with one another. Marcel´s theater brings members of the
audience and characters in the play alike to personal awareness
of questions affecting the quality or the lack of quality in

15

their own individual lives and in the relationships they have with others.

Marcel´s theater is a privileged way of leading spectators to an encounter with mystery. It is precisely this ability to bring people into the presence of the mysterious dimension of human life that is the hallmark of Gabriel Marcel´s theater. This ability to lead people through the tragic aspect of consciousness to a dawning awareness of the presence and light of mystery makes Marcel´s theater a uniquely privileged and invaluable gateway to philosophic reflection.

For those who would study Marcel´s thought, enter into dialogue with it, or simply understand it there are definite advantages to following Marcel´s own example and guidance, adopting an approach that he suggests and that he himself used.

There are significant benefits that can be gained from studying Marcel´s theater as a way of access to his philosophy. Marcel´s plays not only pose the questions that his philosophy later investigates, but his theater enables the audience to personally encounter the mystery under investigation. In addition to these signal advantages, Marcel´s theater spells out concretely and in terms of individual people´s lives the impact of the issues under investigation,--be they war, peace, individual conscience, faith, fidelity, generation gap, or other concerns. The plays also show the various attitudes and stances that different people can adopt toward these issues. In this respect Marcel´s theater begins the process of reflective analysis and interpretation that his philosophy later carries on in a more explicitly reasoned and critical manner. Thus it is an entryway into Marcel´s philosophic thinking.

One who has experienced a Marcel play is moved by its dynamic on a deep and lasting level. One is drawn toward a distinctive light of comprehension and hope. This mysterious light does not do away with the tragedy in people´s lives or the tragic conflicts in people´s fundamental attitudes that underlie their differences of opinions. It does, however, enable people to transcend the conflict in being able to perceive it from a different perspective and then, rather than judging it, to understand it in a different light.

Two more respects in which Marcel´s theater provides an indispensable way of access to his philosophy merit highlighting. One pertains to the distinctive dimension of human life that his thought interrogates; the other relates to the unusual exigencies or high expectations that Marcel held for those who would have dialogue with him.

16

Marcel expects his interlocutors to bring to the discussion a rich, concrete experience of the subject under investigation. He also expects them to become aware of alternate interpretations and to understand the subjective attitudes from which these spring, and further expects that anyone who performs a reflective clarification begins with an encounter with the mystery in question. And, finally, he expects that anyone's interpretation of a phenomenon will be derived from and confirmed against an increasing awareness of the reality present within the person's own life experience. He expects that one's grasp of the authentic nature of a phenomenon and one's cognition of its requisite conditions of possibility are gathered from the intense saturating presence of that reality as it touches and uplifts that person's life.(38) In summary, Marcel expects anyone who philosophizes with him to be constantly in touch with his or her own experience of the reality under investigation, to interrogate it, to experience its features and its essence in its various modes of "givenness," and then to develop and verify one's rational interpretations against the presence of that mystery within one's own life experience. Theater provides a first original experience of this kind of thought as well as food to continually nourish it.

Concrete dramatic approaches enhance one's experience of the kind of reality Marcel's investigations explore. Marcel researches the spiritual dimension of human life. This sacred dimension is accessible primarily by way of inwardness and depth. Its nature and its condition of possibility are best described in the language of subjectivity, which speaks precisely in terms of how this kind of reality presents itself in the conscious experience of incarnate persons.

On this matter, Martin Heidegger, a philosopher so different from Gabriel Marcel in many other respects, agrees emphatically that exploration of one's consciousness of the essential features of human existence is the unique and indispensable pathway for discovering the meaning of Being and the sense this gives to human life. In the preface to "The Invisible Threshold" Marcel affirms that his theater concerns itself with questions of the human spirit. His works explore people's experience of that sacred dimension of human existence, that dimension of spirit that assures absolute worth to individual human lives.(39)

Marcel's thought is concerned with human dignity. To examine this kind of reality one has to encounter it where it occurs, that is, precisely as it reveals itself to the conscious, affective, incarnate persons whose life it affects. Marcel's philosophy deals with matters of the heart. He treats these where they occur, namely within the privacy and depth of a person's being. For it is only there, at the center of a person's spiritual life, that the presence and nature of certain realities can come to light and be acknowledged.(40)

Marcel explores, for example, how within someone's heart a decision is formed that determines the orientation of that person's freedom and the sense that person gives to his or her life. He explores how one accedes to faith, how one struggles with unbelief. He describes how one adopts an attitude of hope or falls prey to the gravitation toward despair. He discloses how individuals influence and become part of one another's lives. He looks at death and the alternate stances people adopt toward it. He explores the possibility of genuine love and the tragedy of its failure. He examines from within the ambiguity of the human condition, and in the face of its tragedy he nevertheless discloses ways of the heart for transcending any condemnation to absurdity or despair.

Marcel's theater shows these dramas of interiority. As characters in the play live through their dramatic awakening, they communicate to the audience something of what they are living and also something of what they live by. As they come to a heightened consciousness of the events affecting themselves, audiences can hear the echoes of this dawning awareness occurring within their own lives.

Marcel's plays enable audiences to experience certain spiritual realities through what he later called existential witness. He had inquired, for himself first but then also for others, how the transcendent, the sacred, or the spiritual dimension of individual lives could become present to him in his unique subjectivity. He inquired as to how, if individuals had not encountered certain spiritual realities directly, they could come to experience them. Marcel recognized that as the lives of others touch ours, we can encounter the transcendent spiritual reality that is operative in these people's lives.(41)

In this respect, Marcel's theater appears once again as a privileged and indispensable way of access for entering into philosophic reflection about these mysteries. Some people may have significant experience and insight into these realities on their own. Others may have less, very little, or almost none to speak of. Yet for all, and especially in the case of those who would study and discuss some of these topics together, Marcel's theater provides a rich and deepening experience in which many can participate both personally and in common with others.

Indeed, in the case of Marcel's work, theater provides a

uniquely valuable and a practically indispensable way of access to philosophic reflection. This relationship is consistent with the metaphor of the three concentric rings. If philosophy is conceived as a function of the theater, then dramas can bring people to that place within themselves where they encounter concretely the precise reality that needs to be present for one's philosophic reflection to be experiential and realistically based. Moreover, if philosophy, the outermost ring, is considered as an outgrowth of music, then the reflective clarification that develops will not only have intellectual rigor but it will also provide, like music, a deep inward assurance of the presence and meaningfulness of the reality entertained.

All this is implied in Marcel's saying, so aptly yet so tersely, in the essay "On the Ontological Mystery," that "it is in drama that metaphysics occurs in concreto." (42)

Philosophy as the third and outermost ring of the three brings a distinctive clarification to the articulation of Marcel's thought, even though, as we continue to affirm, this clarification is most fully appreciated when his philosophy is read in conjunction with his dramatic presentations.

PHILOSOPHY

Philosophy, for Marcel, provides an accurate and explicit articulation of questions in general terms. Philosophy then researches and investigates these questions in a reflective and critically reasoned manner. Philosophic analysis enables one to identify with clarity and rigor, albeit in general terms, the nature of a particular phenomenon that one has been investigating. Critically, philosophy lets one view possible alternative interpretations and discern the subjective attitudes and stances from which these interpretations evolve. In this manner, philosophy's critical reflection not only clarifies the essence of what something is, but in bringing to light the various options and the attitudes from which they spring, it enhances one's opportunity for freedom in the response one makes toward the presence or absence of that particular reality in one's own life.

Philosophy's contribution is distinctive and valuable. As Marcel wrote in Presence and Immortality, philosophy brings to a level of critically reasoned interpretation what was previously present only on the levels of poetry and song.(43)

19

Concrete Approach

Gabriel Marcel distrusted abstractness. He even warned that a spirit of abstraction is at the root of all fanaticism.(44) He insisted on the importance of a concrete approach in philosophy. When he entertained young people who were preparing for careers in the field of philosophy, Marcel insisted that they formulate their ideas as one would if addressing them to a person who was actually living the situation that they wished to discuss. In the case of Marcel´s thought, the need for concrete approaches is not satisfied by simply offering an occasional example as an illustration of a general principle. A concrete approach involves adopting the perspectives of an inquirer whose life is caught up in the issue under investigation, aware that the meaning and worth of his or her life will be drastically affected by the results of one´s investigations. Marcel has affirmed that if individual people in their concrete, incarnate lives are kept central to philosophic reflection one encounters not only the uniqueness of those individuals, but also the infinite depth and richness that are part of their lives.(45) Faithfulness to the concrete approach of one who is, as it were, exploring and charting the terrain of a particular mysterious dimension of human life is of primary importance since the source and data for one´s interpretations should in fact be that mysterious, experiential dimension of human life.(46) It is also important so that the yield of philosophic reflection includes not merely perceiving the essence of something but also encountering the concrete reality in its intense presence and full saturation of givenness.(47) Marcel´s philosophy is distinctive if not unique, in that it not only provides for conceptual clarification, but also strives for the presence of the mysterious reality under investigation as the data source for reflection and as a reality enriching the lives of the questioners.

A Call to Be

There is an ethical dimension to Marcel´s thought that is consistent with its concrete approaches. Marcel expects that people will pose questions about the meaning and value of human life with a view to enhancing the quality of their own lives. So, as dramatic and philosophic reflection clarify certain dimensions of human life, they do so in such a way as to clarify the options and the various subjective dispositions from which they spring. Thus Marcel´s theater and philosophy include a "call to be" that invites individuals in their freedoms to respond and live authentically in the light of the values they perceive.(48)

Neo-Socratic

Consistent with Marcel's concrete approaches, "neo-Socratic" is a term he allowed as validly describing his approach to philosophy. The style of his writing remains personal and conversational, and his philosophic approach is intersubjective and dialogic. He guides readers to investigate questions that arise within their own life experience. Marcel continually invites readers to relate their reasoning and reflection to "recollection" of their own lived experience. He guides readers in reflections on varying and diverse experiences. Through a process of interrogation leading to insight, developed from different standpoints, Marcel leads his reader-interlocutor to perceive within his or her own experience the essential features of the reality in question and also the subjective or intersubjective conditions of possibility requisite for its occurrence. Marcel, through his approach of interrogation toward insight through intersubjective dialogue, intends, like Socrates, to assist at the birth of true ideas and right understanding of the nature of certain realities that can enhance the quality of one's life.

Phenomenological

Paul Ricoeur, who noted at Cerisy-La-Salle the dramatic character of Marcel's thought, also stated that Marcel's mode of reflection would be phenomenological even if Edmund Husserl had never evolved a phenomenological method.(49) What Marcel describes as "recollection" and "reflection" and what he performs as a concrete experiential approach to the clarification of mystery does indeed follow the pattern that the phenomenological method describes.(50) His reflections appear so original in approach, so rich in content, and so artful in execution, that one scarcely has the impression of a disciplined technique being methodically applied. One has rather the impression of a musical composition developed through artful improvisation. One has only to read a masterful work like Marcel's essay "Sketch of a Phenomenology and a Metaphysics of Hope," or, for that matter, "The Mystery of Family" or "The Ego and its Relation to Others" to recognize the positive brilliance and artful care with which he develops a philosophic clarification of topics that concern him.(51) These essays pursue their topic and develop smoothly as an interesting dialogue and a rich, concrete, personal reflection. Yet, if one wishes to verify, one finds that the various steps of phenomenological analysis have been applied. The main interest of this is the verification it offers of the critical rigor of Marcel's analyses. Yet the rigor is evident for most readers from following the process of their own

21

thinking, and the central focus of the reader-interlocutor remains the vitality of the inquiry, the richness of the clarification, and the depth of true and valuable insights.

Marcel´s philosophic essays begin with a preliminary sketch of the reality in question and an evocation of the questions it gives rise to. His approach is consistently personal and experiential, reflecting on the mystery as present in the concrete experience of the interrogators. The process of reflective clarification views the reality from different standpoints and interprets its essential features accurately. Various techniques of entertaining alternate attitudes and interpretations are introduced as part of the process of interrogation toward insight. This critical technique serves not only to bring to light spurious or counterfeit approximations, but also to sharpen and refine one´s understanding of the genuine reality as authentically lived. These essays lead to a recognition of the reality as understood in its essential nature and its subjective conditions of possibility. The mystery is present in the life experience of the investigator and this entails a certain incitement to preserve its worth in our life situation.(52)

As the third and outermost ring of communication, philosophy makes a definite contribution to the expression of Marcel´s thought. Philosophy´s reflection and critical reasoning bring to expression in accurate and general terms the questions and the insights previously present in his theater and music only as poetry and song. The clarity and rigor that characterize philosophic understanding bring one´s consciousness to a new level of explicitness. Philosophy´s understanding also brings a new level of clarity to the sense of uneasiness and inquiry awakened by the unanswered questions of the plays. And philosophy brings a certain completeness to the inquiry and research that theater brought to light and that music foreshadowed. Thus the three concentric circles, music, theater, and philosophy, bring to successive levels of awareness and critically reflective consciousness the questions and the perspectives of light and insight that are part of Marcel´s life´s work and thought.

Once the major part of Marcel´s philosophy, drama, and musical compositions were written, circa 1961 (the date of his last published play), it had become evident to author and various commentators alike that there was a fundamental unity in his life´s work and an important complementarity to be noted in different respects between his works of theater and philosophy.

PROPER RELATIONS BETWEEN THEATER AND PHILOSOPHY

Various authors who have studied Marcel´s writings have illustrated the different ways his theater and philosophy can be interrelated. Charles Moeller, a noted literary critic, sketched Marcel´s theme of hope, fleshing out this portrait with excerpts of dialogue from several plays. In a more extensive study Marcel Belay, an outstanding drama critic, examined the portrayal of death in fifteen of Marcel´s plays. Belay concluded this study with a final essay reflecting on the significance of this theme in Marcel´s thought. Gaston Fessard and Joseph Chenu highlighted the substantial unity and essential complementarity that exists between Marcel´s theater and philosophy. These noted scholars saw Marcel´s thought developing as one route traveled, with theater and philosophy representing the landscape viewed on either side of the road or depicting either side of the same height scaled. Fessard´s work presented this idea principally in terms of dramatic criticism. Chenu developed the idea and with very careful balance showed the essential complementarity that exists between Marcel´s theater and philosophy and traced the progressive development of various themes in Marcel´s thought. Both these authors brought into clear relief the prospective as well as the concretizing role of theater relative to the philosophic thought.(53) Roger Troisfontaines, Kenneth Gallagher, and Vincent Miceli, whose books are classic introductions to Marcel´s philosophy, present his theater as integral to his thought. Each of these writers included in his book a chapter or section developing this thesis. M. M. Davy, in her study of Marcel´s theater, identifies its distinctive qualities and highlights some of its traits and themes that are reflected in his philosophy. Paul Ricoeur, an eminent philosopher, in a conference on Marcel´s philosophy, highlighted the essentially dramatic character of his thought, given his dialogic approach and his essential concern for life as intersubjective.(54)

As Marcel wrote in the preface to (The Secret is in the Isles), the way different authors interrelate his theater and philosophy and the weight of importance these authors attach to one or the other will depend largely on the preference and forte of the individual scholar.(55) This remark seems to have been borne out by the facts in the past, and it seems likely that it will be the case in the future as well.

However individuals may choose to interrelate Marcel´s theater and philosophy, they would be well advised to heed the directives and information Marcel provides in his own writings. For Marcel the essential relation between theater and philosophy is construed in terms of theater´s prospective and concretizing role. In Marcel´s original inquiries, theater was the first stage of research, with philosophy subsequent to it.

Early in his career, Marcel thought that theater alone might suffice as his only form of literary expression. Soon, however, he realized that both the theater and the philosophy were necessary. He began to recognize that there was an essential complementarity, even a substantial unity, between the two.(56)

Marcel recognized that theater and philosophy are distinct and autonomous disciplines. Each has its own proper finality, and neither should be made subservient to the other or to any other purpose. The role of theater is to show life, not to teach or explain. The role of philosophy is to reflect on questions and bring certain perspectives of explanation to light in terms of rational discourse. So theater and philosophy should remain as separate disciplines even though they may have an essential complementarity.(57)

Always Prospective and Concretizing

In Marcel´s writings reflecting on his theatrical and philosophical works he always stressed that the essential complementarity between his theater and his philosophy lay in the concretizing prospective role of his theater. Marcel´s theater is prospective as a first stage of inquiry and exploration. Marcel observed that any question always occurred to him first in terms of the dramatic conflict among people in a concrete situation. He then watched the elements of conflict develop and play themselves out in the lives of the characters of the play. Marcel´s dramatic imagination brought to the light of the theater certain conflicts and fundamental antinomies that were part of his own life situation, and it was thus that theater enabled him to envisage and confront some of the fundamental questions affecting his own life. Marcel´s theater also played a concretizing role in that, in portraying the concrete situation of the dramas, it enabled certain stances to be incarnated and various attitudes to be voiced. This allowed certain questions and themes to become clear in the light of the theater and find expression dramatically long before Marcel ever conceived of any such notions philosophically or became aware of their significance on the level of philosophic discourse. In this fashion theater often anticipated and prepared the way for what philosophy was to discover and reflect upon later.(58) A classic instance of this is Abel´s voicing the word "mystery" in the denouement of (The Iconoclast), written in 1917-1921. The philosophical significance of "mystery" was developed only much later, appearing in the philosophical essay "On the Ontological Mystery" published in 1933 in conjunction with the play The

24

Broken World. (59) On several occasions Marcel emphatically voiced that theater anticipates philosophy, and the scholarly works of Fessard and Chenu amply substantiate it.(60)

Paradox of Philosopher-Dramatist

In his later years Marcel reflected on the paradox he saw in the dual vocation of philosopher-dramatist. For him, the paradox centered in the fact that although his theater was concerned with fundamental conflicts in the concrete situation of individual lives that gave rise to questions and thus consciousness of ideas, his was in no way a theater for ideas in any literal sense. Marcel´s is not a theater that sets out to illustrate a thesis. Nor does his theater propose to proselytize or present propaganda for some ideology. It serves even less as a forum for debate, presenting ideas in the form of reasoned argument. Therein lies the paradox. This theater deals with ideas not philosophically, but dramatically, as dawning in the consciousness of those whose lives are caught up in the issues that give rise to questions about life´s meaning and worth.(61)

When most of Marcel´s major works were complete it became evident that there was an essential complementarity, even a substantial unity, between his theater and philosophy. These were described as the landscape viewed on either side of the one road traveled. And, in another homo viator metaphor, identified as alternate slopes of the same height scaled. From the vantage point of a retrospective view one can see progressively along the path of Marcel´s life different questions explored first dramatically and then philosophically. As he wrote in "An Essay in Autobiography" it appeared to him as if his work is like that of one who charts a territory that he had explored but which territory each individual will want to explore on his or her own.(62)

Looking at Marcel´s work as a whole, one can occasionally consider some aspect of certain plays as illustrative of a philosophic theme or insight. Yet even this risks reversing the dynamic of Marcel´s work and might lead to a misunderstanding or a misrepresentation of Marcel´s thought. This has occurred on occasion.(63) One is therefore rightfully advised to respect the theater´s concretizing and prospective role as foremost to the relationship between Marcel´s theater and his philosophy.

It is hoped that reflection on Marcel´s metaphor of three concentric circles will serve as an attractive and enlightening introduction to the nature of Marcel´s thought. Reflection on the three circles indicates what Marcel considers integral philosophic inquiry should entail and emphasizes the essential complementarity that exists among these three modes of communication. This same reflection should also serve to highlight how and why theater opens up a uniquely valuable, even indispensable, gateway to philosophic reflection.

A right understanding of Marcel´s procedures for philosophic thinking requires concrete approaches that awaken inward experience (as music does), and initiate conscious personal reflection on a reality directly and incarnately encountered (as theater does), so that one can, in a manner that is both realistically based and critically reasoned clarify, as philosophy does, the significance of its presence and/or absence to evaluate the worth of one´s life (as a person seeking freely and responsibly to live an authentic human life does).

All three rings, each in its own way, bring us to a deep center where we can encounter the presence of a mysterious reality within us, a trans-subjective depth of the spiritual dimension of our lives. Music, theater, and philosophy, each in its own way, enable us to clarify the significance of this sacred dimension of humanity so that each of us may live in its light, faithful to its call "to be" and responsive to its incitement "to create."

Notes to Chapter One.   An Introduction to Gabriel Marcel´s
Philosophic Quest Through Music and Theater

1.   Gabriel Marcel, The Existential Background of Human Dignity,
The William James Lectures Delivered at Harvard University
1961-62, Cambridge, MA., Harvard University Press, 1963, 178
pp. Gabriel Marcel, The Mystery of Being, 2 volumes. The
Gifford Lectures Delivered at the University of Aberdeen,
Scotland, translated by G. S. Fraser. Vol. I, Reflection
and Mystery, 270 pp., Vol. II, Faith and Reality, 210 pp.
First published, 1950 by the Harvill Press Ltd., Great
Britain.   A Gateway Edition was published by Henry Regnery
Co. of Chicago, 1960.   Reprinted by arrangement with
Regnery/Gateway by University Press of America, Lanham, MD.,
1982.

2.   Biographic data may be found in: Part Three, Section I,
below, pp. **177-183.**

H. J. Blackham, Six Existentialist Thinkers, London,
Routlege & Kegan Paul, 1951.

I. M. Bochenski, Contemporary European Thought, Berkeley,
CA., University of California Press, 1956.

Seymour Cain, Gabriel Marcel.   New York, Hillary House,
1963; South Bend, IN., Regnery/Gateway, 1979.

Kenneth T. Gallagher, The Philosophy of Gabriel Marcel, New
York, Fordham University Press, 1962, 1975.

Samuel Keen, Gabriel Marcel.   Richmond, VA., John Knox
Press, 1967.

Francis J. Lescoe, Existentialism with or without God, New
York, Alba House, 1974.

Vincent P. Miceli, Ascent to Being.   Gabriel Marcel´s
Philosophy of Communion, New York, Tournai, Paris, Rome,
1965.

David Roberts, Existentialism and Religious Belief, New
York, Oxford University Press, 1957.

Herbert Spiegelberg, The Phenomenological Movement, A
Historical Introduction, 2 Vols., The Hague, Martinus
Nijhoff, 1960.

27

Roger Troisfontaines, De l'existence à l'être. La
Philosophie de Gabriel Marcel, Louvain, Nauwelaerts; Paris,
Vrin, 1952; 1965.

Gabriel Marcel, "An Essay in Autobiography," in The
Philosophy of Existentialism, Secaucus, NJ., The Citadel
Press, 1956, pp. 104-28; En Chemin, vers quel eveil? Paris,
Gallimard, 1971; "An Autobiographical Essay" (Spring 1969)
in The Philosophy of Gabriel Marcel (Library of Living
Philosophers Vol. XVII) ed. Paul A. Schilpp and Lewis E.
Hahn, La Salle, IL., Open Court, 1984, pp. 3-68.

3. An allocution for the Alliance Française, "Le Paradoxe du
    Philosophe--Dramaturge," Réalisations Sonores: Hughes De
    Salle, Collection Française de Notre Temps Nous Confie,
    Sous le patronage de L'Alliance Française, présentation
    écrite sur la pochette de Marc Blancpain. No date.

4. "Foreword" by Gabriel Marcel, pp. VII-X, March 26, 1962, to
    Kenneth T. Gallagher's The Philosophy of Gabriel Marcel, New
    York, Fordham University Press, 1962, 1975, p. VIII.

5. Commemorative medal commissioned by the National Mint of
    France (L'Hôtel Des Monnaies), Presence and Immortality,
    Pittsburgh, PA., Duquesne University Press, 1967, pp. 7, 35;
    Ch. Moeller, Littérature du XXe Siècle et Christianisme,
    Vol. IV, Paris, Casterman, 1960, p. 129.

6. "Musique et littérature," Nouvelles littéraires, jeudi
    17 juin 1948; Existential Background of Human Dignity,
    Cambridge, MA., Harvard University Press, 1962, p. 21; En
    Chemin, vers quel eveil?, Paris, Gallimard, 1971, p. 81;
    Louis Chaigne, Vie et oeuvres d'écrivains, Vol. 4, Paris,
    F. Lanore, 1954, p. 193.

7. Preface à Le Seuil invisible, volume qui contient La
    Grâce et Le Palais de Sable, Paris, Bernard Grasset, 1914,
    pp. 3, 8; Preface to (The Invisible Threshold), an
    introduction to his first two published plays, (Grace) and
    (The Sand Castle).

8. "An Essay in Autobiography," p. 127; "On the Ontological
    Mystery," p. 18 in The Philosophy of Existentialism,
    Secaucus, NJ, The Citadel Press, 1956; The Mystery of Being,
    2 vols., The Gifford Lectures at University of Aberdeen,
    Scotland, Great Britain, Harvill Press, 1950; Chicago, IL.,
    Henry Regnery Co., Gateway Edition, 1960, vol. 1, p. 250,
    pp. 57-58; reprinted by arrangement with Regnery/Gateway,
    Lanham, MD., University Press of America, 1984.

The Philosophy of Existentialism contains "On the Ontological Mystery," "Existence and Human Freedom," "Testimony and Existentialism," and "An Essay in Autobiography." The essay "On the Ontological Mystery" was originally entitled "Position et approches concrètes du mystère ontologique," a conference presented at the Marseilles Society of Philosophy, January 21, 1933, and published in the same volume with Le Monde cassé (The Broken World,) Paris, Desclée de Brouwer, 1933. Etienne Gilson remarked that this essay is as central to an understanding of Gabriel Marcel's work as the Introduction to Metaphysics is to Henri Bergson's.

9. "My Fundamental Purpose" (1937), pp. 13-30 in Presence and Immortality, Pittsburgh, PA., Duquesne University Press, 1967, p. 27. Original French version is "Mon Propos fondamental," pp. 13-26 in Présence et Immortalité, Paris, Flammarion, 1959, p. 24; "The Drama of the Soul in Exile," A lecture given by Gabriel Marcel in July 1950 to the Institut Français in London, published as Preface to Gabriel Marcel: Three Plays, A Man of God, Ariadne, The Votive Candle, trans. with introduction by Richard Hayes, New York, Hill and Wang, 1965, p. 27.

10. Le Quartuor en fa dièze (The Quartet in F#), Paris, Plon, 1925;

    Mon Temps n'est pas le vôtre (My Time is Not Your Time), Paris, Plon, 1955;

    Le Dard (The Sting), Paris, Plon, 1936;

    Le Chemin de crête, Paris, Grasset, 1936, (Ariadne), in Three Plays by Gabriel Marcel, New York, Hill and Wang, 1965.

    Croissez et multipliez (Increase and Multiply), Paris, Plon, 1955.

    The Unfathomable (March 1919), pp. 245-84 in Presence and Immortality, Duquesne University Press, 1967; L'Insondable, pp. 195-234 in Présence et Immortalité, Paris, Flammarion, 1959.

    The Broken World, pp. 19-144 in The Existential Drama of Gabriel Marcel, West Hartford, CT., St. Joseph's College McAuley Institute of Religious Studies, 1974; Le Monde cassé, Paris, Desclée de Brouwer, 1932.

La Grâce (Grace), pp. 9-209 in Le Seuil Invisible, Paris, Grasset, 1914.

Colombyre ou le brasier de la paix (Colombyre or the Torch of Peace), pp. 8-155, Théâtre comique, Paris, Albin Michel, 1947.

11. "The Drama of the Soul in Exile," p. 30; "Les vrais problèmes de Rome n´est plus dans Rome" (The actual problems of Rome is no longer in Rome), in Rome n´est plus dans Rome, Paris, La Table Ronde, 1951, pp. 155-56; Existential Background of Human Dignity, p. 106; Le Secret est dans les îles, (The Secret is in the Islands), Preface, Paris, Plon, 1967, p. 20; "An Autobiographical Essay," (Spring 1969) in The Philosophy of Gabriel Marcel, (The Library of Living Philosophers, Vol. XVII) ed. P. A. Schilpp and L. E. Hahn, La Salle, IL., Open Court, 1984, p. 60; En Chemin, vers quel eveil? Paris, Gallimard, 1971, pp. 235-36.

12. Kenneth T. Gallagher, The Philosophy of Gabriel Marcel, Foreword by Gabriel Marcel, New York, Fordham University Press, 1962, 1975, p. VIII.

13. Présence de Gabriel Marcel, Cahier 2-3, L´Esthétique musicale de Gabriel Marcel, Paris, Aubier, 1980, pp. 1-297; Louis Chaigne, Vie et oeuvres d´écrivains, Vol. 4, Paris, F. Lanore, 1954, pp. 252-53. Cf. ff. Chronological Bibliography of Works by Gabriel Marcel about his Theater, forty titles, pp. 39-42.

14. A Man of God, in Three Plays by Gabriel Marcel, New York, Hill and Wang, 1965, pp. 35-114. Un Homme de Dieu, Paris, Grasset, 1925; reedited, Paris, La Table Ronde, 1950. "La Lumière sur la montagne," an unpublished play (1905) Marcel identified as a childish version of the later work, A Man of God. The child´s version was, however, favorably reviewed by the critic and poet Fernand Gregh. En Chemin, vers quel eveil?, p. 23. Gabriel Marcel´s "An Autobiographical Essay" (Spring 1969), pp. 16-17, published in The Philosophy of Gabriel Marcel, (The Library of Living Philosophers, Vol. XVII), published in 1984, presents much information from En Chemin, vers quel eveil? and makes it available for the first time in English.

15. Cf. ff. Chronological Bibliography of Works by Gabriel Marcel about his Theater, pp. 39-42.
Three full-length books of drama criticism, Théâtre et Religion, Paris, Vitte, 1958; L´Heure Théâtrale, Paris, Plon, 1959; and Regards sur le Théâtre de Claudel, Paris, Beauchesne, 1964.

Marcel´s reviews as drama critic, working for over forty
years for Sept, Temps Presents, La Vie intellectuelle,
L´Europe Nouvelle, and Nouvelles Littéraires, are by far
too numerous to list here. These reviews and others can be
located by using the excellent bibliographic sources listed
in Part Three, Section IV, below pp. 211   citing
especially the works of Roger Troisfontaines, 2 vols., De
l´existence à l´être. La Philosophie de Gabriel Marcel.
Lettre Preface de Gabriel Marcel, Louvain: Nauwelaerts;
Paris: Béatrice-Nauwelaerts, 1953, 2e ed. 1968, vol. 2,
Bibliographie de Gabriel Marcel, pp. 381-464, in particular
III. Articles de Les Nouvelles Littéraires, pp. 427-42,
IV. Journaux, Revues, Avant-Propos, Divers, pp. 442-50,
Conférences, pp. 450-57, Notes, Entretiens, Débats,
Présidences, Interviews, pp. 457-61; and the work of

François H. Lapointe and Claire C. Lapointe, Gabriel Marcel
and His Critics, An International Bibliography, (1928-1976),
New York and London, Garland Publishing, Inc., 1977, Part I,
bibliography of Gabriel Marcel´s writings, pp. 7-107,
arranged by years. Cf. also François H. Lapointe, "The
Writings of Gabriel Marcel," arranged by years, in The
Philosophy of Gabriel Marcel, (The Library of Living
Philosophers, Vol. XVII), pp. 585-609, ed. P. A. Schilpp and
L. E. Hahn, La Salle, IL., Open Court, 1984.

16.   "An Autobiographical Essay," p. 39; Cf. Part Three, Section
      I, Biblio-biography, below, pp. 177-83.

17.   Le Secret est dans les îles (The Secret is in the Isles),
      Preface, pp. 8-13, to the volume of three plays: Le Dard
      (The Sting,) L´Emissaire (The Emissary), and Le Signe de la
      Croix (The Sign of the Cross), Paris, Plon, 1967, 349 pp.

18.   Le Quatuor en fa dièze (The Quartet in F#); Le Coeur des
      autres (The Rebellious Heart) L´Insondable (The
      Unfathomable) Des points sur les I (Dot the I) La Soif ou
      Les Coeurs avides (Thirst or Eager Hearts) La Double
      Expertise (The Double Expertise) Le Regard neuf (The New
      Look), among others treating struggles for communication and
      love, and dealing with challenges to fidelity and situations
      involving infidelity. Un Juste (A Just One); Le Dard (The
      Sting); L´Emissaire (The Emissary); Le Signe de la Croix
      (The Sign of the Cross); Rome n´est plus dans Rome (Rome Is
      No Longer in Rome), among others deal with political
      differences and the struggle of individual conscience.

31

Mon Temps n´est pas le Votre (My Time is not Your Time)
portrays something deeper than the generation gap. Concern
for persons missing in action is portrayed in L´Insondable
(The Unfathomable.) Fear of the menace of war is depicted
in Colombyre ou le brasier de la paix (Colombyre or the
Torch of Peace); and Rome n´est plus dans Rome (Rome Is No
Longer in Rome) conveys reactions to the menace of war. Le
Quatuor en fa dièze (The Quartet in F#), Le Coeur des
autres (The Rebellious Heart), Un Homme de Dieu (A Man of
God), Les points sur les I (Dot the I), Le Fanal (The
Lantern), Le Chemin de crête (Ariadne), and others deal
wih struggles for success and authenticity. La Grâce
(Grace), Le Palais de Sable (The Sand Castle), Les points
sur les I (Dot the I), Le Fanal (The Lantern), Le Dard,
(The Sting), and others deal with faith. Music is a
principal theme in Le Quatuor en fa dièze (The Quartet in
F#), Mon Temps n´est pas le votre (My Time is not Your
Time), and Le Dard (The Sting). In Le Dard (The Sting), Le
Coeur des autres (The Rebellious Heart), Un Homme de Dieu
(A Man of God), and Les points sur les I (Dot the I) the
quest for artistic, professional, and personal integrity
appears. Survival and life after death appear in
L´Insondable (The Unfathomable), L´Iconoclaste (The
Iconoclast), Le Fanal (The Lantern), L´Horizon (The
Horizon), and Le Divertissement posthume (The Posthumous
Joke).

19. The expression "what one lives by" or "what one lives on"
occurs often in Marcel´s works in the sense that comes to
light in the dialogue between Arnaud and Evelyne in La Soif,
Act III, Scene 9, p. 445, and in "An Autobiographical Essay"
(1969), in The Philosophy of Gabriel Marcel, (The Library of
Living Philosophers, Vol. XVII), ed. P. A. Schilpp and L. E.
Hahn, La Salle, IL., Open Court, 1984, p. 61.

20. Le Fanal, Paris, Armand Stock, 1936, Scenes 4, 6, and 7;
especially pp. 38-40. The Lantern, translated by Joseph
Cunneen and Elizabeth Stambler, in Cross Currents, Vol.
VIII, no. 2 (Spring 1958), pp. 129-43, Scenes 4, 6, and 7,
especially pp. 136-37.

21. La Grâce (Grace), pp. 9-209, in Le Seuil Invisible, (The
Invisible Threshold), Paris, Bernard Grasset, 1914,
pp. 202-209. "The Drama of the Soul in Exile," p. 21.

22. "The Drama of the Soul in Exile," p. 27, L´Heure
Théâtrale, p. VI.

23. *Le Seuil Invisible*, Paris, Bernard Grasset, 1914, p. 7; *Le Secret est dans les îles*, pp. 18-19; *En Chemin vers quel eveil?*, Paris, Gallimard, 1973, p. 169.

24. "The Drama of the Soul in Exile," p. 27; "Les vrais problèmes de Rome n'est plus dans Rome," p. 162; "My Dramatic Works as viewed by the Philosopher," p. 111-12; *The Existential Background of Human Dignity*, pp. 5, 53, 107; "On the Ontological Mystery," pp. 26-27, in *The Philosophy of Existentialism; The Philosophy of Gabriel Marcel*, (Library of Living Philosophers, Vol. XVII), "Reply by Gabriel Marcel" to "The Idea of Mystery in the Philosophy of Gabriel Marcel," pp. 272-73.

25. *The Broken World*, Act I, Scene 4, in *The Existential Drama of Gabriel Marcel*, ed. Francis J. Lescoe, translated by Sr. J. M. P. Colla, West Hartford, CT., McAuley Institute of Religious Studies, 1974, p. 36.

26. "Introduction to the Theater of the Broken World," in *The Existential Drama of Gabriel Marcel*, p. 10.

27. "The Drama of the Soul in Exile," pp. 27-28, 33.

28. *The Rebellious Heart*, Act III, Scene 3, in *The Existential Drama of Gabriel Marcel*.

29. *The Broken World*, Act IV, Scene 7, pp. 141-44, especially pp. 143-44.

30. "The Drama of the Soul in Exile," pp. 28-29.

31. Ibid., pp. 30, 32-33; *Le Secret est dans les îles*, p. 20; Preface, in *Percées vers un ailleurs*, Paris, Fayard, 1973, p. 1; "De la recherche philosophique" in *Entretiens autour de Gabriel Marcel*, Neuchâtel, à la Baconnière, 1976, p. 9.

32. *L'Heure théâtrale, De Giraudoux à Jean Paul Sartre*, Paris, Plon, 1959, pp. III, IV; "My Dramatic Works as viewed by the Philosopher" in *Searchings*, New York, Newman Press, 1967, translated from the German *Auf der Suche nach Wahrheit und Gerechtigkeit*, Verlag Knecht, 1964, a conference presented in Freiburg im Bresgau, 1959, pp. 93-118, especially pp. 108, 117.

33. Marcel Belay, in the discussion of "Gabriel Marcel et la Phenomenolgie" presentation by Paul Ricoeur in *Entretiens autour de Gabriel Marcel*, p. 88.

33

34. "De la recherche philosophique," pp. 9-10, 16-17, in
Entretiens autour de Gabriel Marcel; Existential Background
of Human Dignity, William James Lectures delivered at
Harvard University, Cambridge, MA., Harvard University
Press, 1963, p. 93; Le Secret est dans les îles, p. 12;
En Chemin, vers quel eveil? Paris, Gallimard, 1971,
pp. 233-34.

35. Gaston Fessard, "Théâtre et Mystère," published as an
introductory essay to La Soif, Paris, Desclée de Brouwer,
1938, pp. 5-116; Notes de l´auteur: La Chapelle Ardente, in
Trois Pièces, Paris, Plon, 1931, p. 142; "The Drama of the
Soul in Exile," pp. 15, 21-22, 30, 32.

36. Notes de l´auteur: La Chapelle Ardente, p. 142; "The Drama
of the Soul in Exile," pp. 17, 21, 22, 30, 33.

37. "The Drama of the Soul in Exile," pp. 21, 22-23; "My
Dramatic Works as viewed by the Philosopher," p. 115;
L´Heure Théâtrale, p. VII.

38. "Sketch of a Phenomenology and a Metaphysics of Hope,"
pp. 29-67 in Homo Viator, New York, Harper and Bros., 1962,
p. 29. Earlier edition, H. Regnery, Chicago, 1951.

39. Preface, La Seuil Invisible (The Invisible Threshold), p. 8.
This is also the lead argument of The Existential Background
of Human Dignity.

40. "On the Ontological Mystery," pp. 17-22, esp. p. 22; The
Existential Background of Human Dignity, p. 53; Reply by
Gabriel Marcel to "The Idea of Mystery in the Philosophy of
Gabriel Marcel," in The Philosophy of Gabriel Marcel,
(Library of Living Philosophers, Vol. XVII), p. 272.

41. Grâce, in Le Seuil Invisible, pp. 207-209, esp. p. 209;
Les points sur les I, in Théâtre comique, Paris, Albin
Michel, 1947, pp. 142-44; Dot the I, translated by K. R.
Hanley, in Two One Act Plays by Gabriel Marcel, Lanham, MD.,
University Press of America, pp. 1-21; "The Drama of the
Soul in Exile," pp. 22, 27; La Soif (The Thirst), Paris,
Desclée de Brouwer, 1938; reedited Les Coeurs avides,
(Eager Hearts), Paris, La Table Ronde, 1952; later published
La Soif ou Les Coeurs avides in Cinq Pièces Majeures: Un
Homme de Dieu, Le Monde cassé, Le Chemin de crête, La
Soif, and Le Signe de la Croix, Paris, Plon, 1973, pp.
357-450, act 3, scene 9, p. 445; The Drama of the Soul in
Exile, pp. 22, 27; The Existential Background of Human
Dignity, pp. 63, 79, 92.

42. "I am convinced that it is in drama and through drama that
    metaphysical thought grasps and defines itself in concreto,"
    "On the Ontological Mystery" in The Philosophy of
    Existentialism, p. 26.

43. "Presence and Immortality" (1951) pp. 229-44, in Presence
    and Immortality, Pittsburgh, PA., Duquesne University Press,
    1967, p. 232. "Présence et immortalité," (1951)
    pp. 179-93 in Présence et immortalité, Paris,
    Flammarion, 1959, p. 183.

44. Foreword to Kenneth Gallagher's The Philosophy of Gabriel
    Marcel, p. VIII; Postface, Rome n'est plus dans Rome,
    p. 160; The Existential Background of Human Dignity, p. 123;
    Gabriel Marcel's replies passim in The Philosophy of Gabriel
    Marcel, (Library of Living Philosophers Vol. XVII);
    Allocution for the Alliance Française, "Gabriel Marcel: Le
    Paradoxe du Philosophe--Dramaturge."

45. "My Fundamental Purpose" (1937), pp. 13-30 in Presence and
    Immortality, p. 29; "The Drama of the Soul in Exile," p. 27.

46. "An Essay in Autobiography," pp. 104-28 in The Philosophy of
    Existentialism; The Mystery of Being, 2 vols; "The Drama
    of the Soul in Exile," pp. 27-28; The Existential Background
    of Human Dignity, p. 50.

47. "Sketch of a Phenomenology and a Metaphysics of Hope,"
    pp. 29-67 in Homo Viator, p. 29. "This experience, which
    is that of 'I hope...,' must, like the fundamental
    experience of faith, 'I believe...,' be purified; or, more
    exactly, we must pass from this experience in its diluted or
    diffused state to the same experience, touched--I do not say
    absolutely conceived--at its highest tension or again at its
    point of complete saturation."

48. "Les Valeurs spirituelles dans le théâtre français
    contemporian," Orientations religieuses, intellectuelles et
    littéraires, June 25, 1937, Belgium, pp. 768-98, p. 789;
    cited by Gaston Fessard in "Théâtre et Mystère,"
    p. 53; "The Drama of the Soul in Exile," pp. 33-34; L'Heure
    Théâtrale, pp. VII-VIII.

49. Paul Ricoeur, "Gabriel Marcel et la Phenomenologie,"
    pp. 53-74, discussion pp. 75-94, in Entretiens autour de
    Gabriel Marcel, at Cerisy la Salle, August 1973; "Gabriel
    Marcel and Phenomenology" in The Philosophy of Gabriel
    Marcel, (Library of Living Philosophers Vol. XVII),
    pp. 471-94. Reply by Gabriel Marcel, pp. 495-98.

50. "On the Ontological Mystery", pp. 23-26; The Existential Background of Human Dignity, p. 88.

51. Homo Viator Introduction to a Metaphysic of Hope, translated by Emma Craufurd, New York, Harper and Bros., Harper Torchbooks (The Cloister Library), 1962; originally published in English by Victor Gollancz, Ltd., London, and Henry Regnery Company, Chicago, in 1951; reprinted in 1962 by arrangements with Editions Montaigne. "Sketch of a Phenomenology and a Metaphysic of Hope," pp. 29-67; "The Mystery of Family," pp. 68-97; "The Ego and its Relation to Others," pp. 13-28.

52. "Pour un renouveau de la spiritualité dans l´art dramatique," Combat, February, 1937, cited by Gaston Fessard in "Théâtre et Mystère," p. 70; L´Heure Théâtrale, pp. VII-VIII.

53. Charles Moeller, "Gabriel Marcel et la ´mystère´ de l´espérance," pp. 149-279 in Littérature du XXe siècle et christianisme, IV. L´Espérance en Dieu notre père. Paris, Casterman, 1960.

   Marcel Belay, La Mort dans le théâtre de Gabriel Marcel, Paris, Vrin, 1980.

   Gaston Fessard, Théâtre et mystère. Introduction à Gabriel Marcel, Paris, Tequi, 1938.

   Zachary Taylor Ralston, Gabriel Marcel´s Paradoxical Expression of Mystery: A Stylistic Study of "La Soif," Washington, D.C., The Catholic University of America Press, 1961.

   Joseph Chenu, Le Théâtre de Gabriel Marcel et sa signification métaphysique, Paris, Aubier, 1948.

   Guillemine de Lacoste, "The Notion of Participation in the Early Drama and Early Journals of Gabriel Marcel," Philosophy Today, Vol. 19, (Spring 1975), pp. 50-60.

54. Roger Troisfontaines, De l´existence à l´être. La Philosophie de Gabriel Marcel. 2 vols. Louvain, Nauwelaerts; Paris, Béatrice Nauwelaerts et J. Vrin, 1953; 2nd ed., 1968. Preface by Gabriel Marcel. Bibliography.

   Kenneth T. Gallagher, The Philosophy of Gabriel Marcel. Foreword by Gabriel Marcel. New York, Fordham University Press, 1962; 1975.

Vincent P. Miceli, Ascent to Being: Gabriel Marcel´s Philosophy of Communion, Foreword by Gabriel Marcel. Paris, Desclée de Brouwer, 1965.

Louis Chaigne, Vie et oeuvres d´écrivains, IV, Paris, F. Lanore, 1954.

Marie-Madeleine Davy, Un Philosophe itinérant. Gabriel Marcel. Paris, Flammarion, 1959.

Paul Ricoeur, Gabriel Marcel et Karl Jaspers, deux maîtres de l´Existentialisme, Paris, Editions du Temps Présent, 1948; and Entretiens Paul Ricoeur, Gabriel Marcel, Paris, 1968, translated by Peter McCormick as "Conversations between Paul Ricoeur and Gabriel Marcel" in Tragic Wisdom and Beyond, Evanston, IL., Northwestern University Press, 1973; and "Gabriel Marcel et la Phenomenologie" in Entretiens autour de Gabriel Marcel, Neuchâtel, à la Baconnière, 1976; "Gabriel Marcel and Phenomenology" in The Philosophy of Gabriel Marcel (Library of Living Philosophers Vol. XVII) ed. P. A. Schilpp and L. E. Hahn, La Salle, IL., Open Court, 1984.

Simonne Plourde, Gabriel Marcel. Philosophe et temoin de l´espérance. Montréal, Les Presses de l´Université du Québec, 1975.

55. Preface to Le Secret est dans les îles, pp. 7-8.

56. Le Monde cassé: Avant-Propos cited by G. Fessard in "Theatre et Mystere," p. 9; Gaston Fessard, "Theatre et Mystère," pp. 7-9; "My Dramatic Works as Viewed by the Philosopher," pp. 115-18; "Introduction," pp. 7-13 in Paix sur la terre, Deux discours une Tragédie, Paris, Aubier, 1965; The Existential Background of Human Dignity, p. 62; "An Autobiographical Essay," p. 58; En Chemin, vers quel eveil?, p. 139; Reply by Gabriel Marcel to "The idea of Mystery in the Philosophy of Gabriel Marcel," in The Philosophy of Gabriel Marcel, p. 273; Allocution for the Alliance Française, Gabriel Marcel: Le Paradoxe du Philosophe-Dramaturge.

57. "My Dramatic Works as Viewed by the Philosopher," p. 106.

58. "The Drama of the Soul in Exile," pp. 29-30; Notes d´Auteur: Chapelle Ardente, (1950), p. 142; "My Dramatic Works as Viewed by the Philosopher," pp. 115-16; The Existential Background of Human Dignity, p. 62, pp. 13-14; Preface to Percées vers un ailleurs, pp. II-VII.

59. L´Iconoclaste, Pièce en quatre actes, Collection Nouvelle de la France dramatique. (Répertoire choisi du théâtre moderne), No. 13 Supplement to the Revue Hebdomadaire January 27, 1923, Paris, Librairie Stock; Being and Having, pp. 116-20, 111, 141, 101; "On the Ontological Mystery," pp. 19-23; Creative Fidelity, p. 68; "The Drama of the Soul in Exile," pp. 28-30; The Existential Background of Human Dignity, pp. 48, 50-53.

60. Gaston Fessard, "Théâtre et Mystère," pp. 7-9; Joseph Chenu, Le Théâtre de Gabriel Marcel et sa signification métaphysique, pp. 17-18; Part Three, Section II, below pp. 187-96.

61. "Preface," Le Seuil Invisible, pp. 4-8; "My Dramatic Works as viewed by the Philosopher," p. 102.

62. "An Essay in Autobiography," p. 128; "The Drama of the Soul in Exile," pp. 38, 27-28; The Existential Background of Human Dignity, p. 50.

63. "My Dramatic Works as viewed by the Philosopher," pp. 108-109.

64. "My Dramatic Works as Viewed by the Philosopher," pp. 108-09.

CHRONOLOGICAL BIBLIOGRAPHY OF WORKS BY GABRIEL MARCEL ABOUT HIS THEATER

1. "Preface," Le Seuil Invisible, Paris: Editions Grasset, 1914, pp. 1-8.

2. "Réflexions sur le Tragique," L'Essor, No. 13, December 1921.

3. "Remarques sur l'Iconoclaste," Revue Hebdomadaire, 27 January 1923, pp. 492-500.

4. "Tragique et Personnalité," Nouvelle Revue Fraŋaise, January 1924, pp. 37-45.

5. "Notes sur l'evaluation tragique," Journal de Psychologie, January-March 1926, pp. 68-76.

6. "L'avant propos," Le Monde cassé," Paris: Desclée de Brouwer, 1933, pp. 7-9.

7. "Position et approches concrètes du mystère ontologique," Paris: Desclée de Brouwer, 1933, essay published with Le Monde cassé.

8. "Influence du Théâtre," Revue des Jeunes, 5 March 1935, pp. 349-62.

9. "Pour un renouveau de la spiritualité dans l'art dramatique," Combat, February 1937, pp. 458-68.

10. "Réflexions sur les exigences d'un théâtre chrétien," Vie Intellectuelle, 25 March 1937, pp. 458-68.

11. "Les Valeurs spirituelles dans le théâtre français contemporain," Orientations religieuses, intellectuelles et littéraires, Belgium: 25 June 1937, pp. 768-96.

12. "Postface" de L'Horizon, written 1944, reissued in Percées vers un ailleurs, Paris: Fayard, 1973, pp. 367-78.

13. "Le Temoignage comme localisation de l'existential," La Nouvelle Revue Théologique, 78th year, t. 68, no. 2, March-April 1946, pp. 182-91.

14. "De l'Audace en métaphysique," (1947), Revue de Métaphysique et de Morale, reissued in Percées vers un ailleurs, Paris: Fayard, 1973.

15. "Note de l'auteur," La Chapelle Ardente, Paris: La Table Ronde, 1950, pp. 139-42.

16. "The Drama of the Soul in Exile," Lecture given July 1950 at Institut Français in London, Preface, Three Plays, London: Secker and Warburg, 1952; New York: Hill and Wang, 1958, 1965, pp. 13-34.

17. "Les vrais problèmes de Rome n'est plus dans Rome," Conference 18 May 1951; Postface, Rome n'est plus dans Rome, Paris: La Table Ronde, 1951, pp. 149-78.

18. "Théâtre et Philosophie. Leurs rapports dans mon oeuvre," in Le Théâtre Contemporain (Recherches et Debats, no. 2), Paris: A. Fayard, 1952, pp. 17-42.

19. "Postface," Mon Temps n'est pas le votre, Paris: Plon, 1955, pp. 237-48.

20. "Postface," Croissez et multipliez, Paris: Plon, 1955, pp. 201-13.

21. "L'athéisme philosophique et la dialectique de la conscience religieuse," Athéisme contemporain, (Croire, penser, espérer). Genève: Labor et Fides; Paris: Librairie Protestante, 1956, p. 107.

22. Théâtre et Religion, Paris: Vitte, 1958: "Religion et Blasphème dans le théâtre français contemporain," Conference at Brussels, 1956, pp. 9-52; "L'idée du drame chrétien dans son rapport au théâtre actuel," Conference at Cobourg in Germany, 1957, pp. 53-97.

23. "Postface," La Dimension Florestan, Paris: Plon, 1958, pp. 159-69.

24. "Le Crépuscule du sens commun," essay published with La Dimension Florestan, Paris: Plon, 1958, pp. 170-212.

25. "My Dramatic Works as Viewed by the Philosopher," Conference at Freiburg im Breisgau, 1959; Searchings, New York: Newman Press, 1967, pp. 93-118.

26. "Avant-Propos," Présence et Immortalité, Paris: Flamarion, 1959, pp. 7-9; "Author's Preface," Presence and Immortality, translated by Michael A. Machado and revised by Henry J. Koren, Pittsburgh: Duquesne University Press, 1967, pp. 7-10.

27. "Avant-Propos," L'Heure théâtrale, Paris: Plon, 1959, pp. iii-xiii.

28. The Existential Background of Human Dignity, The William James Lectures delivered at Harvard University 1961-62, Cambridge, MA: Harvard University Press, 1963, 178 pp.

29. "Foreword" dated March 1962 to Kenneth T. Gallagher's The Philosophy of Gabriel Marcel, New York: Fordham University Press, 1962; reissued 1975, pp. VII-X.

30. Regards sur le Théâtre de Claudel, Paris: Beauchesne, 1964, 175 pp.

31. "Foreword" to Vincent P. Miceli, S. J.'s Ascent to Being: Gabriel Marcel's Philosophy of Communion, Paris, New York, Tournai, Rome: Desclée Company, 1965, pp. IX-XI.

32. "Avant-Propos," Paix sur la Terre, Paris: Aubier, 1965, pp. 7-13.

33. "Preface," Le Secret est dans les îles, Paris: Plon, 1967, pp. 7-24.

34. En chemin vers quel éveil? Paris: Gallimard, 1971, 301 pp.

35. "Note sur l'attestation créatrice dans mon oeuvre," Archivo di Filosofia, 1972, pp. 531-34.

36. "Préface," Percées vers un ailleurs, Paris: Fayard, 1973, pp. I-X.

37. "Introduction," The Existential Drama of Gabriel Marcel, West Hartford, CT: McAuley Institute of Religious Studies Press, 1974; letter to Francis J. Lescoe, editor, dated February 1, 1973, pp. 6-8, introduction enclosed pp. 9-18.

38. "De la recherche philosophique," Entretiens autour de Gabriel Marcel at Cerisy-la-Salle 24-31 August 1973, Neuchâtel, Switzerland, Editions de la Baconnière, 1976, pp. 9-19.

39. "Le Paradoxe du Philosophe - Dramaturge," Réalisations Sonores: Hughes De Salle, Collection Français de Notre Temps Nous Confie, Sous le patronage de l'Alliance Française, présentation écrite sur la pochette de Marc Blancpain, no date.

41

40. "An Autobiographical Essay" (Spring 1969), and replies to essays in The Philosophy of Gabriel Marcel, The Library of Living Philosophers, Vol. XVII, Paul A. Schilpp and Lewis E. Hahn, editors, La Salle, IL: Open Court, 1984, pp. 1-68, et passim.

BIBLIOGRAPHY OF WORKS ON GABRIEL MARCEL THAT CLARIFY THE NATURE OF HIS THEATER AND ITS RELATIONSHIP TO HIS PHILOSOPHY

Archambault, Paul. "Gabriel Marcel," in Temoins du spiritual, Paris: Bloud & Gay, 1933, pp. 139-76; Colin, 1947.

Bagot, Jean-Pierre. Connaissance et amour. Essai sur la philosophie de Gabriel Marcel. Paris: Beauchesne et ses fils, 1958.

Belanger, Gerard. L'Amour, chemin de la liberté. Paris: Editions ouvrières, 1965.

Belay, Marcel. "Commentaire sur l'Horizon," in Percées vers un ailleurs, Paris: Fayard, 1973, pp. 379-404.

_____. "Commentaire sur l'Iconoclaste," in Percées vers un ailleurs, Paris: Fayard, 1973, pp. 169-97.

_____. "Étude sur Le Mort de Demain," in Entretiens autour de Gabriel Marcel, Neuchâtel: La Baconnière, 1976, pp. 131-38.

_____. "La Grâce dans Le Monde cassé" (Entretiens de Dijon de Mars 1973), Revue de Métaphysique et de Morale, July-September 1974, 79th year, no. 3, pp. 370-75; discussion pp. 376-82.

_____. "La Mort et les morts dans l'oeuvre théâtrale de Gabriel Marcel." Doctoral dissertation, University of Dijon, France, 1977.

_____. La Mort dans le Théâtre de Gabriel Marcel, Paris: Vrin, 1980.

Berger, Gaston. "Constitution de l'univers théâtral," in Mélanges Georges Jamati. Paris: Editions du Centre National de la Recherche Scientifique, Paris, 1956.

Bernard, Michel. La philosophie religieuse de Gabriel Marcel. Etude critique. Le Puy: Cahiers du Nouvel Humanisme, 1952.

Berning, Vincent. "Données et conditions de l'accueil fait en Allemagne à Gabriel Marcel, philosophe et dramaturge," pp. 211-19, discussion pp. 220-37 in Entretiens autour de Gabriel Marcel, Neuchâtel: à la Baconnière, 1976.

Boutang, Pierre. Gabriel Marcel interrogé par Pierre Boutang, followed by "Position et approches concrètes du mystère ontologique." Paris: J. M. Place, (Archives du XXe Siècle), 1977, pp. 7-114.

_____. "Le Souci de la Transcendance," Revue de Métaphysique et de Morale, Vol. 79, No. 3, (July-Sept. 1974), pp. 315-37.

_____. La terreur en question. Lettre à Gabriel Marcel. Paris: Fasquelles Editeurs, 1958.

Bugbee, Henry G. "L'exigence ontologique" in The Philosophy of Gabriel Marcel. Vol. XVII (The Library of Living Philosophers) ed. P. A. Schilpp and L. E. Hahn, La Salle, IL: Open Court, 1984, pp. 81-93, reply pp. 94-98.

Cain, Seymour. Gabriel Marcel. New York: Hillary House, 1963; London: Bower and Bower, 1963; South Bend, IN: Regnery/Gateway, Inc., 1979.

Chaigne, Louis. Vie et oeuvres d'écrivains. 4th series. Paris: Lanore, 1954.

Chastaing, Maxime. "Le langage théâtral de Gabriel Marcel," (Entretiens de Dijon de mars 1973), Revue de Métaphysique et de Morale, Vol. 79, No. 3 (July-September 1974), pp. 354-63; discussion pp. 364-66.

Cheetham, M. "L'actualité de Monde cassé de Gabriel Marcel,"(Entretiens de Dijon de mars 1973), Revue de Métaphysique et de Morale, Vol. 79, No. 3 (July-September 1974), pp. 367-69.

Chenu, Joseph. Le Théâtre de Gabriel Marcel et sa signification metaphysique, Paris: Aubier, 1948.

_____. "Théâtre et Métaphysique," pp. 115-22, discussion, pp. 123-30 in Entretiens autour de Gabriel Marcel, Neuchâtel: à la Baconnière, 1976.

Davy, Marie-Madeleine. Un philosophe itinérant. Gabriel Marcel, Paris: Flammarion, 1959.

De Corte, Marcel. La philosophie de Gabriel Marcel, Paris: Téqui, 1938.

Delhomme, Jeanne. "Un Homme de Dieu," La Table Ronde, No. 24 (December 1949), pp. 48-52.

_____. "Témoignage et dialectique," pp. 117-201, in
Existentialisme chrétien: Gabriel Marcel, Paris: Plon,
1947.

Dubois-Dumée, J. P.   "Solitude et communion dans le
théâtre de Gabriel Marcel," pp. 249-90, in
Existentialisme chrétien: Gabriel Marcel, Paris: Plon,
1947.

De Lacoste, Guillemine. "Man´s Creativity in the Thought of
Marcel," The New Scolasticism, Vol. 48 (Autumn 1974),
pp. 409-23.

_____. "The Notion of Participation in the Early Drama and Early
Journals of Gabriel Marcel," Philosophy Today, Vol. 19
(Spring 1975), pp. 50-60.

Fessard, Gaston. Théâtre et Mystère, Paris: Tequi, 1938.

_____. "Théâtre et mystère. Le sens de l´oeuvre
dramatique de Gabriel Marcel," Etudes, No. 234 (1938), pp.
738-60; and Ibid., No. 235 (1938),
pp. 40-60.

_____. "Théâtre et mystère." Preface to La Soif by Gabriel
Marcel, Paris: Desclée de Brouwer, 1938.

Gallagher, Kenneth T. The Philosophy of Gabriel Marcel, Foreword
by Gabriel Marcel, New York: Fordham University Press, 1962
and 1975.

_____. "Truth and Freedom in Marcel," The Philosophy of Gabriel
Marcel. (The Library of Living Philosophers, Vol. XVII) ed
P. A. Schillp and L. E. Hahn, La Salle, IL: Open Court,
1984, pp. 371-88, reply pp. 389-90.

Gilson, Etienne. Existentialisme chrétien: Gabriel Marcel.
Presentation by Etienne Gilson. Text by Jeanne Delhomme,
Roger Troisfontaines, Pierre Colin, J. P. Dubois-Dumée,
Gabriel Marcel, Paris: Plon, 1947.

_____. "A unique philosopher," Philosophy Today, Vol. 3 (Winter
1959), pp. 278-89.

Gouhier, Henri. L´Essence du théâtre. (Essais et Critiques,
4) Paris: Plon; Brussels: de Klogge, 1943; new edition,
Paris: Aubier, 1968.

_____. "Le Théâtre dans la pensée de Gabriel Marcel," in Savoir, faire, espérer: limites de la raison, 2 volumes published on the occasion of the fiftieth anniversary of the School of Philosophie and Religious Sciences and in honor of Msgr. Henri Van Camp. Brussels: Publications des Facultés Universitaires Saint Louis, 1976, pp. 407-23.

_____. Le Théâtre et l'existence (Philosophie de l'esprit), Paris: Aubier, 1952; reissued J. Vrin, 1973.

_____. "Théâtre et engagement" in Entretiens autour de Gabriel Marcel, Neuchâtel: à la Baconnière, 1976, pp. 95-102, discussion pp. 103-13.

_____. L'Oeuvre théâtrale (Bibliothèque d'Esthétique), Paris: Flammarion, 1958.

_____. "Ou en sommes nous?" Recherches et Débats 2, Le Théâtre Contemporain, Paris: Fayard, 1952, pp. 9-16.

_____. "Philosophie et théâtre" dans L'Encyclopédie fraçaise, t.XIX, Philosophie Religion, Paris: Larousse, 1957, 19. 30 6-8.

_____. "Tragique et Transcendence" in Le théâtre tragique, Etudes réunies et presentées par Jean Jacquot, Paris, Centre National de la Recherche Scientifique, 3rd edition 1970, pp. 479-83.

Hartshorne, Charles. "Marcel on God and Causality," The Philosophy of Gabriel Marcel, (The Library of Living Philosophers Vol. XVII) ed. P. A. Schilpp and L. E. Hahn, La Salle, IL: Open Court, 1984, pp. 353-66, reply by Gabriel Marcel, pp. 367-70.

Hocking, W. E. "Marcel and the Ground Issues of Metaphysics," Philosophy and Phenomenological Research (1954), pp. 439-69.

Keen, Samuel. "The Development of the Idea of Being in the Thought of Marcel," The Philosophy of Gabriel Marcel (Library of Living Philosophers Vol. XVII), ed. P. A. Schilpp and L. E. Hahn, La Salle, IL: Open Court, 1984, pp. 99-120, reply by Gabriel Marcel pp. 121-22.

_____. Gabriel Marcel, London: Carey Kingsgate Press, 1967; Richmond, VA: John Knox Press, 1967.

45

Jouve, Raymond. "Un Théâtre de la Sincéreté, Gabriel Marcel, métaphysicien et dramaturge," Etudes, 5 and 20 April 1932, pp. 21-34; 171-84.

Lescoe, Francis J. Existentialism with or without God, New York: Alba House, 1974, Chapter III, pp 77-132.

_____. (ed.) The Existentialist Drama of Gabriel Marcel, Letter and Introduction by Gabriel Marcel. Introduction by Francis J. Lescoe. The Broken World and The Rebellious Heart, English versions of Le Monde cassé and Le Coeur des autres, translated by Sister J. Marita Paul Colla, R. S. M., and Rev. Francis C. O'Hara, respectively, West Hartford, CT: McAuley Institute, St. Joseph College, 1974.

Miceli, Vincent P. Ascent to Being, Gabriel Marcel's Philosophy of Communion, New York, Tournai, Paris, Rome: Desclée, 1965.

Moeller, Charles. "Gabriel Marcel et le 'mystére' de l'espérance," pp. 149-79, in Littérature du XXe siècle et christianisme, IV, L'espérance en Dieu notre père, Paris: Casterman, 1960.

_____. Man and Salvation in Literature, translated by Charles Underhill Quinn, Notre Dame, IN: University of Notre Dame Press, 1970.

Mesnard, Pierre. "Le Monde cassé" in La Vie Intellectuelle, 15 March 1935, pp. 306-12.

Ngimbi-Nseka, H. Tragique et Intersubjectivité dans la Philosophie de Gabriel Marcel, Mayidi, B. P. 6/224. Inkisi., Publications du Grand Seminaire de Mayidi No. 1, 1981.

Novak, Michael. "Marcel at Harvard," The Commonweal, Vol. 77, No. 2, (Oct. 5, 1962), pp. 31-33.

O'Malley, John B. The Fellowship of Being, An essay on the concept of person in the philosophy of Gabriel Marcel, The Hague: Martinus Nijhoff, 1966.

Parain-Vial, Jeanne. Gabriel Marcel et les niveaux de l'expérience, Présentation, choix de textes et textes inédites, Paris: Seghers, 1966.

_____. "L'Etre et essences dans la philosophie de Gabriel Marcel," Revue de Théologie et de Philosophie, No. 2(1974), pp. 81-98.

_____. "L´Etre et le Temps chez Gabriel Marcel," pp. 187-201; discussion pp. 202-10, in Entretiens autour de Gabriel Marcel, Neuchâtel: à la Baconnière, 1976.

_____. "L´espérance et l´être dans la philosophie de Gabriel Marcel," Les Etudes Philosophiques, January-March 1975, pp. 19-30.

_____. "Sur la paternité selon Gabriel Marcel," Archives de Philosophie du Droit, Tome 20, (1975), pp. 149-62.

_____. "Le Tragique: L´experience existentielle face à la contestation marxiste," Révue de Métaphysique et de Morale, pp. 246-60.

Pax, Clyde Victor. "An Existentialist Approach to God: A Study of Gabriel Marcel," The Hague: Martinus Nijhoff, 1972.

_____. "Marcel´s Way of Creative Fidelity," Philosophy Today, Vol. 19 (Spring 1975), pp. 12-21.

Piguet, J. Claude. "De l´esthétique à la métaphysique," Revue de Théologie et de Philosophie, Vol. 8, no. 1, 1958, pp. 30-41.

Plourde, Simonne. Gabriel Marcel philosophe et temoin de l´espérance, Montréal: Les Presses de l´Université de Québec, 1975.

_____. Jeanne Parais-Vial, René Davignon, Marcel Belay. Vocabulaire philosophique de Gabriel Marcel, (Recherches. Nouvelle Serie - 6) Montreal, Bellarmin, Paris, Cerf, 1985, p. 241.

Prini, Pietro. Gabriel Marcel e la metodologia dell´inverificabile, Pref. di Gabriel Marcel, Roma: Studium, 1950. 125 pp. French trans. Gabriel Marcel et la méthodologie de l´inverifiable, Lettre-préface de Gabriel Marcel, Paris, Desclée de Brouwer, 1952, 129 pp. (2nd ed. Roma: Studium Abete, 1968, 170 pp.).

_____. "A Methodology of the Unverifiable," The Philosophy of Gabriel Marcel, (The Library of Living Philosophers Vol. XVII), ed. P. A. Schilpp and L. E. Hahn, La Salle, IL: Open Court, 1984, pp. 205-39; Reply by Gabriel Marcel, pp. 240-43.

Ralston, Zachary Taylor. Gabriel Marcel´s Paradoxical Expression of Mystery, A Stylistic Study of La Soif, Washington, D.C.: The Catholic University of America Press, 1961.

47

Ricoeur, Paul. Entretiens Paul Ricoeur, Gabriel Marcel, Paris: Aubier, Montaigne, 1968.

_____. "Conversations between Paul Ricoeur and Gabriel Marcel," included in Tragic Wisdom and Beyond, Evanston, IL: Northwestern University Press, 1973, trans. Peter McCormick.

_____. Gabriel Marcel et Karl Jaspers, deux maîtres de l´existentialisme, Paris: Edition du Temps Présent, 1948.

_____. "Gabriel Marcel et la phenomenologie," pp. 52-74, discussion pp. 75-94 in Entretiens autour de Gabriel Marcel, Neuchâtel: à la Baconnière, 1976.

_____. "Gabriel Marcel and Phenomenology," The Philosophy of Gabriel Marcel, (The Library of Living Philosophers Vol. XVII), ed. P. A. Schilpp and L. E. Hahn, LaSalle, IL: Open Court, 1984, pp. 471-94, Reply by Gabriel Marcel, pp. 495-98.

Schwarz, Balduin V. (ed.) The Human Person and the World of Values, New York: Fordham University Press, 1960.

Spiegelberg, Herbert. "Gabriel Marcel as a Phenomenologist," pp. 421-44, Vol. 2, The Phenomenological Movement, A Historical Introduction, 2 vols, The Hague: Martinus Nijhoff, 1960.

Stern, Karl. "Death within Life," Review of Existential Psychology and Psychiatry, (Pittsburgh), Vol. 2, No. 2 (1962), pp. 141-44.

Thevenaz, Pierre. "La Philosophie de M. Gabriel Marcel, Une métaphysique de la présence et de la fidélité," Revue de Théologie et de Philosophie, vol. 26, 1938, pp. 235-43.

Thibon, Gustave. "Une Métaphysique de la Communion: L´Existentialisme de Gabriel Marcel," Revue de Philosophe, 1946, Paris: Téque, 1947, pp. 144-64.

Troisfontaines, Roger. De l´existence à l´être. La philosophie de Gabriel Marcel, 2 vols., Louvain, Nauwelaerts, Paris: Vrin, 1953, 2nd ed. 1968.

_____. "What is Existentialism?" Thought, Vol. 32, No. 127, (Winter 1957-58), pp. 516-32.

Tilliette, Xavier. "Gabriel Marcel et l´Autre Royaume" in Jean Wahn et Gabriel Marcel, Paris: Beauchesne, 1976, pp. 35-56.

_____. "Gabriel Marcel et le socratisme chrétien," pp. 9-47, in Philosophes contemporains: Gabriel Marcel, Maurice Merleau-Ponty, Karl Jaspers, Paris: Desclée de Brouwer, 1962.

Vergote, Antoine. "L´avenement du Je et l´evenement de vérité dans le temoignage," Temoignage, Paris: Aubier, 1972.

Wahl, Jean. Vers le concret, Paris: Vrin, 1932.

addendum: appeared as this work goes to press too late for consultation but in time for mention in bibliographic references:

GABRIEL MARCEL-GASTON FESSARD   CORRESPONDANCE (1934-1971) présentée et annotée par Henri de Lubac, Marie Rougier et Michel Sales, introduction par Xavier Tilliette, Paris: Beauchesne, 1985.

PART TWO:

DRAMATIC APPROACHES TO CREATIVE FIDELITY

Part Two. Dramatic Approaches to Creative Fidelity

53

Chapter II. The Unfathomable: A Search for Presence

On September 13, 1973, I had the privilege of a two-hour conversation with Gabriel Marcel. Our talk had none of the awkwardness of a first meeting. Rather, it had been one of my distinct good fortunes as a philosopher to have first become acquainted with him in Louvain in 1958. Since his four-day visit to Le Moyne College in 1965, I believe it is not presumptuous to have claimed genuine friendship with this great philosopher.

In the foreword, I have recounted some of the topics and tone of our September conversation. Three weeks later, I was back in America and learned to my sadness that the conversation had been our last. Gabriel Marcel passed away on October 8, 1973.

Three topics kept appearing and reappearing in that last conversation--his preoccupation with the presence of loved ones who have gone beyond death; his concern with the continuing fulfillment of life in the light of God; and his assurance of a spiritual bond between loved ones that will not be broken. The topics are so tightly woven to the texture of human life that they were profoundly moving, even as he spoke. With his death they took on new meaning. For the three converge in another theme that was one of Marcel´s richest sources of philosophic reflection--that of death and immortality.

In these pages, I would like to present some humble tribute to one who richly enlarged twentieth-century man´s self-understanding and self-appreciation. The theme I shall consider is that of immortality, from the perspective of love and interpersonal presence. It is a theme that was the subject of a continuing existential quest throughout Marcel´s lifework. I would hope that the following pages not only illuminate his past thought, but also reveal the perspective from which his light may continue to be experienced.

Marcel stated clearly that his concern with death is precisely from the perspective of one who is concerned for a loved one who has died.(1) From his point of view, the existential problem of death is the problem of the conflict between love and death.(2) This unique perspective on death and immortality, which issues in a phenomenological analysis of survival, is intimately linked with his conviction that BEING is fundamentally intersubjective.(3)

Thus, following the lead of Marcel´s own thought, the precise question we shall pursue here is that of seeking the nature of the phenomenon and the conditions that can provide for the continued presence of a loved one beyond death. The principal textual sources we shall draw upon are those published in a book entitled <u>Presence and Immortality.</u> This book, rich in resources and replete with detailed critical analyses, was published in English in 1967 by Duquesne University Press. It includes four works: an essay written in 1937 entitled "My Fundamental Purpose"; entries from Marcel's "Metaphysical Journal for the years 1938-1943"; a 1951 essay entitled "Presence and Immortality," which, significantly, was originally entitled "The Existential Premises of Immortality"; and the script of the first act of an unfinished play, <u>The Unfathomable,</u> written in 1917.

Our procedure will be to first examine the play, as this portrays the existential situation wherein the death of a beloved person occurs. Subsequently, we shall trace Marcel's critical analysis of the existential premises of immortality as he articulates these through his philosophic essays.

For Marcel, it is the art of theater to portray an existential situation. Thus drama communicates a lived experience and allows us to enter into its world. In <u>The Unfathomable,</u> we confront a situation that questions the survival of a loved one. Moreover, the stances of the different characters invite us to consider critically the alternate opinions we may have toward someone's death.

The central event that gives rise to the drama in the first act of <u>The Unfathomable</u> is the fact that Maurice Lechevallier has been reported as missing in action at the end of World War I. The drama portrays the existential situation wherein the various members of his family react to the news of Maurice's disappearance. Each construes and interprets the significance of his fate differently. As the action evolves, it becomes clear that each one's determination of what Maurice's absence means is to a large extent determined by the attitude that individual had toward him and the type of relationship they had shared.

Perhaps, as with the two neighbors, Lise Breton and Francine Vadot, a death may be a subject of curiosity, a topic of gossip. We may remain insensitive to the fact that this event involves a person whom others hold as a loved one. Or the stance may be that displayed by Robert, who proclaims that the facts must be accepted. For him, Maurice is dead and exists no more. Robert's memories fade and appear to fall short of the reality. He even begins to doubt if he ever knew his brother at all. Maurice's wife, Georgette, fearfully worries whether she will have him back, or whether she should start a new life without him. Madame Lechevallier, Maurice's mother, really wishes that he would reappear, for his sake, his wife's, and, of course, also her own. Père Seveilhac insists that Maurice has returned to God and has left his loved ones for good. They can only pray for him.

The various attitudes conveyed by these characters seem to put in relief that of Edith, Maurice's sister-in-law, who accepts that Maurice has died and mourns him, but enjoys the assurance that he continues to live, for she experiences the gift of his presence through love, bestowing refreshment and renewal of life. Three or four of her speeches convey her sense of experiencing his presence and even intimate the subjective dispositions requisite for the continued conferral of intersubjective presence. Her testimony is dramatically poignant.

Edith's speeches in her dialogue with Père Seveilhac are significant for the testimony they present and the description they offer of the type of experience she witnesses.

> Edith (to Père Seveilhac): I can't say to what extent your words chill me ....It seems this prayer to which you invite me exiles me from those for whom it is offered; between them and us, it puts more than space, it puts God himself. One can only pray for those who are truly absent, ... but you can't pretend that death is an absence! There are times when he is more immediately present to me than he ever was in life. No longer is there between him and me this dreadful fear of thinking of one another in a sinful way; no longer is there the disturbing image of third parties...there are no longer any third parties. Don't give me that harsh look, Father; I see too clearly that you don't grasp. And yet, you should remember, you should understand.(4)

> Edith: ...All that is wrong, all that is outside what I feel and live.(5)

> Edith (in a muffled voice): This feeling of absence that a dead loved one could not awaken in us. I experience for my husband with a horrible intensity .... He is always at a distance--and that is not saying enough, for space itself does not separate those who worship one another. He is not with me, we are not together; we are ... I don't know how to explain to you, ... let us say, like objects placed near one another, forever outside one another. And yet, if only you knew how passionately I desired that it be otherwise. (6)

Edith: ... You tell me that nothing outside can
respond to my feeling. I don´t know what you mean by
that. Or rather yes, I think I know. (With sobs in
her throat) Basically, for you, the dead are no
longer there; and your thoughts are in no way
different from those who do not believe. Whatever be
the glorious and unimaginable existence that you
ascribe to them ... for you they are no longer of the
living. But for me ... the truly dead, the only dead
are those whom we no longer love. (7)

Edith: When I think of him in a certain way--with
tenderness, with recollection--there wells up in me
something like a richer, deeper life in which I know
he participates. This life is not I, nor is it he;
it is both of us. Shall I admit it to you? I was
hoping a little that you would be able to take part
in this kind of conversation without words, the
sweetness of which...(with emotion). Why does it
seem to me now that I am violating a sacred
prohibition by telling you that? It is something
about which one must not speak (sternly) with a
stranger. In reality, I have betrayed him.(8)

The lived experience of love and presence, of the assurance
of the survival of a loved one beyond death, an experience that
Edith´s words witness and describe, and an experience that can be
the reader´s own, is the mystery that the philosopher is called
upon to analyze and to clarify. As Marcel writes in another
context: "But the role of the philosopher is to raise to the
level of articulated thought what is here only pre-knowledge and
song."(9)

Marcel carries on such critical analysis and reflective
clarification through entries in his "Metaphysical Journal
1938-1943" and in a phenomenological analysis of survival that
animates his essay "Presence and Immortality."

We can by no means reproduce here the thoroughness of the
detailed analyses and the patient critical probing that Marcel´s
thought brings to bear in questioning the existential premises
for the continued presence of a beloved beyond death. We can,
however, trace the main lines of his thought as he clarifies what
he calls the "presential character" of immortality and uncovers
the existential conditions of its possibility.

The major elements Marcel introduces to clarify the

presential character of intersubjective being are: 1) the overcoming of the categories derived from the model of objects and their relationships, in order to think of presence in terms of intersubjective relationships; 2) a careful investigation of how a subject who is not a physically present object can nevertheless be actually present, affecting and enriching the being of a person; and 3) a reflective examination of the significant difference between possessive desire and the oblative love that animates hope.

Prior to any understanding of the genuine presential character of intersubjectivity, it is necessary to overcome the temptation to think of "presence" in terms of physical objects and those categories proper to their relationships. Marcel effects this correction of thought by inviting those who would give such reductionistic interpretations to recognize the fundamental presupposition implied by their interpretations. The pretension that being physically near or juxtaposed in space constitutes "presence" is belied by our own experience as well as by the sense of Edith´s remarks. One can be juxtaposed to another in space, be near in terms of physical proximity, and yet still be alien or distant, far from either offering or welcoming interpersonal presence. As Edith remarks,

Edith (in a muffled voice): This feeling of absence that a dead loved one could not awaken in us I experience for my husband with a horrible intensity . . . He is always at a distance--and that is not saying enough, for space itself does not separate those who worship one another. He is not with me, we are not together; we are . . . , I don´t know how to explain to you, . . . let us say, like objects placed near one another, forever outside one another. And yet if you only knew how passionately I desired that it be otherwise.(10)

Or as Marcel comments in "Presence and Immortality,"

For instance, we may have the very strong feeling that someone who is in the room, very close to us, someone whom we can see and hear and whom we can touch, IS NEVERTHELESS NOT PRESENT. He is infinitely farther from us than such a loved one who is thousands of miles away or who even no longer belongs to our world. What then is this presence which is here lacking?(11)

Marcel then points out that intersubjective presence, which

is of a completely different order from physical proximity, requires personal openness, that is, a person's availability to the other's appeal or revelation. In contrast to the distance that estranges the opaque and self-absorbed individual from his deepest self and from others, the open person, self-possessed and capable of self-giving, is available to be with and for the other.(12)

In continuing his assertion that physical categories fall short in any attempt to account for intersubjective presence, Marcel points out that material communication may take place between two individuals without the phenomenon of communion that characterizes interpersonal presence. As he writes in "Presence and Immortality":

> It would not be correct to say that we cannot communicate with this individual who is there very close to us, for he is neither deaf, nor blind, nor half-witted. Between us a certain material communication is assured, but only a material one. It is in every way comparable to the kind which can be set up between two distinct stations, one sending and the other receiving. However the essential thing is lacking. One could say that there is communication without communion, and for this reason it is unreal communication.

Marcel continues,

> The other hears the words that I say; but he does not hear me and I can be painfully aware that these words, as he relays them back to me, words which he reflects upon, become for me unrecognizable.(13)

Thus Marcel observes that it is not material communication that creates intersubjective presence. Rather it is the openness and the spiritual exchange of love that create communion. Of an entirely different order from the transmission of material forms is the co-esse or the radiant communication of the being of the other person that constitutes intersubjective communion. In "Presence and Immortality" he writes,

> This experience that I have had a hundred times is one of the most mysterious that exists and it appears to me to be among those to which philosophers have never paid any attention. One could say that it is, in the best sense, existential. For it is not so much what the other says, the content of his words

60

which exercises on me this stimulating action, but it is he himself saying these words, he himself inasmuch as he sustains his own words by all that he is.(14)

As Marcel has clarified in other contexts, this communion is a state of being together in our difference. Such community of being is constituted as an interpersonal event co-authored by freedoms in the dialogue of appeal, availability, receptivity, and commitment. Its enduring quality may be characterized by belonging. Belonging—or the commitment and creative fidelity of intersubjective being—may be phrased in affirmations like these: "I am with and for you." "You have at your disposal all that I am and can be for you." "Your hopes, projects, fullness of life pertain to me as my own." "I am responsive to your new questions and new directions of growth; and I will be responsible for sustaining and supporting them."(15)

Marcel concludes, then, that presence through interpersonal communion is constituted by the distinctive event "that the other, if I feel him present, renews me interiorly in some way. This presence is in such a case revelatory; it makes me more fully myself than I would be without it."(16) Or as Edith´s speech expresses it,

When I think of him in a certain way—with tenderness, with recollection—there wells up in me something like a richer, deeper life in which I know he participates. This life is not I, nor is it he; it is both of us. Shall I admit it to you? I was hoping a little that you would be able to take part in this kind of conversation without words, the sweetness of which . . . . (with emotion). Why does it seem to me now that I am violating a sacred prohibition by telling you that? It is something about which one must not speak (sternly) with a stranger. In reality, I have betrayed him.(17)

Thus, Marcel has shown that although physical nearness and material communication may often be the circumstances in which presence occurs, they do not account for, nor do they constitute, the event of interpersonal presence. Moreover, it has become apparent that presence may occur without these circumstances, for the conditions of possibility and the distinctive event of interpersonal presence arise from an entirely different order of being. The requisite conditions for intersubjective being or events of interpersonal presence are the attitudes that characterize personhood; namely, openness, availability, and

61

especially that unity and luminescent quality of personhood whereby one is capable of self-possession and therefore self-giving. Presence is then constituted by the interaction of people who, in their freedom and grace, can make that commitment of responsible self-gift to be with and for the other. And the "substance" of presence reveals itself to be that event or bond of love whereby the being and life of one and the other are interiorly enriched, inspired, and supported toward a creative fulfillment that is together hoped for.

Turning now to the second perspective of questioning, let us consider what can be the mode of presence of the "thou" to "me," especially when that thou is a beloved beyond death.

Marcel inquires how the other, who is neither a thing nor an objective person, can nevertheless be present. Or, as he phrases it in "An Essay in Autobiography," "Perhaps I can best explain my continual and central metaphysical preoccupation by saying that my aim was to discover how a subject, in his actual capacity as subject, is related to a reality which cannot in this context be regarded as objective, yet which is persistently required and recognized as real."(18)

The challenge is then to think of the way in which a subject can relate to a reality that is in no way an object. Since the relationship of communion is conceived in terms of a bond of spiritual exchange, it is consistent to think of the proper mode of interpersonal presence in terms of spiritual interaction.

This means that the model of subject object dichotomy, or of a transmission linking two stations outside each other, should be radically transcended. These models have a mode of relationship proper to things in a world of objectivity. Love is the relationship proper to persons in the realm of intersubjectivity. Thus the mode of conceiving the interpersonal relationship of presence should reflect the way in which a subject encounters the active influence of another subject who is with and for him.

Reflecting on the spiritual exchange that characterizes participation in intersubjective being, Marcel points out that the subject encounters the spiritual influence of the other by way of interiority or inwardness, as a spiritual influx or an inward accretion that profoundly affects one´s being. Hence the way toward encountering the presence of the other is through one´s own interiority and depth. The other then becomes present in and through an active relationship of spiritual influx that enriches and affects one´s being. Hence the relationship proper to intersubjective being is an encounter of a transcendence by way of immanence. The subject who possesses or recollects himself finds that he may participate in or draw upon personalizing forces that are more and other than his own alone. The subject who invokes the presence of the other may find the active influx of a spiritual influence that bestows benefits that enrich and affect his very being. And this influx can be recognized as originating in the other as its source.

We find Marcel's succinct and positive description of this in "An Essay in Autobiography."

> A presence is a reality; it is a kind of influx; (The word influx, . . . conveys the kind of interior accretion, of accretion from within, which comes into being as soon as presence is effective.) It depends upon us to be permeable to this influx, but not, to tell the truth, to call it forth. Creative fidelity consists in maintaining ourselves actively in a permeable state; and there is a mysterious interchange between this free act and the gift granted in response to it.(19)

One might be inclined to identify the structure of presence in technical terms as the active relationship of encountering an immanent transcendence. Yet Marcel declines technical terminology, preferring to articulate the unique phenomenon in the specific language it presents. I believe this arises from Marcel's determination to analyze and interpret the mystery of presence in a manner faithful to the evidence given within the experience. I find, moreover, that this procedure heightens the originality of his interpretation of presence. He insists on the delicate blending of unity and duality in presence. He acknowledges its predominant unity as communion yet also recognizes the intersubjectivity of its coauthoring and being.

He observes that perhaps the idea of relationship with its strong emphasis on duality is not appropriate to identify presence.(20) He notes that its unity is stressed and expressed by the statement, "This life is not I, nor is it he; it is both of us."(21) And, in speaking of creative fidelity, he points out that the idea of unity of communion in presence is articulated as "you are with me," which transcends the dualistic and problematic categories of "before me" or "within me."

> When I say that a being is granted to me as a presence or as a being (it comes to the same, for he is not a being for me unless he is a presence), this means that I am unable to treat him as if he were merely placed in front of me; between me and him

there arises a relationship which, in a sense, surpasses my awareness of him; he is not only before me, he is also within me--or, rather, these categories are transcended, they have no longer any meaning.(22)

Even if I cannot see you, if I cannot touch you, I feel that you are with me; it would be a denial of you not to be assured of this...With me: note the metaphysical value of this word, so rarely recognized by philosophers, which corresponds neither to a relationship of inherence or immanence nor to a relationship of exteriority. It is of the essence of genuine co-esse -..."(23)

Elsewhere in the same essay he writes:

If presence were merely an idea in us whose characteristic was that it was nothing more than itself, then the most we could hope would be to maintain this idea in us or before us, as one keeps a photograph on a mantelpiece or in a cupboard. But it is of the nature of presence as presence to be uncircumscribed; and this takes us beyond the frontier of the problematical. Presence is mystery in the exact measure in which it is presence.(24)

Marcel thinks of presence as trans-subjective.(25) Presence is the sharing, the active participation in the enriched life and being of intersubjectivity. In this phenomenon the frontier between the I and the thou is transcended; the essence of presence is the unity of communion.(26)

Yet presence brings the other to be with one effectively. The other is really there--in his being, actively constituting the event and contributing from his uniqueness to the enrichment of the life that presence provides.

Marcel shows that the genuine experience of presence is characterized by openness and active receptivity, attitudes that both recognize and highlight the gratuitous and active intervention of the other that is required to effect the co-constituted event of presence.

In speaking of presence, Marcel maintains the delicate balance that "it depends upon us to be permeable to this influx, but not, to tell the truth, to call it forth."(27) The one who retains this openness and active receptivity recognizes that there is a gratuity to the occurrence of that spiritual influx that constitutes presence. For in the same context Marcel writes of creative fidelity:

Creative fidelity consists in maintaining ourselves actively in a permeable state; and (it can be recognized) there is a mysterious interchange between this free act and the gift granted in response to it.(28)

And he further points out that a reciprocal fidelity is required for

an active perpetuation of presence, the renewal of its benefits--of its virtue which consists in a mysterious incitement to create.(29)

Moreover, he continues,

Thus if creative fidelity is conceivable, it is because fidelity is ontological in its principle, because it prolongs presence which itself corresponds to a certain kind of hold which being has upon us; because it multiplies and deepens the effect of this presence almost unfathomably in our lives.(30)

And he points out,

This seems to me to have almost inexhaustible consequences, if only for the relationships between the living and the dead.(31)

For, as he comments in this essay "On the Ontological Mystery" and in entries in his "Metaphysical Journal for the years 1938-1943,"

When I say that a being is granted to me as a presence or as a being (it comes to the same, for he is not a being for me unless he is a presence)....(32)

this involves recognizing that

Revelation is the opposite of inquiry.(33)...and in revealing himself to me the other somehow draws me to himself; and on condition that I consent to it, he lifts me out of this world where I tend to be only a thing among things.(34)

65

By preserving the delicate balance of thinking of presence predominantly as a unity of communion, yet also recognizing its duality--as intersubjectivity of being--through its traits of gratuity and otherness--Marcel metaphysically situates the subject as one open to an influx of participation in being, as in the model of artistic creation whereby "the world is present to the artist, to his heart and to his mind, present to his very being."(35) He thereby transcends the arbitrary limitations of a metaphysics that considers the subject only as an ego, closed on itself, or as a cogito hermetically sealed off from other reality, in which context an immanent experience is interpreted as nothing more than an isolated nomad's lonely, subjective projections--a poor caricature and sad travesty of the genuine phenomenon of presence.(36)

In "Presence and Immortality," Marcel introduces the metaphor of light to further clarify the nature of presence. He points out that it is only in the context of a philosophy of light that we can see emerge the deepest implications of openness for presence and intersubjectivity of being.

He writes,

> One could say that intersubjectivity is the fact of being together in the light. Here as always perhaps, by proceeding negatively one can approach the positive essence toward which it is a matter of directing one's thought. If, in the presence of another person I am burdened with mental reservations about him, or if, which amounts exactly to the same thing, I attribute to him some ulterior motives concerning me, it is obvious we are not together in the light. I put myself in the shade. At once, he ceases to be present to me, and reciprocally, I can no longer be present to him.(37)

However, he observes in "My Fundamental Purpose,"

> the world of the other becomes illumined with an increasingly intense light as the I dispels more of its own darkness and dispels it more heroically.(38)

He continues,

> The more we endeavor to communicate with ourselves--by that I mean with what in us at first appears as most recalcitrant to a certain intellectual penetration--the more we free ourselves

from the automatism which is nothing but a petrifying of our judgment.(39)

So the more closedness is transcended to openness, the more darkness and estrangement are dispelled to disclose the luminous quality of ourselves and the luminescent presence of the beloved, until finally one enjoys a presence that gives rise to an invincible assurance that is communicated by love. As Marcel writes in conclusion to this section of the phenomenological analysis of survival in "Presence and Immortality,"

It expresses itself by some such affirmations as: "I am assured that you are present to me and this assurance is linked with the fact that you do not stop helping me, that you help me perhaps more directly than you could on earth. We are together in the light. More exactly, in moments when I am detached from myself, when I cease to eclipse myself, I gain access to a light which is your light. Surely I do not mean the light of which you are the source, but that in which you yourself blossom, that which you help to reflect or radiate upon me."(40)

Thus, intersubjectivity, or being in the presence of one another, involves an event articulated by freedoms and grace. By presence one´s being and life in its most deeply personal acts is enriched by the active influx of the other in whose light they are inspired, uplifted, supported, and sustained. Being together in the light, the other is really and actively present to me, gracing my being with a light and personalizing force that I cannot but acknowledge as other and more than my own alone. For it should indeed be noted that it depends upon me to remain open and permeable to this gift of presence, but not in fact to call it forth. As interpersonal presence, its conferral comes as a gratuitous influx in response to an openness of appeal.(41)

The third and final perspective we shall explore for its significant illumination of the question of presence and immortality is the difference between desire and hope. Early in "Presence and Immortality," Marcel states that he finds this difference most significant if one is to achieve his aspiration to maintaining a living relationship of active communication with a loved one who has died. In this section we shall first note the difference between desire and hope and then explore its significance to the quest to maintain the presence of a beloved beyond death.

Speaking of the significant difference between desire and

hope, Marcel notes:

> This whole investigation could be articulated only by
> starting out from what came to me as a
> discovery--that of the difference, often ignored even
> by the most distinguished persons, between desire and
> hope.
>
> Desire is by definition egocentric: it tends toward
> possession. The other is then considered only in
> reference to me, to the enjoyments which he can
> procure me if I am full of lust; or he is seen simply
> in relation to the services which he will be able to
> render me. Hope on the other hand is not egocentric:
> to hope, I have written in Homo Viator, is always to
> hope for us. Let us say that hope is never the state
> of wishful thinking which can express itself by an "I
> would very much wish that." Hope implies a prophetic
> assurance which is really its armor and which
> prevents the being from breaking down, internally
> first of all; but it also prevents him from giving
> up, that is to say surrendering or degrading
> himself....(42)

He further elaborates the distinction between desire and
hope by pointing out that, on the one hand, desire is structured
to that mode of relationship of "having," which is geared to the
possession of a thing, while hope, on the other hand, is animated
by generous love.(43) The love that animates hope then is not
possessive and self-centered, but rather self-giving and
other-directed. Thus he writes, "human love--and this word is
broad enough to be applicable also to friendship, to philia
--implies a reciprocity profound enough to let other-directedness
work both ways, to let each become the center for the other.
Thus is created a unity which is no less mysterious than that I
spoke of in relation to incarnation."(44)

Now the attitudes characteristic of "having" must be
transcended if one´s quest for active communication with the
loved one beyond death is not to fall short and fail.

Marcel writes:

> One can affirm in principle, it seems, that the more
> the relationship which has united me to another being
> has been strictly possessive, the more his
> disappearance must come to be likened to the loss of
> an object. True, the lost object can under certain

exceptional conditions be found again, but one cannot attribute to it any presential character.(45)

As one tries to relocate a loved one who has died, there is the inclination to reach for memories or images recalled from the past. Yet if this quest yields to the weight of desire, one's search tries to find something that was lost. One attempts to relocate a person, as an object, to find him again as he was in the past. Yet this temptation is frustrating, for the person is no longer there as an object. And the images or memories one tries to hold and manipulate in this search become fixed and appear as stale replicas or pale counterfeits of the sadly desired loved one. As Marcel observes in entries in his "Metaphysical Journal for the Years 1938-1943," the most this attitude of desire attains is a reconsideration of images, "like photographs that one can handle at will; but which images are inert and passive in my hands."(46) Or, at worst, it may find the object of search as dried bones or as a notary's statistic that inclines one to despair, for these are but hollow substitutes for the person sought.(47)

Images, memories, replicas of events may serve to give focus to an inner activity that seeks the actual presence of the beloved. But it is requisite that the desire for possession be overcome, so that hope may lead one's aspiration to maintain a living relationship of active communication with the beloved beyond death.(48)

The attitude of desire toward "having," having the other there as a subject who is an object, having precise services rendered as demanded in particular circumstances, must be transcended to reach the more genuine attitude of participating in intersubjective being, admiringly and gratefully being with and for the other and reciprocally acknowledging that the other remains with and for me.

Let us consider what there is about hope that makes it indispensible in providing for presence in immortality. Hope is animated by "oblative" love, a love willing to let go of the other, and willing to let the other be in a transformed mode of life, brings with it an assurance of a fullness of life for us. In this, hope affects both the clarification of the conditions of possibility for continued and renewed presence, and also the tone and focus of one's appeal for that presence.(49)

First, hope provides assurance of the grounds for a living relationship of active communication with the actual personal being of the beloved. For hope carries the assurance that the loved one continues to live, "not merely to exist as sealed off but to be capable of awareness and capable of responsibility."(50) So while one acknowledges that the other now lives a transposed mode of life, one is nonetheless assured that his personal being endures and that the living reality of intersubjective being will continue to be renewed.

Second, the attitude of hope affects the aim and the tone of one´s appeal for presence. For hope, with its "oblative" love and the unity of reciprocal other-directed human love it provides, is willing to let the other be in a transposed mode of being, and yet still enjoy the assurance that the beloved will continue to remain an active center of initiative in co-authoring the realization of a fullness of life for us.(51) For hope shows that where there is the reality of an "us," then the fullness of life that the beloved hopes for essentially involves his continued active commitment to the realization of that fullness of life with and for me.

Thus the one who hopes counts on the continued complicity of the beloved´s active intervention of creative fidelity to his personal commitment to bring about the realization of those values that essentially pertain to a fullness of life. In fact, the one who hopes, actively awaits, and confidently expects that the bestowal of presence--radiating his light, supporting, sustaining, and uplifting one´s personalizing forces--will be renewed. For the one who hopes enjoys the assurance that the loved one continues to exist as a actual personhood. As Marcel phrases it, a "for itself for others."(52)

The tracing of a second reflection on Marcel´s theme of presence and immortality enables us to clarify the main lines of this phenomenon and to identify its essential conditions of possibility.

Negatively, it is neither physical juxtaposition nor material communication, nor even the relationship of a subject confronting another person as an object, that constitutes presence. Rather presence occurs through a series of events and relationships that arise specifically within the order of personal being. Its conditions of possibility reside in those qualities of personhood that provide requisite dispositions for the co-authorship of interpersonal events creating the unity of intersubjective being.

Rather than the subject object dichotomy, the structural model for thinking of the mode of presence of the beloved beyond death is that derived from participation in the mystery of being. Openness welcomes the increase of personalizing forces that originate from the other and become resources of one's being by way of inward influx.

Hope emerges as primary in grounding and clarifying the possibility for maintaining the presence of the beloved beyond death. For hope involves a pre-knowledge as well as a prophetic assurance of a fullness of life for us. Hope finds in the other person's being the assurance of his personal commitment and creative fidelity in enduring as an active source working in complicity for the realization of a fullness of life that he wills for us with all his being.

The possibility of establishing and maintaining a living relationship of active communication with a loved one who has died is rooted in hope, which, like all interpersonal acts of spiritual exchange, depends finally on the dialogue of freedom and grace.

One might question the possibility of ever having a living relationship with someone three months, three years, or thirty years after he has died, especially if one has never met or even seen that person face to face. Yet the key to a response to that question is that whether we hope or not depends upon us in our freedom.

In the case of Marcel, I believe there are exceptional invitations to such hope.

The style of his philosophy is so strongly personal that he reveals himself in his concrete approaches, in the articulation of his existential quest, and by the paths he opens up for personal reflection. Moreover, his luminescent quality appears, as he phrases it, in that at times his words seem to be supported and sustained by all that he is.

Furthermore, his life and work, questioning and reflecting upon the human condition, respecting its antinomies yet highlighting its noblest possibilities, is his response to an ontological need for participation in being, and a clarification of its meaning. This is a communication that is not exclusively intended as his, but rather fundamentally intended for an us. This fundamental purpose, I believe, is the root source of his protestations against construing or conceiving of anything as his philosophy. Moreover, this fundamental purpose of communication, I believe, reveals a deep sense of his preference for neo-Socratic as a label, if labelling must be done. For the style of his thought is such that it necessarily respects and awaits the engagement of the other in his or her own personal philosophizing. For while Marcel portrays concrete approaches,

71

articulates existential questioning, offers perspectives of insight, and opens up paths of reflective clarification, still, in order to see the vision each person must travel the distance on his or her own, making the experience part of one´s personal being, explicating the connection between steps of reasoning and perspectives of phenomenological analysis, and deepening a participation in being and clarifying an understanding that becomes truly one´s own.

Thus, to the extent that we aspire to realize fuller and richer forms of creative fidelity to Marcel´s inspiration, there indeed appear to be strong grounds on his part assuring that the presence of his light will be there.

Notes to Chapter II. The Unfathomable: A Search for Presence

1. "Presence and Immortality," in Presence and Immortality,
    Pittsburgh, PA: Duquesne University Press, 1967, p. 230-31;
    "An Essay in Autobiography," in The Philosophy of
    Existentialism, New York: Citadel, Philosophical Library,
    1961, p. 112-13.

2. "Presence and Immortality," p. 231.

3. "Presence and Immortality," p. 239; "My Fundamental
    Purpose," in Presence and Immortality, pp. 24 and 26.

4. "The Unfathomable," in Presence and Immortality, p. 274.

5. Ibid., p. 275.

6. Ibid., pp. 275-76.

7. Ibid., p. 277.

8. Ibid., p. 280.

9. "Presence and Immortality," p. 232.

10. "The Unfathomable," pp. 275-76.

11. "Presence and Immortality," p. 237.

12. "On the Ontological Mystery," in The Philosphy of
     Existentialism, New York: Citadel, Philosophical Library,
     1961, pp. 39-40; "My Fundamental Purpose," pp. 27-29.

13. "Presence and Immortality," p. 237.

14. Ibid., p. 238.

15. Creative Fidelity, New York: Noonday Press, Farrar, Straus
     and Co., 1964, p. 40-42.

16. "Presence and Immortality," p. 38, citing Mystery of Being,
     Volume I, Chicago, Regnery, Gateway Edition, 1960,
     pp. 220-21.

17. "The Unfathomable," p. 280.

18. "An Essay in Autobiography," p. 127.

19. "On the Ontological Mystery," p. 38.

20. "Presence and Immortality," p. 238.

21. "The Unfathomable," p. 280.

22. "On the Ontological Mystery," p. 38.

23. Ibid., p. 39.

24. Ibid., p. 36.

25. "Presence and Immortality," p. 238.

26. "Metaphysical Journal for the Years 1938-1943," in Presence and Immortality, p. 176.

27. "On the Ontological Mystery," p. 38.

28. Ibid.

29. Ibid., p. 36.

30. Ibid.

31. Ibid.

32. Ibid., p. 38

33. "Metaphysical Journal for the Years 1938-1943," May 14, 1943, p. 173.

34. Ibid., May 17, 1943, p. 177.

35. "On the Ontological Mystery," p. 36.

36. "Presence and Immortality," pp. 230, 240-44.

37. Ibid., p. 239.

38. "My Fundamental Purpose," p. 27.

39. Ibid., p. 28.

40. "Presence and Immortality," p. 242.

41. "Metaphysical Journal for the Years 1938-1943," May 3, 1943, p. 153.

42. "Presence and Immortality," pp. 231-32.

43. Ibid., p. 235.

44. Ibid.

45. Ibid.

46. "Metaphysical Journal for the Years 1938-1943," May 31, 1942, p. 79.

47. "Presence and Immortality," pp. 230, 243; "Metaphysical Journal for the Years 1938-1943," p. 209.

48. "Metaphysical Journal for the Years 1938-1943," May 31, 1942, p. 88.

49. Ibid., p. 89-90.

50. Ibid., April 26, 1943, p. 142; May 17, 1943, p. 177; August 7, 1943, p. 207-8.

51. Ibid., August 15, 1943, p. 217.

52. Ibid., August 19, 1943, p. 217.

Chapter III. The Lantern : and The Light of Truth

In the William James lectures he delivered at Harvard University Gabriel Marcel voiced his hope that American audiences might soon know concretely how, in the case of his work, the theater is a privileged way of access to the philosophic reflections. For theater played a privileged role in the development of Gabriel Marcel´s thought.(1)

In this chapter I would like to look with you at The Lantern, a one-act play by Gabriel Marcel that stands in the permanent repertory of the National Theater of France, La Comédie Française.(2) I hope that our analysis of The Lantern will reveal something of the nature of Marcel´s drama and also the peculiar role that theater played in the development of his thought. Through this consideration of The Lantern we also intend to examine a central question raised by the play, namely, "What might it mean to see or to live in the light of Truth?"

Our procedure will be as follows. We will first give a brief synopsis of the play and identify the questions it gives rise to. Then in a second moment of reflection we shall clarify these issues, reconstructing the action of the play to bring to light perspectives of insight on them. And from time to time we shall amplify interpretations by drawing on statements that Marcel articulated years later on the explicitly philosophical level of rational analysis. A third moment will propose some summary conclusions to this study.

The Lantern, written December 26-28, 1935, has as its setting , a Paris apartment, the home of Raymond Chavière. The play explores Chavière´s situation after the death of his mother, Elizabeth Parmentier, and focuses on the question of where and how Raymond will live now that his mother has died. The drama portrays the various options proposed to Raymond, and a surprise ending to the play shows how Raymond makes his own choice. True to the hallmark of Marcel´s theatrical style, the drama presents the heightening of Raymond´s consciousness, communicating it as it were from within, so that audiences too can participate in the mysterious experience that Raymond lived.(3)

The play begins with Madame Andrezy, the housekeeper, showing in Mr. Anton Chavière. She fails to recognize him as Raymond´s father, for he has not come to the house since his divorce from Madame Parmentier. When Raymond enters, father and son greet coldly. Mr. Chavière, who could not get there for the funeral, tells Raymond that he has come now to see if by chance before going she had not left some sort of message for him, and also to ask Raymond if now that his mother has passed on he would not like to come and live with Chavière and Isabelle at their house on Marignan Avenue. Raymond parries this query with the curt statement that this would be awkward now, as he is engaged to be married to Sabine Verdun. There follows a heated exchange between father and son about the mother's approval of this proposed marriage and also about the church's teaching on matrimony.

As Chavière prepares to leave, Sabine Verdun, Raymond's fiancée, arrives. She, for her part, encourages Raymond to go away with her for a holiday of rest and recreation. Raymond becomes angered by Sabine's saying that this is what his mother would have wanted, for certainly such was not the case.

As Sabine Verdun is leaving, Chavière's second wife, Isabelle, who is ravishing, arrives. She asks Raymond to come and live with his father and her, to add a little interest to their lives. And certainly if he came to live with them, she would not hesitate to add some tenderness to his life. Otherwise she is on the verge of leaving with Olivier Guerin, Sabine's former husband, for the Orient. Raymond points out to Isabelle their weakness and the flaw and ambiguity in her proposal.

Anton Chavière returns to see if Raymond has made up his mind about Anton's invitation to come and live with them in the house on Marignan Avenue. Father and son chat, apparent small talk about the apartment, a book by Blondel, the Van der Weyden exhibit this season. Isabelle, feeling herself superfluous, leaves. Then Raymond gently tells his father that Isabelle will be away for a while--perhaps she didn't dare mention it to you, but she had wanted to spend a fortnight with a friend in the country before that friend left on a trip to Japan or India or someplace like that. Anton interjects, "She didn't say a word to me." Raymond continues, "So then I thought . . . perhaps it will seem strange to you . . . " Anton: "What is it, my son?" Raymond: "That while Isabelle will be with her friend . . . you'd come and live here." Anton (with emotion): "It would be just the two of us." Raymond (gravely): "No, father--the three of us, as before . . . as always."(4)

The play ends on that surprising note. It leaves us unsettled and bemused. Marcel plays often have surprise endings. He noted that the end of a play is most important not only for the unity it brings to the whole play but also for the questions it raises.

The end of The Lantern leaves us wondering. What does that

78

ending mean? More precisely, we wonder where that decision came from. Is it an act of compliance or rebellion in reaction to others´ expectations, or is it a genuinely personal choice, one that can be called an act of creative fidelity? We also wonder how Raymond came to that decision. How did he evolve the idea of inviting his father to come home with him? This decision goes against the flow that the proposals and actions of others were suggesting. Where did Raymond´s idea come from? How did it emerge in his consciousness? Or, in other words, how did Raymond come to see in the light of truth?

The end of a Marcel play not only poses questions, it also opens up perspectives of light. Thus the ending of The Lantern stimulates audiences to reflect on the questions raised, not only as these issues influence the lives of characters in the play but also as these mysteries are part of the lives of spectators as well. Thus audiences are invited, by the startling effect of the ending of The Lantern, to reconstruct the play in reverse, in the light of the questions raised, in order to see how Raymond came to the decision he did. This is exactly what we shall do in the second part of this chapter. We shall reconstruct the action of the play to help us clarify, by reflection on the drama, what it might mean to see and live in the light of truth.

The very title of the play, as well as its last lines, suggest that the light of truth refers to Madamee Parmentier´s presence after her death. There is not only the title, The Lantern, and the last lines, "It would be just the two of us?" "No, father - the three of us, as before . . . as always ...," there is also Raymond´s speech wherein he refers to his mother as being for them like a lantern.(5) Raymond´s dawning consciousness in this soliloquy is the crucial moment which change of attitude. It also marks the transition from his perceiving his mother as a sometimes oppressive third person between them (Raymond and Sabine and Raymond and Chavière) to his perceiving her as an intimate light or a presence known by way of interiority and depth.(6)

Let us begin to reconstruct the action of the play. Madame Parmentier is very much present in the action of the first few scenes. In fact, it seems as if Madame Parmentier is a major figure in the play, although she never appears on stage except in terms of the aura of light she seems to radiate into people´s lives.

There is a coolness and a strained sense of distance characterizing Raymond´s meeting with his father after his mother´s death. Raymond has developed a sense of estrangement if not of resentment in relation to his parents´ divorce. In the early conversation with his father, Raymond is defensive of his mother's good name, very protective of his memory of her. The father comes hesitantly and confusedly seeking some closeness, some form of reconciliation. He asks if Raymond's mother might have left some sort of message for him before going. He also asks Raymond to come and live with them, now that his mother is dead. Raymond refuses this invitation rather abruptly, announcing that he is engaged and soon to be married to Sabine Verdun. When Anton asks if Raymond's mother approved of her son's betrothal to a divorced woman, father and son quarrel. Raymond had not told his mother of his plans. Anton and Raymond argue about readiness for marriage and the wisdom of the church's discipline and teaching about the holiness of matrimony. There is a tragic irony about the argument, because basically the ideas the father proposes in advising his son are the very ones the parents' divorce seems to belie. (7)

When Sabine Verdun arrives, Raymond remains upset, deeply troubled by the argument and his father's visit. Sabine's advice to Raymond is that he and she should go away for a holiday together. The rest would do him good, and that is what his mother would have wanted. Raymond reacts. Taken together, his father's question of whether his mother knew and approved of his project to marry a divorced woman, and now Sabine's subtle but incisive observations and even her insistence that Raymond's mother would have wanted them together to enjoy themselves on a holiday, these events get to Raymond. He is angered and then thrown back on his own resources. In reaction to these upsetting references to his mother, Raymond gets in touch with what he really knew her to be. He recalls their relation, the closeness they shared. He begins to remember her as she really was. (8) And in that moment he becomes aware of the deception and rebellion that had come to characterize his life in relationship to Sabine Verdun.

In the famous soliloquy, wherein Raymond refers to his mother's presence as the beam of a lantern, he acknowledges that he and Sabine were deceiving themselves as well as his mother. They were taking advantage of the terrible weakness that death brings. Raymond admits that he was living a rebellion, like a slave taking revenge that he didn't even enjoy. Further, he even recognizes that he, who never lied, had lied to his mother about his relationship with Sabine. He had said, when the mother asked about her, "Oh, Sabine Verdun? A friend, very intelligent. Perhaps a little heartless." He had said that to reassure her. "To say, 'perhaps a little heartless,' about a woman, that was clear proof that one had no intention . . ."(9) He finds that they acted despicably, especially himself, taking advantage of his mother's weakness, waiting for her to die so that they,

80

Sabine and he, could be free for the good life to begin. Recalling his true relationship with his mother, Raymond recognizes his deception of her and of himself, and he sees his resentful rebellion for the foolish act that it was. Raymond now realizes that he will probably not marry Sabine Verdun. Their relation was just a fantasized escape from the demands of an extraordinary woman and the resentful revenge of one who suffered from his parents' divorce.

As Raymond remembers his mother, he begins to perceive his life situation more clearly, and he seems better able to evaluate the different options proposed to him as temporary living arrangements after his mother's death.

We have just seen what is a significant step as one moves to see in the light of truth. Namely, the first moment of coming to see in the light of truth is a moment of recognition that one has previously been living in untruth; that is, one has been deceiving oneself and others. Acknowledgement that one has been living a life of deception, self-deception as well as deception of others, usually occurs as it happened for Raymond. It is in the light of another person's presence that the light dawns. One perceives the self-deception and can begin to be freed from it.

In a philosophical essay written several years after The Lantern, Marcel developed this idea on a philosophical level.(10) A corollary of what he wrote is that the more I am open to the light of the presence of another person, the more I can see and communicate in a light of truth. In proportion as I cease to eclipse myself from their light, I can increasingly live and see in the light of my own truth.(11) It was first through theater and his dramatist's sensitivity to the currents of interaction between various people that Marcel perceived this reality. It was only later, in subsequent reflection, that the idea became clear for Marcel on a philosophic level of analysis.(12)

In the play The Lantern, the concrete portrayal of Raymond's coming to a decision reveals the way one can come to see in a light of truth. Once Raymond, in the light of his mother's presence, recognizes his own self-deception in his attempt with Sabine to deceive his mother, he begins to see clearly into not only that maneuver but also into the other options coming into his field of choice and, perhaps most important, into the true desires of his own heart. We shall see how this develops through the remainder of the play.

In scene five Sabine leaves. There is an air of finality about her departure. After Sabine has left, Isabelle confides in Raymond and exposes the particular idea of how it could be

81

helpful to Anton Chavière if Raymond would come and live with them. Raymond listens and then clarifies by a question what was confused in her proposal. Was it for his father or for her that Isabelle had asked Raymond to come and live with them? Raymond also brings to light what was dangerous in her proposal, the inevitability that if Isabelle and Raymond lived under the same roof, in two months they would become lovers, a disgraceful situation that would not be any real help to any of the three of them.

Raymond sees the accuracy of Sabine's cruel prediction that Anton and Isabelle's household will not survive the death of Raymond's mother. Raymond sympathizes with Isabelle's weakness but also sees through the unconscious treachery of her confusion. Yet while Raymond sees clearly, he does not judge harshly or condemn. At this moment, with great balance, Raymond invokes the memory of his relationship with his mother, a relationship of great intimacy with moments of happiness and also of some suffering, a relationship suffused with admiration yet difficult for fear of the disappointment some show of weakness might cause. So excellent a creature as she is bound to create a great deal of suffering about her.(13) So while Raymond sees where the plans lead and refuses to go along with them, he does not judge the people. He understands why and how the people involved think and feel the way they do. He also sees how the differences among them have contributed to the tragic situation in which they unhappily find themselves. Raymond seems not to judge but rather to understand with a blend of lucidity and compassion.

Raymond seems, in this respect, to incarnate the kind of sympathetic understanding that drama can develop in an audience, a clear-sighted compassion that leads people to see a tragic situation as it were from an overarching perspective, not condemning or judging but rather saying with genuine compassion, "You are understood."(14) And Raymond recognizes that he too is in need of this compassionate understanding as well as being called upon to give it.(15)

As the play moves toward its denouement we can see how Raymond formed his decision. Raymond perceives the options proposed to him as the "apparent goods" that they are. He refuses to follow the direction of others that leads to splitting off from family ties. Not only does he foresee the unhappy consequences prepared by such fragmentation of family, a brokenness of heart and relationships such as he has already experienced through his parents' divorce, but also, and perhaps more important for the sake of good decision-making, he comes very much in touch with those values he wants to love and live by and make his own. In saying no to options proposed by others,

82

Raymond gets more deeply in touch with himself and becomes aware of his own deepest longing for family unity and interpersonal relations that last.

Raymond's initiative in inviting his father home, to come and live together again, is the result of Raymond's progressive clarification of his perspective on the situation. Thanks to his willingness to heed a perspective of light that his mother's presence radiates, Raymond has moved from rebellious self-deception and deception of others to compassionate understanding of a tragic situation that involves oneself and others. He has come to recognize the options of alternate life-styles for what they are and, by way of contrast, to recognize the desires of his own heart for a deep and lasting relationship of love and interpersonal and family relations that abide.

Raymond's decision is no act of conformity or rebellion, merely reacting for or against the expectations of others. Raymond's choice is a genuine act of creative fidelity. There is something spontaneous and original about his offer. Moreover, it springs from his own deep vital center and expresses his personal choice of how he wants to live. Confirmation of these as essential characteristics of genuine acts of creative fidelity is articulated years later on a philosophic level in the book entitled Creative Fidelity. (16)

Raymond, in moving beyond the apparent confines of a tragic situation, has fallen back on his own deepest resources and in drawing upon these has created a new form of fidelity to those persons and values that he wants to restore and preserve in his life. Thus Raymond's personal decision and creative initiative are resourced in his genuine fidelity--his faithfulness in affection and responsibility toward his father, his faithfulness to his own hope for family unity and interpersonal relations that abide, and faithfulness to what his mother longed and lived for, although she did not see it realized during her earthly existence.

In the play The Lantern, the light of truth that illumines Raymond's understanding of his situation and his act of creative fidelity in response to that situation is not just some theoretic knowledge or dialectic argumentation; rather it is the light of a personal presence, the presence of his mother from beyond death.

In Raymond's soliloquies wherein he evokes his mother, he alludes to two different modes of presence, one during earthly life when her presence was like that of a third person who was almost overwhelming, and the other a presence through real intimacy as when we encounter another's presence by way of inwardness and depth. Marcel observed in a private conversation shortly before his own death that he preferred to speak of presence from beyond death as "living in the light of . . ."(17) After death one can sense in a more intense and purified way who the beloved really was and what it was that he or she really loved and lived for. It is in this manner of openness to his mother's presence, who she was and what she loved, that Raymond came to live in the light of truth and to pose his choice of how he would live his life after her death. His choice was consciously and freely his own, yet its inspiration was in a shared light, a light that was other and more than his own alone. As Marcel wrote in reflections on presence from beyond death, after death the loved one can continue to be present although in a transformed way.(18) Privileged moments of renewal of the loved one's presence, which it depends upon us to be open to but not in fact to summon forth, occur by way of inwardness and depth and they bring an uplifting of our being and an incitement to create.(19)

It is in this manner that we can understand that light of truth in which Raymond came to make his startling decision at the end of The Lantern. It is likewise in this context that we can begin to fathom the meaning of Raymond's final remark. "No father—the three of us, as before. . . as always."(20)

An Endnote

It is possible, upon reflection, for someone to see the way Raymond lived in the light of truth as representative of the way one can live life in the light of faith. There are subtle and discrete intimations of this in the play. There is first the fact that while all the other characters situate themselves explicitly in relationship to faith, Raymond simply lives the witness of his. There is also a stage direction indicating a Van der Weyden print as part of the set. This artist was noted for vivid colors, for drawing subjects in three dimensions, and for portraying the religious in everyday settings.(21)

Marcel cautions that he finds it inappropriate for theater in our times to try and show God directly, but he observes that theater can show the working of grace as it operates in peoples' lives.(22) Such witness, he offers, could be an appropriate presentation of religion in theater, but it would be successful only to the extent that this effect was not calculated or intentional.

It is perhaps, as Marcel wrote à propos of his philosophy, as if our reflections are drawn toward a light of a higher order that philosophy perceives from afar and of which it suffers the secret attraction.(23) Marcel´s philosophic reflections do invite another level of personal reflection on the part of those who wish to consider these issues and insights explicitly in the light of religious faith. In the context of Christian faith, the light of Truth is assuredly a personal presence from beyond death. One has only to recall the sacred scriptures celebrated between the feast of Easter and Pentecost.(24)

Notes to Chapter III.   The Lantern: and The Light of Truth

1.   The Existential Background of Human Dignity, Cambridge, MA:
     Harvard University Press, 1963.

2.   Le Fanal, December 26-28, 1935, was commissioned for the
     1937-38 season of the Comédie Française by its director
     Edouard Bourdet. The script was published in Paris, ed.
     Stock, 1938. La Fanal was published in English translation
     by Elizabeth Stambler and Joseph Cunneen in Cross Currents
     Vol. VII, No. 2., Spring 1958, pp. 129-43.

3.   "The Drama of the Soul in Exile" introduction to Three Plays
     by Gabriel Marcel: A Man of God, Ariadne, The Votive Candle,
     New York, Hill and Wang, Mermaid Dramabook, 1965, p. 22.

4.   The Lantern, Scene VII, p. 143.

5.   Ibid., Scene IV, p. 137.

6.   Ibid., Scene IV, p. 137, Scene VI, p. 142.

7.   Ibid., Scene II, p. 133.

8.   Ibid., Scene IV, p. 137, cf. also Scene VI, p. 142.

9.   Ibid., Scene IV, pp. 136-37.

10. "My Fundamental Purpose" (1937) in Presence and Immortality,
     Pittsburgh, PA: Duquesne University Press, 1967, pp. 13-30.

11. Ibid., pp. 26-27. "I shall note in passing that no
     philosophical text has impressed me more strongly than the
     one in which the American philosopher, W. E. Hocking, in his
     book The Meaning of God in Human Experience, has established
     that we cannot really conceive an apprehending of the other
     which is not truly an apprehending of ourselves and which
     confers on our experience its human weight....the world of
     the others becomes illumined with an increasingly intense
     light as the I dispels more of its own darkness and dispels
     it more heroically." Cf. pp. 24, 20, 18, 16.

12. Ibid., pp. 13-15.

13. The Lantern, Scene VI, pp. 141-42.

14. "The Drama of the Soul in Exile," p. 21, "My Dramatic Works
     as Viewed by the Philosopher" (1959) in Searchings, New
     York: Newman Press, 1967, pp. 111, 117.

15. The Lantern, Scene VI, pp. 141-42, cf."The Drama of the Soul in Exile," p. 32.

16. Creative Fidelity, New York: Farrar, Straus & Co., 1964, pp. 107, 109; cf. also Homo Viator, New York: Harper & Bros., 1962, pp. 129-34.

17. The Heights, Le Moyne College, December 1973, pp. 17-18.

18. Presence and Immortality, "Presence and Immortality," pp. 235-39.

19. The Philosophy of Existentialism, New York: Citadel Press, 1956, On the Ontological Mystery, pp. 38, 36, cf. The Lantern, Scene VI, p. 141.

20. The Lantern, Scene VII, p. 143.

21. The Lantern, Scene VII, p. 142.

22. Théâtre et Religion, Lyon, Vitte, 1958, "L´idée du drame chrétien dans son rapport au théâtre actuel" (1957), pp. 76-86, cf. also The Philosophy of Existentialism, "Testimony and Existentialism", p. 98, ". . . testimony is based on fidelity to a light, or to use another language, to a grace received."

23. The Philosophy of Existentialism, "On the Ontological Mystery," p. 46.

24. Philosophic reflection and inquiry are drawn toward the fuller light of faith. Scriptures relating presence beyond death of Jesus Christ from the Resurrection to Pentecost: Matthew 28:1-10, 16-20; John 20:1-18; Luke 24:13-35; John 20:19-23; John 16:7; 14:14-21; 14:16, 17, 26; 14:23-29.

Chapter IV. Dot The I: An Existential Witness of the Light of
                         Truth

A Study in the Theater and Philosophy of Gabriel Marcel.

During his lifetime Gabriel Marcel (1889-1973) often
expressed the hope that his theater and philosophy would be
recognized as essentially complementary, that his dramatic and
philosophic works would be studied together, heard in concert.
Introducing his 1961-1962 William James Lectures at Harvard
University, Marcel expressed his regret that reader awareness of
the substantial connections linking his theater and philosophy
was unfortunately all too abstract. Throughout the course of
these lectures, later published under the title The Existential
Background of Human Dignity, he stressed the importance of
studying his dramatic and philosophic works as complementary
modes of inquiry and clarification.(1)

The theme of this chapter, "Existential Witness of the Light
of Truth," is especially well suited for this integral approach.
The theme, of itself, seems to invite dramatic representation.
Existential witness refers to the fact that a certain quality of
truth is communicated not merely by the words one says, but
rather by the fact that these words are supported by the very
life of the one who speaks them. Communication in the light of
truth refers to the fact that one person can lovingly share a
communication of what he or she lives by in such a way that
another person begins to see in a light of truth what he or she
lives by, or, perhaps even more important, can hope to live by.

Drama can depict existential witness and communication in
the light of truth. Drama can enable audiences to be touched by
existential witness. Drama also lets spectators enter into a
dialogic communication in the light of truth, one that brings
into question not only the lives of the characters in the play
but the lives of individual spectators as well.

Dot the I, Les points sur les i, written November 6-9,
1936, raises questions about the light of truth.(2) The action
of the play shows that existential witness is key in the
communication of a light of truth.

Dot the I portrays the situation of three liberal-minded
adults who attempt to live a three-way marriage. The Girondin
household includes Anatole, the playwright and husband; Irma, his
mistress and muse; and Felicia, his housekeeper and wife. Also
living with them is Aimée, a twelve-year-old daughter of Irma.
Aimée is only there temporarily, having accompanied her mother.
There was no place for Aimée at her father's home in the south
after his new wife, the mother of Aimée's baby brother, moved

89

in.   There´s talk of finding Aimée an "au pair" situation where
she can live and work with a family.

As the play begins it is difficult to figure out who´s who,
how the characters relate to one another, and where they fit in
the household order.   It is evident that there is friction and
irritation between the two women, Felicia, the wife, and Irma,
the live-in mistress.

Each person has a different interpretation of the situation.
Anatole reminds Felicia that when she generously agreed to this
arrangement she became obliged to a civility and considerateness
that is necessary if they are to succeed at living this human
experiment, feasible only for those noble spirits who are beyond
the prejudices and small minded constraints of middle-class
morality.   Felicia reminds Anatole that she likes to keep it
perfectly clear what the situation is.   Irma is there only by
Felicia´s leave.   Felicia can end the experiment just by saying
so, any time she wants.   What´s more, the child will not stay
long.   They´ll find a place for her "au pair." Irma reminds
Felicia that they are all better off now than they were before
Irma came to live with them. The situation then was that Anatole
was gone all night, or coming home at all hours and with "ladies
of the night," or taking off for trips to Belgium. Now at least
he´s home, steady and working. That´s better for all of them.
Aimée is not complicated and does not bother her head trying to
sort out or explain that level of situations. She tries to fit
in, be helpful, and not bother others, who she knows really don´t
want her around.

The fragile fiction that the adults have fabricated is
threatened when Felicia hears that Irma and Anatole plan to spend
the weekend in the country passing as Mr. and Mrs. Girondin and
staying at the estate of a socially prominent couple, Lucien and
Blanche Foucard. This they propose on the pretense of wanting to
gain political influence to promote the production of Anatole´s
play Robespierre so that it will premiere at the National
Theater.   Felicia is furious that things have gone too far. She
senses that she is powerless now that events are beyond her
control.   She has been ignored and excluded. Moreover, she is
humiliated to the breaking point when, in her own home, she is
not introduced or presented as the person she really is. Irma
introduced her to the Foucards as Mrs. Rosary, a relative who is
unfortunately suffering from painful facial neuralgia.

After the two couples have gone out, Felicia sends Aimée
to run and tell her mother that Felicia says she is going to tell
Aimée the whole truth, everything. She says she is going to
dot the i´s..., give the full and complete explanation.

While Aimée runs to catch up to her mother and give her the message, Felicia goes to the window, looks out and then abruptly closes the shutters and the drapes and turns on the electric lamps, even though it is broad daylight outside. Felicia sits in this semiobscured, artificially illuminated room. When Aimée reenters the living room, the stage is set for the final confrontation.

We are prepared to hear Felicia tell Aimée the harsh facts of life, projecting her own perceptions and sense of rejection onto the child, informing her that she is unwanted and unloved. But we find that the conversation takes a surprise turn and moves in unexpected directions. With dramatic irony the child becomes mother to the woman, and the light of truth appears to be not the dreadful harsh light of resentment, recrimination, and rejection, but rather a childlike light of faith communicating a remarkably mature experience of forgiveness and love.

The conversation starts out very tentatively, then moves to kindly, friendlier sharings, and finally yields some startling exchanges of confidence and understanding love.

At first the exchanges are touchy if not hostile. Aimée inquires about Felicia's health and apologetically assures her that she doesn't mean to bother her. Aimée asks Felicia not to speak harshly, for Felicia has nothing for which to reproach Aimée. Aimée has done nothing to hurt Felicia, at least not deliberately.

When Felicia asks whether Aimée didn't really want to get to Paris, Aimée reveals the truth that she would have liked to have stayed at her father's house with her baby brother, but that there was no room for her after her father remarried. When Aimée shows pictures of her baby brother and dissolves in tears, telling of her fear that he'll forget her if she is never able to go and see him, Felicia shows kindness and pity and assures the girl that they'll arrange some way for her to go and visit.

The conversation continues in a friendlier vein. Aimée asks what "dot the i's" means, and Felicia responds that it is only a cliché that does not really mean much. Aimée asks what kind of work she might do "au pair," to which Felicia replies in a motherly tone that maybe she'd take care of little children. She'd love that, Aimée exclaims. She adds that when she's married she's going to have twins right away, a boy and a girl. It seems that one can choose. Mother Simone's friends talk that way, and they seem to decide and choose. Felicia states that it´s not always a question of choice and blurts out that she´d lost twins and was told by the doctors that if she tried to bear children again she´d die in childbirth.

Aimée commiserates with Felicia and then, trying to console her, affirms that Felicia´s twins are angels in heaven. This draws a joking and mocking reaction from Felicia. Aimée asks Felicia if she doesn´t ever repent and confess. Felicia´s reply is that she has no need to, that she has nothing for which to reproach herself. Aimée declares her need. She says that if she didn´t confess she´d die. It would be as if she couldn´t breathe, as if her soul would suffocate and die. But, she adds, the soul doesn´t die because the soul is immortal. Entangled in language, Aimée leaves off theological discussion to share a confidence.

Aimée admits that when she heard that she´d have to leave her father´s house and not see her brother for a long time she felt shocked and hurt. She even wished that her stepmother would die so that Aimée could stay with her father and be a little mother to her baby brother. But then she was ashamed, for some feel that a thought is something real, like a weapon, that can hurt people. Aimée felt guilty and ashamed, and didn´t dare to look at her stepmother or to go to confession. But the priest who´d helped her prepare for confirmation saw something in her eyes and was kind to her. That helped her find courage to go to confession. Then she affirms, "Those thoughts left me, I felt light and happy."

Felicia protests but breaks down, letting tears flow and a new light of truth be born into her life. She protests that she´s beyond reproach. She did what was best. Few would have had that courage. It is the others who are wrong. Aimée interjects, "Those others who hurt you." Felicia continues, "If I´d only had a child like you. The little bit I had I wanted to keep." Aimée asks, "Those others who have hurt you, cousin, are they....?" Felicia shakes her head as if to convey that she cannot answer. Aimée continues and gets tearful nods from Felicia. "That is none of my business? I shall never know? I have perhaps guessed, you know."

The dialogue continues:

> Felicia: No.
> Aimée: You don´t want me to guess?
> Felicia: I don´t want it, I don´t want it anymore.
> Aimée: You´re crying now like a child...like a little child, my cousin. (She drops to her knees; she puts her arms around Felicia´s neck.) (3)

Marcel´s plays usually have a surprise ending. The final scene is most important, both for dramatic unity and for the questions it raises for the audience. At the end of this play we find many questions raised. What does it mean to "dot the i´s"? Can one give the full and complete explanation of a human situation especially as it involves freedoms in interpersonal relationships? What is it to see and judge in the light of truth? Is it to see with childlike simplicity or with adult sophistication? Is it to judge blame, fault, and incrimination, or is it to come to a compassionate understanding through forgiving love?

The one question the limits of this chapter allows us to focus on, and that only with a cursory view of its highlights, is: What is the nature of the existential witness and the communication in the light of truth that we see happening in the lives of Aimée and Felicia in the last scene of Dot the I ?(4) In the final scene Aimée shares an existential witness that enables Felicia to begin to see her life and revise its meaning in a new light of truth.

In a loving and confiding manner Aimée tells Felicia her secret. Aimée, like Felicia, knew rejection and felt the pain of love´s loss. She was so terribly hurt that she bitterly resented the one who replaced her, hated her and almost wished that she´d die. Yet Aimée adds that these thoughts of hatred and resentment and the feelings of shame and guilt that accompanied them almost suffocated her. Then someone was compassionate toward her, and that helped her find the courage to confess. When she confessed and renounced those feelings, the thoughts that had hurt her left and she felt light and happy.

Aimée´s witness includes the story she tells, but it also conveys the reality and light of truth she lives by. Aimée shares this communication in a genuinely loving way. She feels compassion for Felicia and hopes that Felicia too can be set free. It is in this spirit that Aimée shares her message that to let go of hatred and judgments of condemnation lets one be free to live and feel love. Aimée shares with Felicia the very reality she promises--forgiveness opens the way for love and hope to reenter one´s soul.

The communication of a light of truth touching both their lives was enabled by a genuine spirit of love and trust. Felicia´s opening to the light of truth Aimée communicates also entails Felicia´s opening by way of inwardness and depth to her own light of truth.(5) Though at first she protested, Felicia is able gradually to let go of judgments of resentment and condemnation. With Aimée's compassion, Felicia is able to acknowledge that the real grief she holds is the hurt of rejection, the pain of loss and the desperate fear of never being able to love or be loved again. With Aimée's communication of love awakening in Felicia a feeling and a hope for love, Felicia says, "I don't want it anymore." She doesn't want it anymore--the hurt, the hatred, the three-way marriage, the impossibility or unavailability of love. Felicia's confession in the light of truth is not as explicit or complete as Aimée's, but she has begun the reversal, from hatred to love, from suffocating to breathing, from the artificial light of deception to a genuine light of truth.

Aimée's existential witness communicates not only her story but also the incarnate expression of the reality and light of faith she lives. Aimée, who is apparently unwanted and unloved, yet whose name means the loved one, enjoys an assurance since her solemn communion that she is loved. This has been renewed in the forgiving love of reconciliation and in her remembrance of these. It is Aimée who, by her assurance of being loved, is able to love Felicia in such a way as to communicate to her the assurance that she too is loved. That assurance is communicated through Aimée's loving yet ultimately is found also within Felicia's own being. A certain regard of love awakens within the other person her own sense of divine filiation.(6)

Theater lets this communication of mystery touch our lives as well.

Notes to Chapter IV.   Dot the I: An Existential Witness of the
                        Light of Truth

1. Gabriel Marcel, The Existential Background of Human Dignity,
    Cambridge, MA, Harvard University Press, 1963, p. 179.

2. Les points sur les i, Paris, Editions Grasset, 1936.

3. Dot the I trans. by Katharine Rose Hanley in Two One Act
    Plays by Gabriel Marcel: Dot the I and The Double Expertise,
    University Press of America, Lanham, MD, 1986, pp. 1-21.

4. "Testimony and Existentialism" in The Philosophy of
    Existentialism, Secaucus, NJ, Citadel Press, 1980,
    pp. 91-103.

5. "My Fundamental Purpose" (1937) in Presence and Immortality,
    Pittsburgh, PA, Duquesne University Press, 1967, pp. 11-30.

6. "The Dangerous Situation of Ethical Values" in Homo Viator,
    New York, Harper Torchbook, Harper & Bros., 1962, p. 160.

Chapter V. The Rebellious Heart: and Human Creation

The Rebellious Heart is the title Marcel insisted he wanted
for the English version (1974) of the play he originally wrote in
French with the title Le Coeur des autres (1921).(1) The
Rebellious Heart tells the story of Daniel Meyrieux's attempt to
achieve theatrical success as a playwright. The Rebellious Heart
also portrays the tragic parody Daniel creates as he fails to
live a genuine communion of love and creativity in his intimate
family relations.

The setting for the play is the home of Daniel and Rose
Meyrieux in Paris in 1921. With them is Daniel's natural son
John, whom Rose insisted that they adopt when the child's mother
died. John has not been told, however, that Daniel is his real
father. The play presents the struggles and conflicts that
accompany Daniel Meyrieux's efforts to find his identity through
artistic creativity.

In the first act we see Daniel and Rose all caught up in
efforts to achieve theatrical success. Their preoccupation with
critics' reviews and their own reflections of what creativity
involves have only two interruptions. The first is the signal
visit of Rose's mother, Madame Chambley, who comes to protest
Daniel's outrageous exploitation of Aunt Solange's story and to
request that Daniel withdraw the play or at least delete those
parts that are so personal that they really should remain
private. Daniel and Rose refuse this request. Although Rose
protests to her mother that she, Rose, is completely in accord
with what Daniel is doing, it seems that she does protest too
much. She has gradually increasing misgivings about the
psychological exploitation involved in Daniel's literary
creations especially the play Daniel is currently writing that
capitalizes, obviously with artistic embellishments, upon John's
situation in their own household. The second interruption occurs
after Madame Chambley has left and Daniel is back at work writing
The Silent Child the play about which Rose is so uncomfortable.
John returns from lunch at the home of a friend. When Rose
chides John for not congratulating his foster father on the
success of his play's première, John retorts that he doubts if
anything can hurt his father if it doesn't affect theatrical
works. John then confides to Rose that one of the maids has told
him that Daniel is not merely his foster father but is in fact
his real father. On the heels of that stirring confidence Daniel
enters. He peremptorily dismisses John and proceeds to read to
Rose the dialogue that he has just written for his new play. It
is the scene wherein Gilbert, the silent child, reveals to his
foster mother, Therese, that he has learned that his so-called

97

foster father is indeed his real father. In that same scene Gilbert goes further and declares his romantic feelings for Therese. Stunned, Rose can only listen. She cannot even react.

In the second act Daniel is concerned only to find some way of dealing with John so the latter doesn't think badly of him and doesn't pursue any lines of embarrassing questioning. When father and son finally converse, John asks Daniel why he has not acted as a real father toward him, why he did not marry his mother. Why was he not kind and caring toward John and his mother? John is revolted by Daniel's cruelty and still holds fast to the sacredness of his mother's love. Daniel summarily dismisses John's questions with the rejoinder that John is simply too young to discuss or understand the issues. Daniel turns his anger into blame that he transfers onto John for reading The Silent Child without permission. John responds that he thought it a good way to get to know his father, and he was right—it was a good way.

When Daniel tells Rose that John has read The Silent Child on the sly, Rose ironically informs John that this action was like a breach of trust. Alone with Rose, John confides that Daniel, by his heartless dealings, has spoiled the only beautiful thing in his life, his relationship with Rose. John reveals to Rose that he is disgusted by Gilbert in The Silent Child, especially by the romantic feelings that Gilbert professes for Therese. John, afraid lest others construe Gilbert's feelings to be his own, distances himself from Rose while resenting the loss of the only genuine affection left in his life.

At the end of the second act Daniel, on his own without consulting either Rose or John, decides that John will start the following week as a resident student at St. Louis Academy. Alone with Daniel, Rose feebly warns him, "Take care."(2)

The third act of The Rebellious Heart shows the success that Daniel's dramatic works have won him. It also reveals the failure of his intimate relations with his family.

The act opens with Daniel receiving accolades including even a personal visit from an important critic, Paul Thomas. Daniel reproaches Rose for not being more enthusiastic about this tribute to his success. Rose, grieved by John's suffering, has become conscious of what Daniel is doing. She protests what has become of their love. There is no genuine communion. She finds she is no longer someone, but rather has become merely a provider of tenderness and an inspiration for plays. Daniel has completely eclipsed her. He has annexed her. Since she doesn't count as a person, they no longer are two but have merely become

98

one. In her rebellion, Rose has now identified with John's suffering and she asks Daniel to withdraw The Silent Child. Moreover, she warns Daniel that if he refuses her request she will leave him.

While Daniel goes off to deliver corrected proofs to his publisher, Rose converses with John, who is home visiting after several months away at boarding school. Rose is ready to leave Daniel in order to mother John.

When Daniel returns from his publisher's, he seems anxious lest Rose really think of leaving him. He is ready to make some minor concessions in the future, although he reminds Rose that her situation is most fortunate compared with that of other writers' wives. Thereupon he is content that they are reconciled. He embraces her and calls her "his treasure." Rose, conscious of the tragic in their situation, resigns herself to it hopelessly.

> Rose (with the deepest sadness): Understand me, Daniel, I am giving up myself; I know it. And I know also that I cannot do otherwise. After ten years of our life, I am no longer strong enough to think of myself. When a being has come to this...go ahead, you are right. Take me. And when you are short of subjects... Curtain.(3)

The Rebellious Heart has a very sad ending. It ends, as it were, on a muted note of despair. Rose's spirit is crushed. She has given up. It is as if her soul has died, though she will continue to go through the motions of life. John's life too already seems on the way toward tragic ruin. He has given up any hope for genuine love or happiness in life. He is ready, perhaps without even realizing it, to go the dissolute way of his father. Daniel, by way of contrast, seems quite content with his life, elated as he is by his recent theatrical success. He remains quite insensitive to the tragic loss in the lives of those around him, the ravaging of the lives of those closest to him--or as the French title, Le Coeur des autres, implies"the hearts of others." The play has a tragic ending indeed.

Marcel noted that The Rebellious Heart is a play with a most somber ending. Still, he remarked that even those of his plays with somber endings bring a certain light for the audience. It appears that the quality of light that the ending of The Rebellious Heart brings is not a direct light dawning explicitly in the consciousness of any of the lead protagonists, but rather a diffuse light that is reflected, as it were, from beyond them.(4)

99

This, like any other Marcel play, leaves us with questions. There are first the questions affecting the characters of the play, questions that even awaken among spectators certain feelings of rebellion or revolt. For example, why is Daniel so insensitive to his wife and son? How can he be so caught up in his theatrical success as to remain insensitive to the toll that it has taken on the real lives of those closest to him? Why does Rose dissolve and give up, abandoning all hope and any effort toward achieving a genuine communion of love with Daniel or a better life for John? Why doesn't Rose leave Daniel to care for John? The prospects for life after the end of this play are bleak, in fact quite hopeless. That is perhaps why the play leaves audiences with a deep and lingering sadness. Gradually, however, the haunting quality of the play gives rise to another level of questioning. On reflection spectators begin to wonder about Daniel's success and creativity. One questions whether Daniel's theater was genuinely creative or successful only for its borrowings from the lives of real persons? It would be an awful irony if what caused such suffering and loss in the lives of the people close to him did not even contribute to his producing real art or genuinely creative theater. Is it possible that Daniel failed to be genuinely creative artistically as he failed to be creative and loving in his family life?

Indeed, reflection on The Rebellious Heart invites us to consider the question of what is genuine creation, both human and artistic. The play also invites us to inquire what is required in order for someone to be genuinely creative.

Marcel explored these questions both in his dramatic and his philosophic works. For the remainder of this chapter we shall trace how Marcel pursued his inquiry into these questions and brought to light essential perspectives of insight, first through dramatic inquiry and then through philosophic analysis. To retrace the development of Marcel's thought on human creation, we shall refer to aspects of The Rebellious Heart, which was written in 1919 and staged and then published in Paris in 1921. We shall also refer to philosophic essays written and published in France between 1932 and 1944, principally several chapters in his book entitled Creative Fidelity, English translation of Du Refus à l'invocation, and also several chapters in his book entitled Homo Viator, Introduction to a Metaphysic of Hope, English translation of Homo Viator, prolégomènes à une métaphysique de l'espérance. (5)

We find in The Rebellious Heart many comments that attempt to clarify the nature of artistic creation. Patently, Daniel's efforts to produce literary work that achieves theatrical success

100

also illuminate to a certain extent what artistic creation involves, although Daniel's life gives us more of a reverse image of creativity than a direct illustration of what genuine creation might involve. Theater presents the first moments of inquiry. Philosophy, as drawn from several chapters in Creative Fidelity and Homo Viator, will guide a subsequent moment of tenacious reflection with critically reasoned analysis of the nature of genuine creativity, particularly as this can be manifest in the life of the artist and the parent.

Throughout the play we hear many comments that attempt to clarify the nature of human creation. Clearly in the play creation appears to involve taking a lived situation and adding something of oneself and one's inspiration to it so as to make of it a new situation with different people.(6) Throughout the play we hear various characters trying to identify what artistic creation is. First John asks whether to create is to make a medley of fact and fiction, the true and the false, the real and the unreal, what is mine and what is someone else's, to fashion from that something new.(II, 7, pp. 186-87)(7) And Rose wonders whether to create is not to give over, to consecrate, what is sacred and most precious in our lives.(I, 2, pp. 157-58; III, 3, p. 205)(8)

Finally, Daniel wonders whether to create doesn't mean to save, to make eternal something of oneself because one has expressed it.(I, 1, pp. 149-50; I, 2, pp. 157-58)(9) Still, Rose's mother and John affirm that people should not be sacrificed for the sake of art or ideas. What is sacred in their lives should be held secret and should not be profaned by distorting it for public display.(I, 2, pp. 153-58; II, 7, pp. 185-90)(10)

Throughout the play Daniel displays what appears upon reflection to be a reverse image of creativity. Genuine creation involves a deeply personal act. It is resourced at the spiritual center of the person whom it expresses and engages. Daniel's efforts fall short of this. His artistic inspiration is drawn not from the depth of his own being but from the lives of others--Rose, John, Aunt Solange. He uses his literary talent to embellish what was real and vital in the lives of others close to him. At times he distorts, even warps, personal aspects of the private lives of those close to him for their titilating or shocking effect.

In another respect too Daniel presents a reverse image of genuine artistic creation. His efforts as a playwright find their direction by seeking the approval of others, Paul Thomas, the public, or other drama critics, instead of being guided by a profound urge or a strong personal inspiration. Marcel warns that one can be misled if one takes the direction of one's life or work from outsiders. One may even become estranged from one's true source of inspiration, the depth of oneself, and profane one's productivity, letting it become merely compliance to the critics' tastes and the public's expectations.(11)

In his philosophic reflections Marcel noted that genuine creations arise from the depths of a person. Creativity springs from the spiritual center of oneself. So for one to remain creative it is necessary to maintain vital contact with what is alive in oneself and to resist the temptation to profane oneself, thereby becoming alienated from one's true self. One must instead remain simple and in touch with one's true self, preserving a real intimacy of presence with oneself. For the center of personhood, that particle of divine creation that reveals itself only to love, is that depth of self that resources genuine creation.(12)

Marcel even maintains that it is finally only the artist who can truly evaluate his or her creation. For only the artist can know whether he or she has responded faithfully to a particular inner call. Only the author can estimate the extent to which the creation measures up to, corresponds to, or incarnates the original inspiration that gave rise to the created work.(13)

Our reflections thus far enable us to see that human creation involves taking something given, adding something of oneself and thereby producing something new.(14) We also see that genuine creation springs from the spiritual center of the person.(15) And we may add that the more creation flows from the very depth of who a person is, the more that creation has the characteristics of freedom, spontaneity, originality, and value.(16)

As we continue our consideration of Daniel's efforts toward successful creativity and insights from Marcel's later philosophic reflections that clarify these dramatic situations, we shall continue to identify some of the requisite conditions ·for genuine human creativity.

As we consider Daniel's efforts in human creation, we see that like his attempts at artistic creation, while they may at first appear to be successful, they reveal themselves upon reflection to be in fact failures.

Daniel, for his part, feels elated with his theatrical success and equally content with the way he has "managed" his relations with those closest to him. Yet the end of the play suggests the tragic failure that characterizes the intimate family relations in the Meyrieux household.

Daniel's failure as a father is clear both from reflection on the play and from the perspectives of thought developed in the philosophic essay "The Creative Vow as the Essence of Fatherhood."(17) Once again the characters and situation of the play offer, as it were, a reverse image of what genuine fatherhood or genuine human creation would involve, and the philosophic analysis pursues further the question of what the nature and possibility of genuine human creativity would involve.

While Daniel did beget a son, this happened as a mere biological act. Daniel's relationships were devoid of any of the characteristic dimensions of genuine human creation. Daniel begot a child, but although he had several opportunities to acknowledge John as his son, that is "to be a real father" to him, Daniel declined or refused all of these. Other than the biological act, Daniel denied any responsibility for the creation of the child. Daniel did not acknowledge John as his son and refused to marry or support John's mother. The decision to adopt John into the Meyrieux family after the death of his mother was entirely at the insistence of Rose, the foster mother. Daniel only went along with it for Rose's sake, he himself never understanding why she wanted such a situation. Even when John had been adopted, Daniel never accepted or loved him, but rather belittled and distanced him, sometimes in not too subtle ways. He just couldn't believe the genuine affection that existed between Rose and John. Then when John learned that Daniel was his natural father, Daniel thought only of finding some way of reestablishing himself in the boy's esteem. When challenged and confronted by embarrassing questions, Daniel immediately exercised his parental authority by sending John away...to boarding school.

Daniel patently fails in his human creativity or responsible parenting. This appears to have occurred for lack of what Marcel called "availability," a disposition or willingness to be there with and for another and to care for the life of that other.(18) Daniel appears as a rather shallow, egotistical, and self-absorbed person. He showed himself incapable of the deep personal commitment and the generosity of love that genuine fatherhood entails. Marcel discovered personally and then disclosed through philosophic reflection that the essence of human parenting is a creative vow. As he clarified in "The Creative Vow as the Essence of Fatherhood," parenting is not a mere biological act, nor is it some casual or impersonal gesture. It requires a deeply personal act of commitment. Parenting involves a vow of commitment to be with and for another, guiding that other through growth toward fulfillment in human personhood.

Parenting is a generous act of sharing life. The sharing is not casual or occasional but should rather be generous and personally responsible. Human creation springs from the conviction that life is a rich gift, and it expresses a willingness to share that gift. The creative vow calls forth a commitment to another to support that other in the adventure of life and to offer one´s guidance and inheritance toward the development of that life.(19)

In other essays, "The Mystery of Family" and "The Ego and its Relation to Others," Marcel points out that it is one´s experience of a family of origin that assures a child that he or she is the object of love and careful attention, shareholder of a wealth in life that is to be developed so that it can be received in turn by one´s own children.(20)

To see the lack of hope that John has for any happiness in life is to appreciate the extent to which Daniel´s parenting has failed. John, rejected by his father, effectively makes his way unwittingly and ironically to follow in his father´s own tragic footsteps.

Rose´s rebellion against Daniel because of what is happening to John and because of what has become of their marriage reveals the root source of Daniel´s failure in human creativity. Daniel, it appears tragically, is incapable of any genuine communion of love.

What Rose and Daniel have lived is a love of fusion. She has enriched and has gradually been absorbed into his life. As Daniel said, they are not two but one. Yet Rose realizes that this is finally not a good thing because he has annexed her. She no longer counts as a person. There is no longer any need to consult her wishes, to consider her for herself, or to care for happiness in her life. Daniel´s response is merely to remind her that she is better treated than the wives of many writers he knows so she ought to be thankful for that.(21)

What Rose desires is a genuine communion of love, wherein, as in any genuine communion, the two are together in their difference.(22) Or as Edith expressed it in another context in The Unfathomable, "it is not his life, nor is it my life, it is our life."(23) Rose seems to aspire toward this genuine communion of love first for the sake of John, so that his life not be sacrificed and merely used, but that he be appreciated for his real worth, that Daniel recognize as Rose does that John has real sensitivity and depth. Rose wishes and for a moment insists that Daniel put aside his work and do something to protect their son and to promote his happiness and well-being in life.

Daniel, for his part, is incapable of this kind of love. Or at least he is unwilling now to consider Rose and John as others, people whose life and happiness call for respectful care and the involvement of self-giving love on the part of Daniel. Daniel either simply cannot hear or simply refuses this call to love. Moreover, he takes Rose´s son away from her. Her heart is broken, so that finally and tragically she knows that their union, which exalts Daniel, is neither happy nor fruitful.(24)

Marcel shows in the tragedy of The Rebellious Heart and further clarifies through reflections in Creative Fidelity that genuine creativity is resourced in a communion of love.

For Marcel creative fidelity is a requisite condition for any artistic or human creation. Reflection on the mystery of human and artistic creation reveals that creativity is rooted in fidelity. Ideally, creative fidelity is lived as a communion of love. It involves a fidelity to oneself, a fidelity to others, and a fidelity to an Absolute Other.(25)

In the essay "Obedience and Fidelity," in which Marcel showed that genuine creativity requires a living fidelity to the spiritual depths of oneself, he also explained that this fidelity to oneself seems almost inseparable from a fidelity to another. For, paradoxically, one finds fulfillment as a person through self-giving. And genuine creativity is lived also as a response to a call. Thus a communion of love is the ideal context in which human creation can occur.(26)

This situation is a far cry from the pitiable marriage that Rose laments at the end of The Rebellious Heart. Creative fidelity is a communion of love. Creative actions are realized as incarnate gestures in response to the appeal of the loved one to whom one has consecrated one´s life. It is the actual presence of the beloved that invites and inspires human creation. In a genuine communion of love, each partner remains available to hear and willing to respond to the other´s appeal. It is through a permanent physical/spiritual presence that the members of that community of love invite and inspire one another´s creativity.(27)

The Rebellious Heart was staged and published in 1921. The philosophic essays, "On the Ontological Mystery," "Obedience and Fidelity," and "Creative Fidelity" appeared in 1932, 1940, and 1944. It was over the course of twenty years that Marcel developed the notion of creative fidelity, a central theme in his work and a leading idea in his life. Marcel discovered this notion in an original manner. As he expressed it, his life

105

traveled one road, yet theater and philosophy depicted the scenery on either side of the territory through which he traveled.(28) Theater presents the concrete approach to the lived situation, and philosophy offers a reflective analysis of the drama portrayed. Marcel also maintained that theater often showed the tragic situations in life that communicate an inclination toward despair, but that also bring a certain light that opens onto mystery and hope.(29) Philosophy, through a process of critical reflection, can then bring to light a positive identification of what genuine human creation entails.(30)

The dual reflection shows the dangers and difficulties but also highlights the positive value and possibility of an authentic creativity that calls for freedom's choice of a way of living that draws on humanity's deepest resources and makes the noblest uses of a person's potential. Still, it is theater that lets us enter into the lived situation that enables us to follow the consciousness of the tragic and opens onto the ontological mystery where we reach for our ultimate recourse.(31) One finds in Marcel's thought the idea that in situations wherein despair is a real temptation, there hope may appear in its intense purity.(32) This is reminiscent of Alfred de Vigny's saying that our cries of distress are often our most beautiful songs.

Marcel is convinced that only a most patient, probative, and also most painful reflection can lead to the discovery of an Absolute that reveals itself as our ultimate recourse and whose fidelity is the foundation of our own.(33) For Marcel this Other, this Absolute Thou, becomes part of the integral reality of our life and our creation.(34)

He sees human creation as a free and deeply personal act that is rooted in fidelity: fidelity to oneself who lives, fidelity to the other who inspires and invites, and fidelity to an Other who enlivens, invites, inspires, and illumines genuine creativity.(35)

Notes to Chapter V.   The Rebellious Heart: and Human Creation

1. Le Coeur des autres, Paris, Grasset, 1921, pp. v-132. Play
    premiered March 17, 1921 at the New Theater in Paris. The
    Rebellious Heart in The Existential Drama of Gabriel Marcel,
    ed. F. J. Lescoe, McAuley Institute, West Hartford, CT.,
    1974, pp. 145-215, cf. p. 4.

2. The Rebellious Heart, Act II, Scene IX, p. 191.

3. Ibid., Act III, Scene VI, p. 215.

4. "The Drama of the Soul in Exile" in Three Plays by Gabriel
    Marcel: A Man of God, Ariadne, The Votive Candle, New
    York, Hill and Wang, 1965, p. 21.

5. The Rebellious Heart, Paris, Grasset, 1921, pp. v-132; The
    Rebellious Heart in The Existential Drama of Gabriel Marcel,
    ed. F. J. Lescoe, McAuley Institute, West Hartford, CT.,
    1974, pp. 145-215. Creative Fidelity, New York, Farrar,
    Straus and Company, 1964, xxvi-261; Du Refus à
    l'Invocation, Paris, Gallimard, 1940, pp. 326; Homo Viator
    Introduction to a Metaphysic of Hope, New York, Harper and
    Bros., 1962, pp. 270; Homo Viator Prolégomènes à une
    métaphysique de l'espérance, Paris, Aubier, 1944,
    pp. iii-369.

6. "Testament philosophique" (Vienna, Sept. 1968) in La Revue
    de Métaphysique et de Morale, tome 74, July-Sept., 1969,
    pp. 257, 258, 259. Reprinted in Présence de Gabriel
    Marcel, Cahier 4 Gabriel Marcel et les injustices de ce
    temps. La responsabilité du philosophe, Paris,
    Aubier-Montaigne, 1983, pp. 127-37, cf. pp. 130-34.

7. The Rebellious Heart, Act II, Scene 7, pp. 186-87.

8. Ibid., Act I, Scene 2, pp. 157-58; Act III, Scene 3, p. 205.

9. Ibid., Act I, Scene 1, pp. 149-50; Act I, Scene 2,
    pp. 157-58.

10. Ibid., Act I, Scene 2, pp. 153-58; Act II, Scene 7,
     pp. 185-90.

11. "Obedience and Fidelity" in Homo Viator, pp. 129-32.

12. Ibid., pp. 131-32.

13. Ibid., p. 130.

14. "Testament philosophique," pp. 257, 258, 259.

15. "Obedience and Fidelity" in Homo Viator, pp. 131-32.

16. Ibid., pp. 129-34; "The Creative Vow as the Essence of Fatherhood" in Homo Viator, pp. 105-106; "Observations on the Notions of the Act and the Person," Ch. V, in Creative Fidelity, pp. 108-109.

17. "The Creative Vow as the Essence of Fatherhood" in Homo Viator, pp. 98-124.

18. "Belonging and Disposability," Ch. II in Creative Fidelity, pp. 38-57, esp. p. 53.

19. "The Creative Vow as the Essence of Fatherhood," in Homo Viator, pp. 113-15.

20. "The Ego and its Relation to Others," in Homo Viator, pp. 13-28; "The Mystery of Family," in Homo Viator, pp. 68-97.

21. The Rebellious Heart, Act III, Scene 3, p. 204.

22. Introduction to Creative Fidelity, p. 8.

23. The Unfathomable in Presence and Immortality, Pittsburgh, PA., Duquesne University Press, 1967, p. 280.

24. The Rebellious Heart, Act III, Scene VI, p. 215.

25. "Obedience and Fidelity," in Homo Viator, pp. 132-34.

26. Ibid., pp. 132-34; "The Ego and its Relation to Others," in Homo Viator, pp. 22-23; "The Creative Vow as the Essence of Fatherhood," in Homo Viator, pp. 104-106, 117-20.

27. "The Creative Vow as the Essence of Fatherhood," in Homo Viator, pp. 117-20.

28. The Existential Background of Human Dignity, Cambridge, MA, Harvard University Press, 1963, pp. 60-62; "An Essay in Autobiography," in The Philosophy of Existentialism, Secaucus, NJ, Citadel Press, 1956, p. 128. "Gabriel Marcel: Le Paradoxe du Philosophe-Dramaturge," Paris, no date, Alliance Française.

29. "Le Secret est dans les îles," in Le Secret est dans les
    îles, Paris, Plon, 1967, p. 21.

30. L'Heure théâtrale, de Giraudoux à J. P. Sartre, Paris,
    Plon, 1959, avant-propos, p. xi.

31. The Existential Background of Human Dignity, pp. 64-69; "Les
    vrais problèmes de Rome n'est plus dans Rome," in Rome
    n'est plus dans Rome, Paris, La Table Ronde, 1951, p. 162;
    "On the Ontological Mystery," in The Philosophy of
    Existentialism, Secaucus, N. J., Citadel Press, 1956,
    pp. 23, 26, 32.

32. "On the Ontological Mystery," in The Philosophy of
    Existentialism, p. 32; "Sketch of a Phenomenology and a
    Metaphysic of Hope" in Homo Viator, p. 36.

33. Preface to Le Seuil Invisible, Paris, Grasset, 1914,
    pp. 6-8; "On the Ontological Mystery," pp. 23, 24, 32, 34,
    38-39; "Sketch of a Phenomenology and a Metaphysic of Hope,"
    in Homo Viator, pp. 60-63, 66-67.

34. "Meditations on the Idea of a Proof for the Existence of
    God," Ch. IX in Creative Fidelity, pp. 182-83.

35. "Creative Fidelity," Ch. VIII in Creative Fidelity,
    pp. 147-74; "Meditations on the Idea of a Proof for the
    Existence of God," Ch. IX in Creative Fidelity, pp. 175-83;
    "From Opinion to Faith", Ch. VI in Creative Fidelity,
    pp. 120-39.

Chapter VI.   The Double Expertise: Fidelity and Infidelity

The Double Expertise, a one-act comedy, portrays the tragicomic situation that develops as Gilbert Marquiset, mustering all the help he can, tries to find grounds for marrying his third wife. The setting is an elegant bachelor apartment, Gilbert´s home in Paris, 1937.(1)

Since Gilbert´s mind muddles when he must decide on something like marriage, he has invited his first wife, Georgette, to advise him. Georgette´s second husband, Stani Zürcher, accompanies her. Kate Leliégeois, Gil´s second wife, drops in unexpectedly. She has come to claim something toward overdue alimony payments. She decides to stay, feeling that she too should have the right to vote on Gil´s choice.

When Miss Hedwig Frühling, Gilbert´s intended, arrives, she is accompanied by her uncle, Mr. Edward Zürcher, an appraiser with a double expertise. The conversation that ensues inquires about Hedwig´s likes and dislikes both for the sake of small talk and to ascertain whether she is a suitable partner for Gil. Meanwhile Ed Zürcher wanders around the apartment, inspecting its furnishings as one might preview a gallery prior to an art auction or an antique sale.

Protesting against Zürcher´s estimation of Gil´s lack of taste, Georgette and Kate reveal that each of them was married to Gil for a brief time, Georgette for three years and Kate for fourteen months. On the strength of that, Zürcher advises Hedwig to leave. To everyone´s amazement, Hedwig, whose name means strife, remains and takes charge. She proclaims an ultimatum. Either they all remain as a harmonious group, or the others will have to leave and she will stay there alone with Gil.

Noticing the familiar tone Stani uses with Zürcher, and learning that they are father and son who became estranged over an inheritance settlement, Hedwig announces that those two will go out onto the balcony and settle their differences. Before that, however, there must be a moment of "recollection." Hedwig announces the procedure they will follow. Each is to listen in silence to his or her conscience and then write his or her inspiration on a piece of paper.

Hedwig reads the statements aloud and comments on each one. To Georgette and Stani´s statement that they want to see prospectuses on Hedwig´s father´s hotels, Hedwig exclaims triumphantly, "There no longer are any hotels. They were sold in order to found a commune to regenerate life among those who can

111

no longer live, nor work, nor love."(2)

Georgette and Stani's reaction to that news is clear-cut. No hotels, no marriage contract. As Georgette and Stani leave, they shake Gil's hand as one might at graveside after a funeral ceremony. Kate, for her part, takes a Dufy painting to cover back alimony payments. Zurcher drifts out, babbling about how this experience has aged him ten years.

Hedwig and Gil are alone. Hedwig coos enthusiastically to Gil. "You'll see, we'll lead a very restful life ...green vegetables ...fresh air ...long walks ...soothing naps.... Gradually you'll learn to live a natural healthy life." Gil, dumbfounded, groans his response, "a life that restful, I'm afraid it might kill me."(3)

The Double Expertise is an artful, cleverly written comedy. It is amusing in many ways, yet it also has a disquieting effect. Marcel referred to his comedy as a "yes...but" part of his work. It is precisely this unsettling aspect of the play that we will investigate.

On an obvious level, the play is a satirical farce. Its theme of matchmaking with family and friends assisting fits comfortably into the tradition of situational comedies. Comic characters are caught up in the ridiculous task of trying to find grounds for matrimony where patently none seem to exist. There is, moreover, the comic device of concealed identities becoming revealed and overlapping relationships becoming embarrassingly clear. There is also the parody of caricatures. As the identities of the jury--Gil, Georgette, Stani, and Kate--and the appraiser--Ed Zurcher--are disclosed, it becomes clear that they in no way have qualities of expertise that would inspire confidence in their abilities to evaluate grounds for matrimony, advise about good relationships, or guide harmonious living. There is furthermore the farcical, almost slapstick, ending as the hope for a good match fizzles and the gathering breaks up. The others leave in a surprising reversal of the movement toward a merger that characterized the direction of the play up to that point. Finally, there is the ironic and disonant note as Gil and Hedwig find themselves alone together. Hedwig proclaims what an idyllic life they'll lead, and Gil responds that a life that restful could kill him.

The Double Expertise is a clever and amusing farce. Upon reflection, however, we can notice that there is a shadow side to the whole play that has a haunting effect. At the play's end, it is apparent that the matchmaking has failed. Hedwig and Gilbert appear ill suited, and as appraiser and jury leave, the verdict seems to read "no deal." Still there is a melancholic note of nostalgia. For Gilbert needs a wife, someone to care for him, and Hedwig needs someone to take care of. Clearly Gil needs to learn to live, to love, and to work, and Hedwig is all ready to rehabilitate him. The prospect seems vain. Yes...but. Perhaps it could work. It is unlikely, yet there is a trace of disappointment. So the play ends on a disconcerting note. There is a similar feeling of uncertainty about the appraiser´s and the jury´s attempts to evaluate. Not only do appraiser and jury agree, no deal. There is an uneasiness about their attempt to find criteria by which to evaluate. Thus a deeper question is unearthed, one that begins to emerge and haunt us. Are there grounds that can motivate a choice and substantiate a prediction for a happy, stable marriage? If not, then are the serial marriages of Gilbert, Georgette, Stani, and perhaps Hedwig, or the marred and broken relationships lived by Kate and Mr. Ed Zurcher the only fate left? If so, that is a sad fate, a disappointingly narrow set of options, an unsettling prospect for those who might still hope for something more stable in human and familial relationships.

Clearly the play gives rise to questions in the minds of its audience. Marcel observed that the last scene of a play is most important both for the unity it brings to the play as a whole and for the questions it raises in the minds of the spectators.(4) Certainly the final scene of The Double Expertise raises the question of whether or not Gil and Hedwig will marry. With that it reopens at a deeper level a whole series of questions about whether or not there are grounds for marriage. The end of the play leaves us with these questions and invites us to reflect on our own and consider whether or not there are grounds for matrimony and criteria that would enable us to foresee whether there are grounds for a solid marriage that might last.

The way we will proceed in our consideration of these questions is first to trace how they are defined in the dramatic action of The Double Expertise and then explore the clarification that philosophic reflection can bring to these questions as Marcel discusses them in "Obedience and Fidelity" and in chapters II, VIII, and IX of Creative Fidelity. (5)

Characters in the play illustrate different attitudes and stances that can be adopted on the issue of criteria for matrimony and for a good and lasting marriage. They bring to light the various interpretations these standpoints suggest. They also occasionally disclose some of the presuppositions of these various stances and attitudes. The characters and action of the play further bring to light certain avenues of investigation that seem worth exploring. In this way The Double Expertise not only raises questions, it brings them more clearly into focus and thus prepares the task of reflective

113

The question of marital criteria runs throughout the entire play. It is clarified and explored but left unanswered. It is up to the audience to critically clarify and personally resolve the issues raised. Right from the start, Georgette and Gilbert compare their successive domestic economies, noting advantages and disadvantages of frugal versus prodigal, calm versus agitated, stable versus changing. Then Georgette and Stani try to help Gil recognize his own estimation of this latest prospect. Is she pretty? Does she suit you? Is she modest, or old fashioned? Is she a nurse? Will she be a good companion for Gil in his old age? In response to a query from Stani, Georgette remarks that marrying is like buying an apartment or even a house. It's quite a permanent arrangement. When Stani retorts that it can always be resold, Georgette admits that that is true, but sold at a loss, so one keeps it.

A propos of Gil's second marriage, with Kate, Georgette affirms that this was merely a parenthetical break. It's as Doctor Zürcher-Solomon says--each person has one serious illness, emotional as well as physical, in his or her lifetime. Gil's marriage to Kate really was a bad precedent. One really shouldn't go against one's deepest feelings. What matters now is to get Gil nicely settled.

A propos of households, finances, and living arrangements, Gil blurts out that Hedwig's father owns three big hotels in Engadine, Switzerland. Stani and Georgette agree that Gil should ask to see the prospectuses on these hotels. No need to be embarrassed, just say that a friend is considering vacationing in that area.

With Kate's arrival on the scene, the importance of financial status in marriage contracts becomes evident. Kate comes to claim something from Gil's apartment as security for late alimony payments. The others really wonder what Kate lives on; her phone has already been disconnected. Both Gil and Stani admit they are financially embarrassed, temporarily a bit short. Georgette has money, and Kate is very nearly bankrupt. Obviously Gil's need for a financially advantageous marriage is capital. The bride-to-be must offer him financial security.

When Miss Hedwig Frühling and her uncle Mr. Edward Zürcher visit, the ensuing conversation searches out points of compatibility and incompatibility. Preferences in life-style vary widely. Personality differences are also significant.

114

Hedwig is a naturalist. Health foods, wildflowers, and the high Alps suit her tastes. She unabashedly states her dislike for cities and for modern art in which nothing is recognizable. She concedes that if one must live in a city one can adjust. Fortunately, however, there are the weekends when one can get out into the country for long walks. On the strength of her own say-so she is very much the doctor and the person in charge. Gil is quite the opposite. He is a city sophisticate. Long walks tire him. The mere prospect of them discourages him. He's also apparently stunned by this enthusiasm for wildlife and nature that the Swiss Miss is exuding.

Uncle Ed, who is not only Hedwig's escort but also an appraiser, inspects the furnishings of Gil's apartment and his impression is quite negative. He judges that there's not much money or class there and so concludes that Gil is not an interesting prospect.

If experience were a criterion for good matches and lasting marriages, Gil might qualify as an expert, since he's been married twice.. Apparently, however, something more than experience, like wisdom, art, or prudence is needed to produce good judgments. Gil has lots of experience, but as Georgette stated , "Gil appears very observant without actually being so."(6) If it comes to making a decision or a well-founded choice, Gil is lost. His mind muddles and he loses his bearings.

Hedwig, who has the least marital experience, is surest of her judgment. She wants to marry. Gil is available. So that makes him eligible. Despite evidence to the contrary, Hedwig hopes for the best. She has complete self-confidence. She looks forward to the marriage and feels sure that it will succeed. The success she envisions, however, involves Gil being transformed to her wishes and desires. He needs to relearn how to live, to love, and to work. They'll proceed gradually. Gil will adjust, even come to enjoy it. After all, as she says, "she's the doctor." Her criteria are her self-confidence and her tenacious desire that things be the way she wants them to be.

Hedwig proposes a method of "recollection"--silent listening to one's own conscience--as a means for discerning and decision-making. In the context of the play, however, this procedure is hardly taken seriously. What we see is a mere parody rather than an authentic exercise of genuine recollection.

Throughout the play, jury and appraiser alike seek by various criteria to estimate whether the proposed match between Hedwig and Gil would be a good and lasting one. A variety of criteria are brought to light. The relevance of taste,

115

life-style preference, harmony or complementarity of personality, financial status, deep feelings, experience, appraiser´s expertise, even "recollection" for discernment were all considered. Yet these criteria did not reach a conclusion in the case of Hedwig and Gil.

The fact that the play ends with every indication that a marriage will not take place, but without assuring that conclusion, raises the question of whether or not the criteria considered by jury and appraiser are adequate. The disconcerting ending to the play seems to raise the question whether grounds for a decision to marry and grounds for a stable and lasting marriage are not of a distinctively different sort. We begin to glimpse that if a marriage occurs, this happens as a result of an interpersonal dialogue that creates a commitment by mutual and reciprocal consent. A decision to marry one another is a free choice created in interpersonal dialogue. If reasons conclude or if criteria compute is this not finally because of a personal element of free choice that intervenes? Is it not the case that no matter how an evaluation process is calculated and tallied, what really counts is that personal element of whim, preference, or commitment that determines what the free choice will be?

As the play ends, who knows if Hedwig and Gil will marry or not? The choice will be determined by their decision or their lack of decision. Ultimately, it is Hedwig and Gil themselves who will create their decision to part company, or to marry or perhaps even to love one another, as unlikely as that may at first appear.(7)

The criteria that surfaced in the play are certainly valid indicators of various kinds of compatibility. Yet these kinds of compatibility are not adequate grounds for matrimony. If marriages are based on these kinds of affinities then the relationships cease to exist when the compatibility is no longer there. Since any and everyone can change regarding the various criteria highlighted in the play, no commitment would be stable if based only on affinities of this sort.

Grounds for matrimony are drawn from a whole different order, namely the distinctively interpersonal order of love, freedom, commitment, and intersubjective communion. Marcel clarifies this point prior to investigating the nature of genuine interpersonal commitments and the possibility of living interpersonal relations with creative fidelity. When Marcel does investigate these issues philosophically, the questions he raises are even deeper and more difficult than those raised by the play, for it is in the context of human freedom´s authenticity that Marcel inquires about the possibility of interpersonal commitments and the possibility of living out these commitments as creative fidelity.(8)

Marcel's philosophic analysis brings into focus the following questions. He inquires whether interpersonal ground for a deep and lasting commitment to marriage can be found. He also seeks to clarify what the nature of such an interpersonal commitment might be. Articulating his questions with reference to human freedom, Marcel wonders how both freedom and fidelity can be preserved within the context of a marriage commitment. Specifically he inquires as to how freedom can commit itself without enslaving the person so committed? He also asks explicitly how one can reasonably commit oneself to love another in the future when circumstances, one's own feelings, and the other person may have changed. For one might be left merely living out routine compliance, fulfilling a promise begrudgingly and not loving genuinely and wholeheartedly. Marcel inquires as to the manner and the conditions in which one can voice a commitment to a lasting interpersonal relationship. He likewise explores how one can live out creative fidelity to such a commitment in a manner that is genuinely faithful and at the same time respectful of freedom and human dignity?

Marcel explores the questions raised by The Double Expertise philosophically in several essays, especially "Obedience and Fidelity" in Homo Viator and chapters of the book entitled in English Creative Fidelity. (9)

When Marcel considers the possibility of a marriage or of any lasting interpersonal commitment, he raises several questions that are intellectually exacting and personally demanding. Can one responsibly commit one's freedom? Has one the right to bind one's freedom in a lasting way to love and be faithful to another person? Does one have the right to engage one's liberty for the future, when circumstances, others, even one's own feelings may have changed? It is these questions that we shall examine in the context of Gabriel Marcel's reflective clarifications of intersubjectivity.

Can one responsibly bind one's freedom, committing oneself to love another with a steadfast love in the future? Certainly one cannot responsibly abdicate freedom, getting rid of responsibility for the use of one's freedom by disposing of that responsibility into the hands of another. Freedom cannot be bound or given away. Nor can freedom be committed to demeaning or enslaving causes without falling beneath the level of human dignity.(10) One cannot responsibly give one's freedom away, but one can validly commit one's freedom, definitively claiming responsibility for that lasting will. One can commit one's

117

freedom responsibly, knowing that one continues to have authorship and responsibility for that commitment. One can commit one´s freedom authentically when one recognizes that to commit oneself to this cause or person is enobling and is in fact the best use one can make of one´s freedom.(11) Only conscious, responsible commitment is worthy of human freedom.

A commitment then that binds people in an interpersonal relationship would have to be made as a mutual agreement of two liberties to be worthy of these people´s dignity. Such a commitment should also evolve through a dialogue of freedom. We will see shortly a sketch of how this commitment can occur.

Still on the side of freedom Marcel pursues the question of whether or not one can validly engage oneself to love another in the future. Would not such a commitment involve a risk of compromising the genuineness of love and the self-determination of freedom? Would not such a situation also introduce the possibility of hypocrisy, since one can easily imagine changes in circumstances and even in character that could cause one to regret the commitment and comply with its demands only in a begrudging way.(12) If a bond were founded only on feelings, circumstances, and compatibilities that can readily change, or even if the relationship were founded on a pledge of freedom that reserved its right to renege, then the commitment would not last if any of these factors changed. Certainly some of the basic factors will alter, and it is all the more likely that a relationship will not last when the commitment is envisioned as being essentially only a conditional one. So Marcel has set forth the challenge to think about how freedom can commit itself without denaturing itself. He further asks, once a pledge is made, how it can be lived out in a manner respectful of freedom´s essential self-determination.

Marcel´s approach to this type of question is usually to reflect critically, exploring various concrete situations until he finds the subjective attitudes that are requisite for certain events or relationships to become possible.

For a valid interpersonal commitment to occur, or even to be possible, several conditions are requisite. The first requisite condition is that there be two persons involved, not just two individuals but rather two persons. What does Marcel mean by that distinction? A person is someone who is available. In order to be capable of self-disposition, one must first have a certain degree of self-possession. A person is one who knows what he or she loves and lives for.

In chapter II of Creative Fidelity on "Belonging and

118

Disposability" Marcel offers a lengthy excursus on belonging.(13) The person who recognizes what he or she wants to be is someone who belongs to himself or herself and who is capable of self-gift. By contrast, someone who does not belong to himself or herself cannot give himself or herself. It follows that the one who says, "I belong to no one, to no cause, I belong only to myself," errs. If one belongs to no one, he does not belong to himself or to anything. As a matter of fact, it is an anarchy beneath the level of liberty to try and maintain that one does not want to devote oneself to any cause, value, or person. Such a person is committed to nothing, consecrated to nothing. Such an individual cannot promise his allegiance or fidelity from one minute to the next. Someone like that pretends to belong to himself or herself alone, but actually he or she belongs to no one, is committed to nothing. By contrast, an authentic person is capable of commitment, devotedness, consecration, self-gift, in brief: love. Such a person knows what he or she loves and lives for. Because of belonging and disposability, such a person has something to give in response to the appeal of another person. We meet here a paradox. To possess oneself is to be capable of giving oneself.(14)

There can be no commitment or self-gift between individuals who do not possess themselves. Availability and belonging are capabilities only of persons who possess themselves, determine and know what they love and live for. The unavailable individual has not determined what he or she values and belongs to, and so that individual is incapable of self-gift. Such an individual is unavailable or indisposable, incapable of consecrating, giving, or commiting himself or herself. All the more so the unavailable individual is incapable of pledging or promising faithfulness in love, now or in the future.

Gilbert is a fine example of someone who does not know who he is or what he wants out of life. He never can decide. He hasn't determined what he loves and lives for, so he hasn't enough self-possession to be capable of self-disposition. He may appear self-centered in his instinct for survival. Still he is not conscious and resolved, or self-possessed enough to be capable of a commitment. Likewise, he is not self-possessed enough to welcome or assume responsibility for another.

Hedwig displays another kind of unavailability. She knows what she wants and is overly determined to get it. She wants the marriage with Gil. She desires it tenaciously. Yet she is unavailable in the sense that she is not disposed to welcome others, be receptive to them, let them be as they are. She is not open to accepting Gil as he is. Instead she is committed only to what Gil will be when he has relearned to live, to work,

119

and to love--under the tutelage of Dr. Frühling, of course. Hedwig doesn´t give the impression that she is capable of receptivity, or that she can love and accept another as he or she is. She is so filled with her own plans that she has no room to welcome another with his or her particular individuality and life projects. To be available, or to be capable of belonging, is to be open and receptive to the presence of the other person. Once again we see a paradox. Giving oneself entails receiving others.(15)

Looking at Gil and Hedwig´s situation from the perspectives that philosophy brings to light, we can begin to understand why the play doesn´t disclose grounds for marriage. Such grounds need to be of an interpersonal sort, and neither Hedwig nor Gil, where they are in the action of the play, seems to show signs of the requisite attitudes necessary in order for a genuine interpersonal relationship to occur.

For an intersubjective relationship to occur, there must be two persons with knowledge and self-determination of who they are and what they live for, two persons capable of availability or disposability and belonging, two persons capable of an act that commits their freedoms and that also creates and confirms their resolve to be loving and available for one another. When these conditions are provided, then an interpersonal relationship can be created by a dialogue of freedoms. First there is an appeal, concretely expressed, of one person inviting the other to be with and for him or her. Then there is the other´s response. It may be yes, no, maybe, no way, later, etc. If the response is affirmative, then the I-Thou encounter occurs, a spiritual bond is created by the reciprocal self-gift of two persons. The spiritual exchange of that reciprocal self-gift to be with and for one another is what authors the I-Thou encounter and constitutes an I-Thou relationship.(16)

An I-Thou relationship is a spiritual exchange of persons willing to be with and for one another. Normally an I-Thou encounter grows into a stable interpersonal relationship of love and friendship. Furthermore, this interpersonal relationship can develop to constitute a veritable co-esse, a stable communion of intersubjectivity, or an interpersonal bond of love. The logic of love wants a relationship to be permanent. As Marcel wrote, "To say to someone, ´I love you´ is to say to that person, ´You...you will not die.´" To love someone is to want that person to be and to be a presence for me.(17)

How can one promise love that is lasting? Obviously such a commitment can only be made under certain exacting conditions and with the noblest of human attitudes.(18)

What are the requisite conditions? And how can a lasting commitment be validly founded? As we said earlier, a commitment requires two persons who know what they want from life. It is also requisite that these two persons be sufficiently transparent to reveal themselves to one another. It is likewise necessary that they be sufficiently respectful of one another to invite and grant disclosure to one another of who they are and what they live for as their relationship grows and meets the challenges of change. Those who propose to commit themselves to one another know what they love and live for. They also know that with all their being at their disposal, it is their will to promote the essentials of life with and for one another. Moreover, they also know that both of them wholeheartedly will to live out their commitment to love one another in the future. And so a vow is made. They consecrate themselves to live with and for one another.

The vow to love one another in a lasting way can indeed be well founded, even if in some respects it partakes of the nature of hope in that it refers to the future that has not yet come to be and so is not yet fully determined, and also in the respect that it recognizes that its grounds of assurance are interpersonal. Marcel points out that one should never underestimate the determination and strength that one receives toward living out one's promises from the very fact that one resolves to remain faithful.

> The fact is that when I commit myself, I grant in principle that the commitment will not again be put in question. And it is clear that this active volition not to question something again intervenes as an essential element in the determination of what in fact will be the case....My behaviour will be completely colored by this act embodying the decision that the commitment will not again be questioned. The possibility which has been barred or denied will thus be demoted to the rank of a temptation.(19)

Some view the future as if it were an event that happens to us without our being in any way able to influence its significance. Such an attitude looks at one's pledge from the outside as would a distant spectator. (20) Yet such distancing from one's act can be the beginning of one's disowning it. In fact this attitude entails, whether consciously or not, the betrayal of a mystery that one is part of and reduces that mystery to the status of a problem from which one is disengaged.(21) By contrast, it is possible to see that one's attitude and resolve now can greatly influence one's future stance and choices. So what is capitally important is to recognize that once one's troth is pledged, once one's life is committed, then one considers as a temptation to betrayal any inclination toward infidelity that might occur. The sense of freedom's living in love is to refresh and renew this commitment of love, to complete it and to enjoy fulfilling it. Any idea of abandoning this commitment or bond of love appears as a betrayal of one's beloved, oneself, and one's life and not in some distorted way as a chance for a new life or a second career. Marcel even goes so far as to ask whether one may not pledge as part of one's original commitment the intention that, even if on some level one's feelings alter, one's behavior would nonetheless remain consistent with one's original commitment. Marcel observes that in certain instances this can even be a higher form of fidelity.(22)

Marcel observes that the vow of interpersonal commitment is sacred, essentially because it springs from freedom. It is I myself who create it, will it, pledge it, offer it as a gift to another person. The more the act is free, the more it is personal, that is acknowledged by its author.(23) The vow is also sacred because it is addressed to another person whom it engages and affects. The more I realize that the other is incapable of exacting compliance and is in fact powerless against me if I should forsake my pledge, the more I see the other as vulnerable and recognize the sacredness of the trust for which I am responsible. Furthermore, the more the act is free, the more it becomes an act of self-giving love, not a selfish act of covetous desire that seeks principally the advantages the other may provide.(24)

It is finally significant that the vow is spoken as an act of hope that is also the beginning of a prayer. "May it be given to us to find the means to remain faithful to the love we now vow."(25)

A vow of unconditional and permanent love is a vow that strives to be absolute. It thus anticipates and calls upon the help of an Absolute Thou as the ultimate source of our strength and hope. As Marcel wrote in Homo Viator, the statement of hope in its ultimate intensity and purity is "I hope in Thee for us."(26)

As Marcel sees interpersonal relations evolve, they develop through dialogue and growing engagement of freedoms whereby persons commit themselves more and more to be fully and permanently with and for one another. The relationship is initiated through a dialogue of freedoms: appeal, response, and gratuitous conferral of presence. This reciprocal agreement

122

constitutes an I-Thou encounter. If an interpersonal relationship develops, the spiritual exchange of presence and availability increases. If friendship, marriage, or religious commitment evolves, it comes to the point of commitment that Marcel describes as "belonging."

In chapter two of Creative Fidelity, "Belonging and Disposability," Marcel inquires as to what can it mean to use the term "belonging," not in the context of things, but in the order of intersubjectivity? To say "you belong to me" certainly does not mean that you belong to me like a slave or a bicycle. To say "you belong to me," means that I take to heart everything that affects you and your well-being, as affecting me. To say "I belong to you" rejects any connotation of possession or abdication of autonomy. It affirms that all I am and have is at your disposal. There is a trust fund in your account that you can draw on in support of your hopes and projects.(27)

It is this sense of belonging and assured availability that is affirmed in a commitment of love--in friendship, marriage, or religious promises. A pledge of commitment formalizes the belonging, it actualizes the commitment of freedom in an explicit way and clarifies the nature of the relationship and the legitimate expectations it includes. A commitment of matrimony aspires to be a total and complete self-giving. The intimacy, depth, and completeness of that reciprocal self-gift calls for a commitment that is interpersonal and lasting. And the living out of a lasting commitment of belonging in an authentic fashion is what Marcel calls "creative fidelity."

Marcel reflects on how it is possible to live fidelity in a manner that is respectful of the dignity of freedom and also of the exigencies of genuine communion of love. The following discussion clarifies the authentic manner of living creative fidelity. The description also clarifies an authentic manner of founding a vow of marriage as an interpersonal commitment.

Marcel purifies our understanding through a negative clarification. Creative fidelity is not merely certain forms of conformity or unswerving compliance. Creative fidelity is the willingness to invoke the actual presence of the beloved and to expect in relation to gratuitously conferred renewals of the actual presence of that loved one, an incitement to create, that is to love faithfully in new and fresh ways.

So Marcel clarifies. Creative fidelity is not merely keeping one's promises no matter what, even though it is good to keep one's promises. Nor is creative fidelity merely a question of fulfilling contractual obligations one has agreed to, though it is good to be true to one's word. These forms of compliance can become impersonal, mechanical, routine observances. They can also become merely annoying demands to which one responds grudgingly and finally with bitterness and resentment. Fidelity is not simply a question of constancy in one's behavior or consistency in complying one's behavior to one's principles or promises, or one's reputation or popular image. Nor is creative fidelity a simple compliance to what one believes others expect of him or her.(28)

Marcel points out that it is difficult to ascertain to what or to whom one is faithful. It is difficult to discern whether fidelity is lived first as faithfulness to oneself, or faithfulness to another. It is likely that normally one lives faithfulness to the other in the appeal he or she is and to oneself in the response that one is to that invitation, and in the joy that one has to be a response of creative fidelity to that call to be.(29)

Fidelity is certainly not merely repeating certain words or gestures. Nor is it merely a question of obeying orders, observing laws, and following rules. In the essay, "Obedience and Fidelity," Marcel notes that obedience may be commanded by a chief or officer with authority to direct certain functions, but fidelity cannot be ordered merely by dint of office or authority. Fidelity must be merited, and it is addressed to a person, not an office, idol, or role.(30)

Actually the form of fidelity that is authentic and well founded, that form of fidelity that can renew itself and remain creative, is a fidelity that invokes the actual presence of the other person. Conferred gratuitously, it is the presence of the other person that incites love and inspires incarnate gestures expressing love, that is, acts of creative fidelity.

The renewals of presence that refresh love and fidelity are also acts of intersubjectivity. Marcel notes in his essay "On the Ontological Mystery" that it depends upon me to invoke presence, to remain open, receptive, permeable. But in point of fact it does not depend totally on me to summon it forth. When presence is renewed, that revelation, a correlate to invocation, inevitably manifests itself as gift and always brings an inspiration to create. Presence always has its characteristic traits of gratuity, altereity, and incitement to create.(31)

This positive sketch of the nature of an authentic interpersonal commitment and a life of creative fidelity that we have drawn from Marcel's philosophic reflections goes far beyond what we might have imagined from the options depicted in the tragicomic farce The Double Expertise. In this instance again we see that theater and philosophy complement one another remarkably for those willing to reflect on existential issues that affect our lives.

After both dramatic and philosophic reflections we can see that an adequate, although by no means automatic, foundation for an interpersonal commitment and a lifetime of intersubjective communion requires the following attitudes and subjective dispositions:

1) That one is capable of self-possession and self-disposition.

2) That both persons recognize one another as willing the same essentials for life, and as being willing to share and provide these essentials of life for one another and eventually for others too.

3) That the interpersonal commitment to be with and for one another for life is coauthored by a dialogue of freedoms, thus co-constituting a spiritual exchange that becomes a communion of intersubjectivity, a veritable co-esse.

4) That people express this mutual and reciprocal self-gift in a resolve of freedoms that expresses itself as a vow that includes a note of hope and a tone of prayer.

5) That people renew this spiritual exchange by acts of presence one to another, as privileged and tangible moments of the intersubjective communion that founds and renews their life of creative fidelity.

Notes to Chapter VI. The Double Expertise: Fidelity and
Infidelity

1. La Double Expertise in Théâtre comique, Paris, Albin
    Michel, 1947; Two One Act Plays by Gabriel Marcel: Dot the I
    and The Double Expertise, Lanham, Maryland, University Press
    of America, 1986, pp. 23-38.

2. The Double Expertise, Act I, Scene 3, p. 37.

3. Ibid, p. 38.

4. "Drama of the Soul in Exile," in Three Plays by Gabriel
    Marcel, New York, Hill and Wang, 1965, p. 30; Le Secret est
    dans les îles, Paris, Plon, Preface, pp. 12, 20-21.

5. Creative Fidelity, New York, Farrar, Straus and Co., Ch. II,
    "Belonging and Disposability," pp. 38-57; Ch. V,
    "Observations on the Notion of the Act and the Person,"
    pp. 104-19; Ch. VIII, "Creative Fidelity," pp. 147-74; Ch.
    IX, "Meditations on the Idea of a Proof for the Existence of
    God," pp. 175-83. Homo Viator An Introduction to a
    Metaphysic of Hope, New York, Harper Bros., 1962, Chicago,
    Henry Regnery Co., 1952, "Obedience and Fidelity,"
    pp. 125-34.

6. The Double Expertise, Act I, Scene 1, p. 28.

7. L'Heure théâtrale, Paris, Plon, 1959, avant-propos,
    p. iv.

8. Creative Fidelity, Ch. I, "Incarnate Being as the Central
    Datum of Metaphysical Reflection," pp. 26, 30; Ch. II,
    "Belonging and Disposability," pp. 147-74; Homo Viator,
    "Obedience and Fidelity," pp. 125-34.

9. Cf. note 5 above.

10. "Obedience and Fidelity," p. 129.

11. Creative Fidelity, Ch. II, "Belonging and Disposability,"
    pp. 47-49.

12. Ibid., Ch. VIII, "Creative Fidelity," pp. 153-64.

13. Ibid., Ch. II, "Belonging and Disposability," pp. 38-47.

14. Ibid., "Belonging and Disposability," pp. 51-55; Homo Viator, "The Ego and its Relation to Others," pp. 13-28; The Philosophy of Existentialism, Secaucus, New Jersey, Citadel Press, 1956, "On the Ontological Mystery," pp. 24-25.

15. Creative Fidelity, Ch. II, "Incarnate Being as the Central Datum of Metaphysical Reflection," pp. 27-29.

16. Ibid., pp. 32-34; "On the Ontological Mystery," p. 39.

17. Trois Pièces, Le Regard neuf, Le Mort de demain, La Chapelle ardente, (Three Plays, The New Look, Tomorrow's Dead, The Votive Candle), Paris, Plon, 1931, Le Mort de demain (Tomorrow's Dead), Act II, Scene 6, p. 161; cited by Joseph Chenu, Le Théâtre de Gabriel Marcel et sa signification métaphysique, Paris, Aubier, 1948, p. 97.

18. Creative Fidelity, Ch. VIII, "Creative Fidelity," pp. 157-59, 160-62.

19. Ibid., p. 162.

20. Ibid., Ch. I, "Incarnate Being as the Central Datum of Metaphysical Reflection," p. 31.

21. Ibid., Ch. VIII, "Creative Fidelity," pp. 163-64; "On the Ontological Mystery," pp. 28-30, 35.

22. Ibid., Ch. VIII, "Creative Fidelity," p. 158.

23. Ibid., Ch. V, "Observations on the Notions of the Act and the Person," pp. 107-109, 113; "Obedience and Fidelity," pp. 132-33.

24. "On the Ontological Mystery," p. 39.

25. "Obedience and Fidelity," p. 133.

26. Creative Fidelity, Ch. VIII, "Creative Fidelity," pp. 166-67; "Obedience and Fidelity," p. 134; Homo Viator, "Sketch of a Phenomenology and a Metaphysic of Hope," pp. 29-67, especially pp. 60-61.

27. Creative Fidelity, Ch. IV, "Phenomenological Notes on Being in a Situation," pp. 97-100; "On the Ontological Mystery," p. 40.

28. "Obedience and Fidelity," pp. 128-32.

29. Ibid., pp. 129-32; Présence Gabriel Marcel Cahier 4, Paris, Aubier, 1983, Gabriel Marcel et les injustices de ce temps. La responsabilité de philosophe, "Testament philosophique," (Vienna, September 1968), pp. 130, 132-33.

30. "Obedience and Fidelity," pp. 127-28.

31. "On the Ontological Mystery," pp. 37-38.

Chapter VII. Colombyre or the Torch of Peace: The Role of
Person-Communities in Living Creative Fidelity to Values.

Creative fidelity is one of the central and most significant
themes in the thought of Gabriel Marcel. The present chapter
examines one aspect of this exceedingly rich theme, focusing upon
Marcel's inquiry into the possibility of living with creative
fidelity to humanizing values in the face of a situation
threatening their survival.

To retrace Marcel's reflective clarification of this topic
this chapter will examine the development of his thought through
his dramatic and philosophic works: Colombyre or the Torch of
Peace, a comedy in three acts written in 1937, and "The Dangerous
Situation of Ethical Values," an essay of philosophic reflection
written in 1943.(1) This fresh approach to studying Gabriel
Marcel's work is intended both to illustrate the important
interconnections between his dramatic and philosophic works and
to permit a faithful portrayal of the clarification he brings to
the question of the possibility of creative fidelity to values in
a dangerous situation wherein their survival is menaced.

The procedure of the study will be as follows. First, the
distinctive features of Marcel's drama will be summarized with a
view toward identifying its relation to his philosophic
reflection. Second, the play Colombyre will be examined in order
to sketch the situation it conveys and to summarize the questions
it raises. Third, the essay "The Dangerous Situation of Ethical
Values" will be seen to illustrate the clarification philosophic
reflection brings to questions underlying an existential
situation. Fourth, the findings on the significance of dramatic
approaches to philosophic reflections will be summarized as well
as the clarification they bring to our understanding of the
indispensible role of person communities in providing for the
survival of values.

Existential theater, as Marcel conceives it, communicates a
concrete situation that enables the author and the audience
consciously to participate in it. The development of the
dramatic action evokes an awareness of the fundamental antinomies
characterizing the human condition. The drama evolves among
persons whose attitudes and alternate stances of interpretation
the audience can recognize as being on some level their own. The
distinctive dramatic element in existential theater is the
emergence and heightening of consciousness for both the drama's
characters and the audience. The successful final act of an
existential drama is not one that settles all the problematic
elements of the situation, but one that brings a certain dawning
of light.(2)

Marcel´s theater focuses on the dramatic issue of whether, in a given concrete situation, a certain quality of life or more precisely a certain quality of interpersonal communion is possible. At the end of his plays, author, protagonists, and audience alike arrive at a certain consciousness of this existential issue, the awareness of which enables them to be beneficiaries of a certain diffuse light in which to carry on the pursuit of their existential inquiry. The complementary role of philosophic reflection is to bring this awareness of existential questions and light to another, higher level of consciousness and clarification.(3)

Marcel´s philosophic essays interpret the existential situation and articulate its existential questions in more general and fundamental terms. The critical analysis and dialectical reasoning of philosophic reflection shed light on the fundamental antinomies of the human condition by identifying their root sources. At the same time, phenomenological analysis clarifies the requisite attitudes and conditions of possibility for gathering ontological resources that would enable one to transcend these antinomies and authentically realize one´s noblest and deepest possibilities.

Philosophic reflection continues the questioning to which existential drama gives rise and through a more rigorous style of inquiry brings it to a level of critically reasoned clarification. Yet, philosophic reflection continually draws on the personal engagement in the quest and the concrete approaches to reflection which existential theater can provide.

Let us now consider Marcel´s dramatic approach to a situation wherein the survival of values is dangerously imperiled. Colombyre or the Torch of Peace is set in a Swiss mountain resort in the summer of 1937, that ominous period before the outbreak of World War II. The play represents in farcical fashion a caricature of a peace colony, tracing the complacent vanity of its members, the vagaries of its spirit and goals, and the fragmenting dissolution that becomes its fate. Its style is marked by clever wit, deftly drawn caricatures, sharp-edged humor, ever-present irony, and a comic sense of the ridiculous. The play satirizes the flaws and foibles that undermine the "Colombyre" project´s goal of being "A Torch of Peace." Yet, ironically, its final scene of dissolution touches a chord of nostalgia for the possibility of what might have been, or what perhaps someday might be.

The first act introduces a strange collection of characters who have bought shares in a Swiss mountain villa called

"Colombyre." While this international group seems in some vague way to have as its ambition the preservation and promotion of peace, it quickly becomes apparent that there are sorely lacking any bonds of fraternal love, any kind of consensus about the nature of this collectivity, and any common commitment toward the realization of its goals.

The second act reveals the vanity of "Colombyre"'s pretentions. The various plans for radiating peace fail, while the animosity and open hostility among its members increase. "Colombyre," instead of being a hearth of peace, becomes a hot-bed of strife.

Act three traces the final fragmentation of the "Colombyre" experiment. Its dissolution develops apace with the unraveling of the mystery of the old Russian's violent death. Speculations, accusations, recriminations, plots of assassination, and startling betrayals abound. As the specter of violent death approaches, the option of flight rather than fight wins popular consent. A note scribbled before the cook's hasty departure warns of immanent disaster, and the deciphering of its message spreads panic for fear of a time bomb. All flee in disarray, deserting "Colombyre." Silent in the aura of sunset, "Colombyre" appears to two young lovers as an idyllic setting for a haven of peace. They leave. Explosion. Curtain.

The experiment at "Colombyre" failed. Its pretentions of being a refuge and a radiating center for peace were farcical and doomed. Instead of promoting peace and life, the experiment fomented dissension, destruction, and death. The end of Colombyre certainly raises the issue as to whether all such efforts to ensure the survival of peace are equally ridiculous. Yet, the irony of the final scene, wherein the young couple envisions this site as one day being a radiating center for international peace, does raise the question of whether a person-community could ever contribute effectively to the survival and radiance of peace.

At face value Colombyre seems to ridicule the possibility of a person-community actually resourcing and effectively radiating peace in this world. However, Colombyre is no mere farcical comedy, it is also a satire. Thus, as Colombyre sketches the tragicomic flaws of a ridiculous caricature of a peace center, it also brings into relief and focus paths of inquiry about what the essential features and distinctive traits of a genuine community of creative fidelity might be.

Questions are raised about the possibility and nature of an international community with a bond of fraternal love, a person-community animated by a spirit and light from above, and about the requisite conditions and attitudes for resourcing fidelity to values and extending their realization in this world.

In a subsequent essay, "The Dangerous Situation of Ethical Values," written in December 1943, Marcel articulates his philosophic reflections on the possibility of living creative fidelity to humanizing values in a situation wherein their survival is seriously threatened.

The preliminary sketch in this reflection stresses that person-community is the indispensible context for genuine creative fidelity to values. Values are real and not merely ideas when they are incarnate, that is, realized and embodied within the lives of individual human persons. One's response to values is incarnately expressed toward the concrete reality of individual human persons with, and for whom, values are to be realized. Consistently, one's ethical response is a personal commitment to promote the realization and embodiment of humanizing values and is addressed to that cause as a suprapersonal reality. Thus, one's commitment to promote value with and for other persons engages one in a particular type of unity, which holds together a number of persons within a life they share. In a spirit of loyalty, one's engagement in the cause of a suprapersonal reality, promoting the realization and embodiment of life's values with and for persons, leads to the inclusion of all members of the human community as those with and for whom one strives to see values realized and embodied.(4)

Marcel shows that it is man himself in the unity of his life who is in danger of death. This peril, he notes, applies equally to the concrete individual person as a whole, and to the human race considered as a flowing out or expansion of an essence. Man is threatened and in danger of death by severance from the ontological foundation of life, and also by the separation that alienates him from humankind.(5)

Many forces contribute to the perilous situation. For over four hundred years atheism in our civilization has continually undermined the natural foundations of life upon which faith and virtue grew. For the last century and a half, naturalist and reductionist philosophies have desacralized and profaned life. A general spirit of abstraction has removed the reality of life and concrete approaches to its values from the sphere of philosophic study. Techniques of control, leveling, and debasement have aided man in diminishing his humanity. Thus, man has lost both contact with the dignity and depth of his life and faith in himself and humankind.(6)

132

Marcel warns that any attempt to save values must be clearly envisioned and lived with constant vigilance, lest by oversimplification or facile schematization, it should tend to aggravate the fissure that is developing at the center of the human mass. Marcel then proceeds to envisage various alternative stances that propose to promote values. He indicates the difficulties and dangers that accompany each alternate stance, and evaluates their appropriateness in function of their ability to enhance those dimensions of unity, depth, and dignity in human life that are in need of restoration and renewal. By successively analyzing alternative positions and identifying both the presuppositions that underlie and the consequences that flow from them, Marcel evolves a critical identification of the requisite conditions of possiblity for the survival of values. The descriptive clarification that accompanies his critical investigation also develops a phenomenological sketch of appropriate ways to provide for the survival and regeneration of values.

To the proposal that would count solely on social, economic, and political techniques to effectuate humanization, Marcel warns that such strictly tellurian mystiques do not draw on resources capable of regenerating the moral quality of life. He also warns that the operationalization of such tellurian mystiques carries the danger of aggravating the fragmentation of humanity into opposing groups of domination and subjugation and establishing relations of envy and resentment in the struggle for possession of the world.(7)

In view of the dangers and risk of compromising the moral quality of life involved in such collaboration, there is a temptation to withdraw from such efforts. Yet, to abandon the effort to promote values entails a betrayal of life and the very notion of hope for its salvation.(8)

Pursuing another direction, Marcel inquires as to what the stance should be of those who believe in values in a situation that includes others who are either non-believers, indifferent, or desire to merely survive a bad situation with the least possible harm.

Should the believer patronize and attempt to bestow values on less fortunate individuals? Should the believer preach particular truths to others who are still in the darkness of ignorance or error? No attitudes could be more likely to incite envy and spite and thus deepen the rift of misunderstanding and resentment. Furthermore, these stances falsify the reality of the situation. The believer cannot claim to give something he has, for the reality of light and grace is not something one has.

To act as if it were is to denature and distort its reality. Faith or grace is genuine on the condition that it inhabits a person, not only as radiance, but also as humility. Even this attitude may seem hypocritical to the unbeliever. The believer must practice constant vigilance lest he merely make a gesture of what he imagines humility to be.(9)

Marcel suggests that there is a Christian maieutic more appropriate to healing rifts and more fruitful for communicating an experience of values. A regard of love can awaken the other's consciousness of his divine filiation. One does not bring or give the other anything, rather one addresses one's act of adoration to God's presence within the other's life. This is more difficult to the extent that a person remains closed in his self-complacent vanity.(10) Yet, to communicate thus serves not only to strengthen the suprapersonal community that binds one with this other, but also to strengthen the bonds that make universal community possible.(11)

Marcel observes that upon further reflection even the division between believer and unbeliever is belied when one recognizes those vast regions within one's own life wherein the gospel has not yet been preached. Such resistant dimensions of one's self and action are often the most, and sometimes the only, part of life that is visible to others.(12)

A proper approach toward providing for the survival of values now begins to emerge. It is creative of that unity in life which is indispensible for resourcing a renewal of values. Individuals who are concerned for the survival of values can together, and in the context of a person-community, explore and rediscover the natural foundations of human life and values. Such an exploration of the peri-Christian or natural foundations of life's values is capital. The survival and renewal of values depends upon the restoration of that vital contact. Seeking humbly together to rediscover the natural foundations of human life opens a viable way to experience anew the present grace and revelation of values carried by human life.

Within the life of a person-community that exercises the Christian maieutic of love, the vital contact with the unity and depth of human life can be restored. Through that the renewal and communication of human and ethical values can occur. Individuals living a communion of fraternal love and exercising a Christian maieutic can come to share what is essential in each one's experience and heritage. Together they can deepen the discovery and enrich the communication of the values they come to share. Living this spirit of truth in the openness and depth of their quest, the individual members can achieve a unity with a suprapersonal reality of light and love that will make possible the gathering and communication of those values they seek to embody with and for one another and all humankind.

Marcel envisages the development of many small groups, relearning how to live in conditions that are real, and in a light that illumines the group they form at the summit with each other and the things supporting them. He envisages this as the proper and indispensible way in which the lacerated tissue of human life can be regenerated. The guarantee of success for such undertakings is bound up with the humility in which they originate and which shapes their first objectives.(13)

Person-communities can effectuate and philosophers help to formulate this regeneration of the lacerated tissue of human life and the renewal and communication of values. Without this, man will be condemned to an infra-animal existence of which our generation has the painful privilege of witnessing the first apocalyptic symptoms.(14)

Marcel´s essay identifies precisely the forces that menace, the nature of what is at stake, and the stances that threaten to aggravate rather than ameliorate the imperiled situation of human values. Hence, Colombyre can be viewed as a dramatic representation of humankind´s plight. It traces the inadequacies in the attitudes of its membership as the reason for the alienation and destruction which become the fate of life at "Colombyre."

Marcel´s essay identifies person-community as the appropriate and indispensable manner of effectuating the survival and regeneration of values in human life. More important, the essay identifies the essential traits of life and spirit which enable a person-community to realize a genuine creative fidelity to values. In this, success depends upon humble and heroic realization of man´s noblest possibilities, which only the dialogue of freedom and grace can assure. This clarification of the spirit and life which animates a genuine person-community´s realization of creative fidelity to values stands in stark contrast to the tragicomic caricature satirized in Colombyre.

Dramatic imagination and critical conceptual clarification are mutually illuminating. They further the ongoing human effort to achieve concrete awareness of the existential situation and bring questions to that level of conscious elucidation that should characterize human understanding and enlighten ethical response.

135

Notes to Chapter VII.   Colombyre or the Torch of Peace: The
Role of Person-Community in Living Creative Fidelity to
Values

1.   Gabriel Marcel, Colombyre ou le brasier de la paix, in
     Théâtre Comique, Paris, Edition Albin Michel, 1947,
     pp. 7-154. Colombyre or The Torch of Peace, English version
     by Joseph Cunneen scheduled to appear in Two Plays by
     Gabriel Marcel: The Lantern and The Torch of Peace,
     University Press of America, Lanham, MD, forthcoming.
     Gabriel Marcel, "The Dangerous Situation of Ethical Values"
     in Homo Viator, an Introduction to a Metaphysics of Hope,
     trans. by Emma Craufurd, New York: Harper Torchbook, 1962,
     pp. 155-65.

2.   Gabriel Marcel, Le Seuil Invisible, Paris, Edition Grasset,
     1914, Preface, pp. 1-8.

3.   Gabriel Marcel, "De la recherche philosophique" in
     Entretions autour de Gabriel Marcel, Neuchâtel, La
     Baconnière, 1976, pp. 9-19.

4.   Gabriel Marcel, "The Dangerous Situation of Ethical Values,"
     pp. 155-56.

5.   Ibid., p. 156.

6.   Ibid., pp. 156, 161, 164 passim.

7.   Ibid., pp. 157-58.

8.   Ibid., p. 159.

9.   Ibid., pp. 159-61.

10. Ibid., p. 160.

11. Ibid., p. 156.

12. Ibid., p. 160.

13. Ibid., p. 164.

14. Ibid., p. 165.

Chapter VIII.   The Sting: Threatening the Foundations of
                             Fidelity

Through   the   William   James   lectures   that   he delivered at
Harvard University in 1961, Gabriel Marcel amply illustrated that
he considered his theater a privileged way of access to his
philosophic inquiries.   Marcel developed this idea repeatedly,
not only in his Harvard lectures, The Existential Background of
Human Dignity, but also in works of drama criticism and in his
two major essays of autobiographical reflection.(1)

     The works we shall focus on in this chapter are The Sting, a
play written in 1936 and staged in 1937, originally entitled Le
Dard, and Man Against Mass Society, a collection of philosophic
essays first published in French under the title Les hommes
contre l'humain in 1951 and then published in English in Great
Britain in 1952 and in the United States in 1962. These works
proceed in distinctively different though quite complementary
fashions to identify the forces of degradation that undermine
human dignity and threaten the survival of individual persons by
demeaning spiritual values.(2)

     While Marcel's earlier works usually focused on questions
that affect the emptiness or fullness, inauthenticity or
authenticity of individuals' lives, The Sting is perhaps
prophetic in that it focuses on the mood and temper of a society
wherein the survival of spiritual values is seriously threatened.
Yet, whatever topic an investigation researches, Marcel's
approach is always the same. He inquires as to how the lives of
individual persons will be concretely affected by the particular
issue at hand.

     Marcel felt that drama let audiences enter into the life
world depicted on stage and even into the inner consciousness of
certain characters who communicated their growing awareness of
the tragic dimension within their lives. Since the dramas often
highlight questions and open perspectives of light, especially in
their denouements, audiences have access to the life situation of
others and can thus enter into a shared experience of the mystery
occuring on stage.   The dramas present questions as these
challenge individual lives. Theater's role is not to demonstrate
or explain, but rather to present life. Marcel's theater invites
reflection on certain issues that philosophy can subsequently
investigate critically and then interpret through rational
analysis.

     In this study we shall look first at the play, The Sting,
considering an analysis Marcel gave to it in the preface to (The
Secret is in the Isles).(3)   Then we shall examine Marcel's

subsequent philosophic consideration of some of the issues the play brings to light. These philosophic issues we take from the several essays included in the book Man Against Mass Society. (4)

Gabriel Marcel´s Analysis of The Sting, excerpted from (The Secret is in the Isles).

"The Sting, written in 1936 and staged in 1937, reflects the disorientation of mind and spirit affecting people before the outbreak of World War II. I must say also that in the case of this drama as in most all of my plays, the creative inspiration came in terms of two exceptional individuals who in their reciprocal relationships imposed themselves on my imagination. Around these main protagonists other people of secondary importance grouped themselves. These are presented in a somewhat satirical fashion. One might say there was a center and an epicenter. Surely the center is Eustache Soreau, an intellectual who came from more than modest circumstances. Though he has attained a certain social status, he cannot allow himself to accept his success, which he views as somehow involving a betrayal.

"The epicenter is Werner Schnee, a German artist, who has become a refugee in France, not so much out of necessity as out of solidarity with a Jewish friend who was persecuted and who will probably not live long after the terrible treatment he received.

"These two, Eustache and Werner, knew each other in Germany when Eustache was a teaching assistant at Marburg University. They became friends, but what will become of that friendship? Will it withstand the stresses of a cohabitation during which each of them will experience, as it were, the other as a sort of judgment or condemnation of what he lives or aspires to be?

"Eustache and Werner are not the only protagonists in the play. First of all, there is Beatrice, Eustache´s wife. And there is her father, M. Durand-Fresnel, a narrow-minded politician, a conservative socialist, who would just fit as a chairperson of a masquerade committee.

"There is no question that Eustache has loved Beatrice for herself and not because of but rather despite the advantages that accrued from their marriage. But his love has been, one might say, poisoned by the idea that their marriage has been advantageous for him, and by that very fact liable to be considered as a sort of desertion. Should Beatrice have refused to accept the dowry that her parents gave her? Should she now, in order to please Eustache, break off relations with her family

138

under the pretext that they are secure bourgeois? She has too much good sense for that, and her family means too much to her (even though she recognizes their mediocrity) for her to yield to a demand that she finds excessive and quite unreasonable. She has mixed emotions about this. She admires, to a certain extent, Eustache's detachment and disinterestedness, but on a deeper level she considers suspect what is impure in Eustache's protestations. And it is here that Gertrude Heuzard, a grammar school teacher, an extremist of the radical left, comes into the picture. She and Eustache were close comrades before Eustache's marriage. She has just recently been suspended from her job on the allegation that she has disseminated antipatriotic propaganda among her students. In that respect she can be considered a victim, and Eustache envies her more than he pities her. She has the merit of having conformed her actions to her ideas. Eustache feels judged by her as a deserter. She is a personification of his bad conscience. But Beatrice, who is intelligent and sensitive, perceives what is essentially equivocal about this woman. Beatrice suspects that basically Gertrude is in love with Eustache and considers Beatrice as a rival. She tells her husband this feeling of hers, but he simply refuses to acknowledge it. Eustache has only disdain for the realm of affectivity; in this, as in other matters, he reasons only as a function of his ideology. To Beatrice this would be mere childishness that would make her smile, if it were not for the fact that the rift between her husband and herself was growing. The arrival of Werner Schnee and his wife Gisela only serves to widen the gap.

"Werner is essentially an artist--not a composer, but a singer, a gifted and impassioned interpreter of the songs of classical musicians. He was never active politically. As a matter of fact, he is not interested in politics and probably even disdains it. He left Germany, as I have said, in sympathy with the persecuted Jewish pianist who was his accompanist. What matters for him are individual persons and relationships between people. He distrusts the abstractions with which fanatics nourish themselves. In such circumstances, how could a conflict not inevitably erupt between him and Eustache, who is precisely a man of abstractions, a man of "isms"? Eustache reproaches him for not establishing contact with other political refugees, for not joining one of the organized groups that already exists. For Eustache there is a category of refugee that implies certain obligations that one must meet. But, in Werner's eyes, that category as such is nonexistent. There is no reason to affiliate himself with people whom he doesn't know and who probably would be uncongenial if he did know them. But Eustache judges such individualism as reactionary and consequently scandalous. Is it only an ideological difference that sets these two men off in opposition to one another? Eustache, without admitting it, is

139

annoyed by the admiration that Beatrice obviously manifests for
Werner. Can one speak of jealousy in the strict sense of the
term? Perhaps not. But Eustache has a vague presentiment of
usurpation, which offends him. Moreover, he will discover with
profound irritation that Beatrice and Werner talked about him in
his absence, doubtless to discuss his situation and maybe even to
criticize him. He cannot bear being treated as a third party by
those two, and there is here a particularly meaningful
illustration of one of the fundamental themes of my philosophic
reflections.

"It seems unnecessary to me to literally tell the story of
the whole play. I merely wanted to clarify the essential
elements of its dramatic structure. This play is, in my opinion,
one of the most characteristic of all the plays I have written.
It is not merely a psychological drama; rather it portrays, as I
have said, a definite and important moment in our history. But
even more important, it is hard for me not to find a prophetic
dimension to this play. Here I am thinking, of course, of the
concluding lines of the final scene.

"Werner has decided to return to Germany, certainly not to
accept the comfortable position that an impresario offered to
him, which would have presupposed his surrender to an execrable
regime. He has discovered that there is something within himself
and his songs that is his way of participating in life
creatively, something that touches people and by which he can
help them to live. As he is essentially a noble person, he is
repulsed by the idea that these gifts could become merely a means
for social success. He asks himself--and the author asks with
him, without in any way answering the question--if he has not to
some extent become infected by the contagious sickness that
plagues Eustache. But there is more; he discovers that he loves
Beatrice and that probably his love is reciprocated. But how can
he live with the idea of betraying Eustache, who, after all, has
been his friend? On this basis he feels the obligation to leave,
to tear himself away from a temptation which, in the long run, he
is not sure that he could resist. The moment of decision is all
the more critical since Eustache has become Gertrude's lover, and
Beatrice is at the end of her strength and just about ready to
leave him. Still there would be something base and despicable in
taking advantage of this set of circumstances.

"Werner: You cannot abandon him. You must always remember
that you are the wife of a pauper...Poverty is not a lack of
money, nor is it lack of success. Eustache has had money, he's
had success; yet he remains poor and keeps getting poorer.
Probably he will never recover from his kind of poverty. It's
the great evil of our times, and it's spreading like the plague.
They haven't yet found a physician who can heal it. They don't

140

even know how to recognize the illness. There´s a chance artists may escape, even if they do go hungry. And also the faithful who by their prayer...All other people are in danger.

"Beatrice: You are asking me to live with a leper...
"Werner: The leprosariums are going to proliferate on this earth, I fear. It will be a grace reserved for very few to live there, knowing that they are living with lepers and yet not hold them in horror. Even more than a grace. How do you say? Via-te-cum, a viaticum.
"Beatrice: I am not brave enough, Werner, I assure you.
"Werner: You will think of me, as I think of Rudolf. Later on I shall be in you a living presence, as Rudolf still is in me. You will remember then what I told you here a few weeks ago. If there were only the living, Beatrice...

"The words he spoke were these: ´If there were only the living, I think life on this earth would be quite impossible.´

"Those who have read Man Against Mass Society will have no difficulty in recognizing that this prophetic word not only announced the ideas that were developed in the essays that I collected under that title, but also pictured in advance the terrible situations that developed in France and other countries after the Second World War. But what I want to underline here, appropriate to this introduction, is that the subsequent reflections developed in connection with an individual person, namely Eustache, who came to me with his particularity, and also from imagining someone who was oriented in the opposite direction and what one might think of the other. Nothing is less like an argument, or a demonstration of a thesis. It is a question rather of showing and awakening, by means that are not unlike those the musician uses to awaken consciences concretely to a terrible disorder, yet beyond that an order that transcends conceptualization, but which each one of us can attain by means of recollection and prayer".(5)

Marcel identifies The Sting as one of his most significant dramas. It deals, he writes in "The Drama of the Soul in Exile," with the suffering of our contemporary world.(6) What is this suffering? It is a kind of spiritual poverty, a sickness that threatens the survival of humanity on earth. When Marcel discussed The Sting as he did in The Existential Background of Human Dignity in Chapter VII on "Human Dignity," and in a preface to the reedition of (The Sting) along with (The Emissary) and (The End of Time) in the book (The Secret is in the Isles), he quoted the final dialogue between Beatrice and Werner from the final scene of The Sting .(7) These final exchanges let us hear in the words of people who are living the dramatic challenge their concrete perception of the tragic sickness affecting the masses today and the heroic action required of those who must live in that situation but who hope to do so without succumbing to its poisonous sting.

Our procedure in the second part of this chapter will be similar. Recognizing that Marcel's theater is a privileged way of access to his philosophic thought, we shall reconstruct scenes from the play and perspectives from the philosophic analyses collected in Man Against Mass Society, as together these clarify questions about what the Sting is, and how people can be preserved from its infection.

Early in the book Man Against Mass Society Marcel observed that between Frederich Nietzsche's declaration that "God is dead" and the current phenomenon that "man is in his death throes," there is no logical connection, but there is a connection that is concrete and existential.(8) A spiritual poverty such as is presented in The Sting and commented upon in Man Against Mass Society is only possible where belief in God and transcendent values is absent.(9) Yet Marcel also stated that "it is perhaps by starting from the statement 'man is in his death throes' that we may be able to question once more the statement, 'God is dead,' and to discover that God is living after all."(10)

In that same essay, "What is a free man?", Marcel clarifies that: "To say that man is in his death throes is only to say that man today finds himself facing, not some external event,...but rather possibilities of complete self-destruction inherent in himself...(possibilities) of a spiritual destruction wrought by techniques of human degradation."(11)

With these preliminary perspectives noted, let us take up our analysis of the play and Marcel's philosophic commentaries about the sickness plaguing our civilization.

In the first two scenes of Act One, Eustache Soreau shows his dis-ease about his poor social origin, evidenced by his irritation over the contrast between his mother's obvious lack of cultural refinement and the mannerly affectations of his wife's family. Yet it is Eustache's contact with Gertrude Heuzard that precipitates his showing symptoms of that particular form of bad conscience that Marcel saw as a malady of our times. The bad conscience that Eustache displays is, Marcel noted, very like the phenomenon of resentment as Max Scheler and Frederich Nietzsche have described it.(12)

It is Eustache's interaction with Gertrude that discloses the dynamics of bad conscience. Eustache felt uncomfortable about his humble origins, but he also felt guilty about having risen above them. Yet it is Gertrude who, judging him in terms of a militant's ideology, convicts him of guilt. Eustache, by a strange complicity, interiorized Gertrude's judgment, and in a spirit of condemnation convicts himself of betraying the people by having deserted their condition for the sake of bourgeois privileges.

The degradation of others, and the overthrow of values through the phenomenon of resentment works as follows. The "oppressed" convict the "elite" of guilt, thus degrading them and removing them from positions of privilege. By this process of condemnation, the oppressed become the powerful, and the elite become powerless.

Indeed Beatrice perceived rightly that Gertrude not only disdained Eustache in the light of her militant ideology, but that she also wanted to gain power over him and possess him and thus considered Beatrice her rival.(13)

Marcel observed that in many radical socialist and peoples' democratic parties, although the phenomenon is not limited to these groups, the ideal of equality is one that envisages reducing everyone to the lowest common denominator. Such an ideal of equality, he notes, is not congruent with either liberty or fraternity. This claiming of equality strives to eliminate spiritual values by degradation and to surpress any admiration of excellence. The struggle for equality is often founded on a spirit of envy and meanness, not on a reverence or admiration for the human dignity of persons as created by God, imago Dei. (14)

Scene 4 of Act I, the scene wherein Eustache engages his in-laws in conversation, shows further how spiritual degradation spreads. Eustache now becomes the agent inducing bad conscience, a technique of which he was so recently a victim. This scene also shows ideas that Marcel explores quite thoroughly in Man Against Mass Society. We see that the spreading of an ideology does not proceed by carefully reasoned analyses of concrete situations, nor is it communicated through civil rational discourse. Conversations are more like diatribes of partisan politics. The techniques used are those of propaganda. A militant claims to possess the truth, and he or she is willing to coerce others until they adhere to that conviction. Conversations exchange slogans of propaganda that resemble battle cries more than ideas. Marcel also notes that most often these slogans are adhered to more by passion than by intelligent understanding. Propagandizing manipulates ideas for the sake of power and does not operate in a spirit of truth. It also attempts to manipulate opponents, to find their weak points and exploit them, to confound their arguments and make them appear foolish and vain.(15)

From the time of Eustache´s conversation with the Durand-Fresnels, act I, scene 4, and then the arrival of Werner Schnee and his wife Gisela, the difference between Eustache and Werner becomes clear, as does the tension of opposition that will develop in this cohabitation, even though these two men were once friends at Marburg University. Through this contrast and the interaction of Eustache as point and Werner as counterpoint it becomes evident what on the one hand contributes to the process of spiritual degradation and what on the other hand serves as a basis of resistance to such dehumanization. Eustache is an intellectual animated by a spirit of abstraction, caring only for political goals and ideals. Werner is a dedicated artist, who cares for music and individual persons. A spirit of abstraction and a disdain for life are part of the process of spiritual degradation. Care for individual persons and a faithful commitment to creatively communicate the transcendent values of life to others are the lifelines of a strength that can resist such dehumanization.

Act II begins with Werner singing a Goethe song, Gisela accompanying him at the piano. In the conversation that ensues, Eustache affirms that he does not like music, finding it valuable only if it promotes the spirit or goals of the party. Eustache goads Werner to join a political alliance or a refugee action group. Werner avows that he finds politics distasteful. What he cares about now is music and Rudolf Schontal, his accompanist--a real person, who has suffered terribly from political persecution and probably will die as a result. Gisela offers that she does not want to battle with a dead man, she wants to go home to Germany where she had a life, her house, her family, her friends. Werner muses, "Oh Gisela, if there were only the living, I think this world would be quite uninhabitable."(16)

In a lecture entitled "The Paradox of a Philosopher-Dramatist"(17) Marcel affirmed that a spirit of abstraction is at the root of all fanaticism and fratricide. He develops that idea in Man Against Mass Society´s essay "The Spirit of Abstraction as a Factor Making for War."(18)

A spirit of abstraction is necessary in order to regard another human being as "the enemy." Through a spirit of abstraction one can kill a "Nazi," a "commie," or a "whatever" not envisioned as an individual human person. A spirit of abstraction is, moreover, a factor for waging war in that often one kills or maims for the sake of an abstraction, "the People," "Justice," "the Party," or even "peace." A spirit of abstraction is an essential part of the process of propagandizing and the development of a fanaticized consciousness. A spirit of abstraction is radically opposed to a concrete approach that considers every issue as it affects the lives of individual

144

persons, whom one continues to regard as individuals created by God, even imago Dei whose being includes a particle of the divine reality. This latter perspective allows one to perceive that sacred dimension of persons that reveals a true universality concretely present in persons, one disregarded by a spirit of abstraction that falsely fires up fanaticism and incites the masses.(19)

The path that Eustache and Gertrude's relationship follows indicates the role of disdain for life in techniques of degradation. Gertrude comes to Eustache's home to tell him that she is going to commit suicide. Her life has led her to a point where she expects nothing more from it, and so she plans to end it. Eustache, though aware that there may be some sort of blackmail involved, goes to be with Gertrude. In taking this decisive action, he insults, soils, and repudiates everything he had previously held as valuable. He refuses a promotion, insults his "friends" in the ministry of education, profanes his house and marriage, bringing Gertrude to be there with him in his wife's absence and telling his father-in-law that this is just the beginning of militant action yet to come. In "Techniques of Degradation," Marcel cites reports from World War II concentration camps that indicated that techniques of degradation were intended to shame the victim so that he or she appeared worthless in his or her own eyes, felt wholly at the mercy of another, ceased to be an opponent worth reckoning with, and provided to the executioner a feeling of delight and exaltation comparable to the delight and exaltation of sacrilege.(20)

In the third act of The Sting, it appears as if all is lost. Everyone associated with Eustache's household is to some extent afflicted by the sting. Eustache has gone over to be with Gertrude and live out her militant ways. M. Durand-Fresnel is offended by insult and ingratitude. Eustache's mother and brother feel rejected and deeply hurt. Beatrice, upon her return, finds that Eustache is effectively planning to leave her and everything of their life together, to go and be with Gertrude. And then Werner comes to announce his imminent departure for Germany.

When Werner tells Beatrice of his plans to return to Germany, she protests that it's suicide and pleads, asking how he can leave her alone in this most terrible moment. And Werner explains his mind to her. It is not a question of suicide; he plans to be with the oppressed and, by sharing his gift of song, serve to quicken their sense of their human dignity. Both Beatrice and Werner are intelligent and loving people who care for individuals thoughtfully. Werner recognizes that he must go his way, faithful to his commitment, and Beatrice must continue in hers though the persecution and suffering may be excruciating for them both.

Werner acknowledges that indeed he and Beatrice do love each other. Their love does not exempt them from the temptation to give carnality full reign, yet in this case, their fidelity to higher values will protect them. Thus Werner encourages Beatrice to stay with Eustache, to be faithful to him and care for him even though the situation may be horribly painful.

Werner adds that it is a grace given to very few to live among those infected by the sting of spiritual poverty and degradation and not hold them in disgust. Marcel wrote in Man Against Mass Society, "Individual goodness is inconceivable without grace."(21) He adds that it is an extraordinary grace that enables a person to break the hellish cycle of reprisals and counter-reprisals that spiritual degradation sets in motion.(22) Werner's decision to affirm human dignity in concentration camps and his encouragement to Beatrice to do likewise in her household is just such a decision to transcend the force of spiritual degradation.

Werner's life as an artist witnesses how creative fidelity to higher values is possible. Marcel observed that Werner, as an artist consecrated to music, has his life totally given over to creatively communicating this value with and for others. By thus living creative fidelity to that spiritual value he is protected from the sting of spiritual degradation.(23) Furthermore, his willingness to give his life, even to the point of martyrdom, so that a spiritual value will be present among others shows how one person's life, even after his death, can resource creative fidelity in other people's lives. Werner witnesses that communion with his friend Rudolf helped him to make his decision. This communion he knows will also sustain him in his suffering and death. On the strength of this witness he assures Beatrice that not only an artist but also a true believer who can pray will be spared from destruction by the spiritual sickness that menaces our time. Werner's life and words assure Beatrice that she will not be alone. She will find, through tender remembrance and prayer, a communion of love and an assurance that he is with her, as Rudolf was with him. He even assures her that, later on after his death, he will be for her like a via te cum, a viaticum sharing his life in a way that a loved one from beyond death can be here with us, strengthening us in our weakness in time of persecution and death.(24)

The Sting ends on a note of hope. Even in the face of the tragic situation wrought by spiritual poverty and degradation, we discover that it is indeed possible to resist the sting by drawing on transcendent spiritual resources deep within ourselves that enable even heroic forms of creative fidelity. Reflection assures that the grace to live such heroic fidelity will not be lacking to those whose creative lives--like those of artists and true believers who pray--will be resourced by the continuing life of someone who has died before us yet continues to live on.

The study of Gabriel Marcel's theater and philosophy in concert has enabled us to see in an existential and concrete way that a concern for human beings in their death throes can bring us to the center point within ourselves where we can recognize that in fact "God is not dead but living"...beyond death, yes, living with and for us.(25)

In the process of his reflection as philosopher-dramatist Gabriel Marcel has revealed something of his notion of personhood. His notion is one that transcends by far the idea of equality of individuals as alloted by materialist psychologies, philosophies, or ideologies, and exceeds by far the level to which cultural propaganda of 1937, 1950's, 1960's, 1980's, or 2000's would reduce people's self-images. Marcel has let us share in his perspectives that allow us to perceive persons as imago Dei, and even experience the sacred depth and possibility of interpersonal communion that assure the true existential background of human dignity.(26)

The fidelity of the living finds its basis in the enduring fidelity of martyrs. By their self-sacrificing love, their self-gift for others, they continue to live on in survivors nourishing and supporting the fidelity of the living despite the epidemic proportions of spiritual poverty in this world.

147

1. "An Autobiographical Essay" (Spring 1969) in The Philosophy
    of Gabriel Marcel (Library of Living Philosophers Vol. XVII)
    ed. Paul A. Schilpp and Lewis E. Hahn, LaSalle, Illinois,
    Open Court, 1984, pp. 1-68; "An Essay in Autobiography" in
    The Philosophy of Existentialism, Secaucus, New Jersey, The
    Citadel Press, 1956, pp. 104-28; Introduction to The
    Existential Drama of Gabriel Marcel, ed. F. J. Lescoe, West
    Hartford, Conn., McAuley Institute, St. Joseph College,
    1974; "My Dramatic Works as Viewed by the Philosopher" in
    Searchings, New York, Newman, 1967, pp. 93-118; "The Drama
    of the Soul in Exile" (July 1950) in Three Plays by Gabriel
    Marcel, London, Secker & Warburg, 1952; New York, Hill &
    Wang, 1965; The Existential Background of Human Dignity,
    Cambridge, Mass., Harvard University Press, 1963.

2. (The Sting), A Play in Three Acts. Le Dard, Paris, Plon,
    1936, reedited in Le Secret est dans les îles, Paris,
    Plon, 1967, pp. 25-153. Les Hommes contre l'humain, Paris,
    La Colombe, 1951; Man Against Mass Society, Great Britain,
    1952; Chicago, H. Regnery, Gateway, 1962.

    (The Secret is in the Isles), including a preface ("The
    Secret is in the Isles") and three plays, (The Sting), (The
    Emissary), and (The End of Time), Paris: Plon, 1967, has not
    yet been translated into English. Even though (The Sting)
    has not yet been translated and published in English, its
    title has been underlined in the text of this chapter to
    enable readers to easily recognize by the conventional sign
    that The Sting is the title of the play analyzed in this
    chapter. This underlining is a departure from the system
    employed in Part Three of this book, wherein titles in
    English are not underlined in order to indicate that a work
    has not yet been translated and published in English.

3. Le Secret est dans les îles, Paris, Plon, 1967, pp. 14-19.

4. Man Against Mass Society, Chicago, H. Regnery, Gateway,
    1962. "The Universal Against the Masses," I, II, pp. 1-11,
    257-73; "What is a Free Man?" pp. 13-25; "Lost Liberties,"
    pp. 26-36; "Techniques of Degradation," pp. 37-75;
    "Technological Progress and Sin," pp. 76-101; "The
    Philosopher and the Contemporary World," pp. 103-32; "The
    Fanaticized Consciousness," pp. 133-52; "The Spirit of
    Abstraction, as a Factor Making for War," pp. 153-62; "The
    Crisis of Value in the Comtemporary World," pp. 163-92.

5. Le Secret est dans les îles, pp. 14-19, quotes from (The
    Sting), Act III, Scene 8, pp. 152-53.

6.   "The Drama of the Soul in Exile," p. 32.

7.   The Existential Background of Human Dignity, Ch. VII, p. 122.

8.   Man Against Mass Society, "What is a Free Man?" pp. 14-15.

9.   Ibid., pp. 22-23; "Techniques of Degradation," p. 67.

10. Man Against Mass Society, "What is a Free Man?" p. 15.

11. Ibid., p. 14.

12. Max Scheler, Ressentiment, New York, Schocken Books, 1972.

13. (The Sting), Act I, Scene 3; cf. Act II, Scene 9; Act III, Scenes 2, 3, 6.

14. Man Against Mass Society, "Lost Liberties," pp. 27, 28, 29, 35-36; "Techniques of Degradation," p. 67.

15. Man Against Mass Society, "Techniques of Degradation," pp. 37, 49-52, 69, 73, 75.

16. (The Sting), Act II, scene 10, p. 121.

17. Gabriel Marcel: Le Paradoxe de philosophe-dramaturge, Réalisations Sonores: Hughes De Salle, Collection Français de Notre Temps Nous Confie , Sous le patronage de l´Alliançe Française, présentation écrite sur la pochette de Marc Blancpain, no date.

18. Man Against Mass Society, "The Spirit of Abstraction, as a Factor Making for War." pp. 153-62.

19. Man Against Mass Society, "The Spirit of Abstraction,..." pp. 156-58, 160; "The Universal Against the Masses," pp. 4, 259, 262, 267, 273; "Techniques of Degradation," p. 67.

20. (The Sting), Act II, Scene 6; Act III, scene 6. Man Against Mass Society, "Techniques of Degradation," pp. 42-45, 46, 47, 48; "Technological Progress and Sin," pp. 79, 92-93.

21. Man Against Mass Society, "Lost Liberties," pp. 30, 93; Jeanne Parain-Vial, "La Grâce dans Le Dard," to appear.

22. Man Against Mass Society, "Techniques of Degradation," p. 48.

23. The Existential Background of Human Dignity, pp. 124-25; Man Against Mass Society, "Technical Progress and Sin," p. 100; "Degradation of the Idea of Service," p. 203.

24. "The Sting," pp. 152-53. The Existential Background of Human Dignity, pp. 124-25.

25. Man Against Mass Society, "The Universal Against the Masses," pp. 15, 259, 266-67.

26. Man Against Mass Society, "What is a Free Man?" pp. 22-25; "Lost Liberties," pp. 29, 35; "Techniques of Degradation," pp. 57, 67; "Technical Progress and Sin," pp. 79, 92-93; "The Spirit of Abstraction," p. 160; "The Universal Against the Masses," pp. 4, 266-67, 273.

Chapter IX. Rome Is No Longer In Rome: Challenge for Creative
             Incarnations of Fidelity

     Rome Is No Longer in Rome is a play that in its own time
created quite a stir both for its timeliness and the power of its
message.   It was originally produced at the Hébertot Theater in
Paris, April 19, 1951.(1) Its composition was occasioned by the
atmosphere in France and other parts of Western Europe, where
people had lived through two major wars in close succession.
People felt the impending advent of a political or military coup
that would introduce a Soviet or at least a "popular front"
regime.   Still, the situation depicted in the play has
counterparts in our current situations.

     Significant questions are brought to light, questions that
are personal and that have relevance to the current plight of
western civilization.   How can one be genuinely faithful to one's
heritage of spiritual values and communicate them or creatively
incarnate them in a world where these kinds of values are
foreign?   The foreign land in question may be a territory or
nation or it may mean a material civilization where spiritual
values are unknown, devalorized, or forgotten.

     After a brief summary of the play we shall reflect on a few
questions to clarify their significance with reference to the
drama and the philosophic writings of Marcel.

     Rome Is No Longer in Rome depicts the Laumière family as
they live out their decision to emigrate to another land rather
than be destroyed by the events that menace their survival in
France.

     This play is certainly one of Marcel's finest works. Rather
than depict barricades and trenches, Marcel portrays in five acts
the psychological drama that some individuals undergo as they
evolve a decision and struggle to find its meaning in the trying
circumstances of their lives.

     The first three acts deal with the drama of making the
decision to leave France.   The last two reveal the drama of
giving meaning to that move.

     Renée Laumière, without consulting her husband, Pascal,
has made arrangements for him to be offered a teaching position
at a newly founded university in San Felipe. When Pascal learns
that there is a professorial appointment and a welcome for him
and his family in San Felipe, he is disconcerted. Certainly he
wants his wife and children to be safe, but he himself had not

151

planned to leave France.

He is helped in his decision by his nephew Marc André, who
announces his plan to leave France with a friend whose father can
get them jobs in Africa. Marc André begs Pascal to take care
of his mother, Esther, so that she will not feel forsaken. While
they exchange views on various topics, Marc André wants to test
his uncle's strength. Would Pascal subscribe to the following
commitment by one of his friends' fathers, Professor Moreuil?

I don't know what that moment will make of me, perhaps
a rag. I'm not presuming on my own strength alone.
I'm counting on God, that he will not abandon me, that
he will save me from a final disaster. Either he will
take me to himself, or he will give me the strength to
withstand the torture. (Act II, Scene I)(2)

Pascal responds that in all honesty he cannot state that
conviction as his own. He sees that he has only the more
abstract notion of his sense of integrity and the hope of his
loyalty to French "honor" and "patriotism." Marc André then
inquires whether the orphaned children inherit this sense of
"honor" by proxy.

After a sharp exchange between Pascal and his wife Renée,
it seems that there are no solid reasons left for remaining in
France. Reason seems instead to suggest leaving while they can
move to a land where life seems possible. This is all the more
true since Marc André just learned that his plan for Africa has
fallen through. Pascal, then, looks upon Brazil as an
opportunity to give his family, including Esther and Marc
André, a chance for a good life.

The last two acts take place in Brazil at the home of the
Martinezes. The setting is a spacious living room that opens
onto a patio.

When we arrive in Brazil, it is immediately and painfully
clear that the Laumières are considered refugees. They are
expected to respect the sensitivities of their host country and
to follow the ways of its culture. This behavioral compliance is
requested in the name of politeness or the common courtesy that
is due in exchange for the hospitality they enjoy. Expectations
become increasingly oppressive, in both professional and personal
life. Compliance is of course expected of refugees. Pascal
feels undone. Marc André, by contrast, feels as if life has
just begun. Esther appears, carrying a letter with news of her
brother, Robert, who has disappeared. Probably he has been put
out of the way because he staunchly, perhaps even

uncompromisingly, championed a "French" communism.

Pascal and Esther discuss the death of Robert. They reminisce about him, as if death let others see more clearly into his character. Unloved, rejected by his mother, he forced everyone else to despise him.

Renée and Carlos Martinez beg that no mention be made of Robert´s death, nor of his communist affiliations. News of these would create scandal among their friends. Carlos informs Pascal that his weekly broadcast will be from the Martinez home, since Pascal appears tired and somewhat weakened.

Pascal confides in Esther that curiously, almost paradoxically, the scandalously persecuting manner of the Martinezes and their priest friend from the university gave him a vivid sympathy for Christ. It was as if behind the threatening words of those torturers was an infinitely discrete appeal of Christ, a distinct call--"not to betray." Later that same day, in sharp contrast with the Martinezes´ pagan priest friend, a young monk approached Pascal. This young monk´s face had the gentle look of Christ´s.(3)

Esther asks if Pascal has decided to submit. When he responds that he definitely has not, she interjects that she, for her part, has decided to return to France to care for Robert´s baby since the infant´s mother, Robert´s mistress, wants no part of raising the child.

Marc André joins them, startled to see that his uncle doesn´t look well. Pascal comforts him, explaining that now he can make Professor Moreuil´s statement his own.

Pascal begins his weekly broadcast back to the people in France with a quote from Sertorius, a Roman general in one of Corneille´s tragedies. Sertorius claims that "Rome is no longer in Rome" but instead lives on in the hearts of those outside her walls who keep her heritage alive.

Pascal cries out, "That verse is false. The claim is false." He staggers but continues. "Stand fast. Stay....And if you don´t feel you have the strength. Or if you think you won´t have the strength." He staggers and falls faint.

Esther runs to revive him. A young monk with a kind smile and a gentle manner enters and moves toward Pascal. "Let me go to him. I know he´s waiting for me."(4)

The end of the play is stunning; its theatrical impact is

153

powerful. The curtain falls, and the audience is left facing a darkened stage with only a radio facing them.

We are surprised, disconcerted. We are left with questions that call for reflection about the possibility of fidelity and the possibility of communicating our values to others.

The play gives rise to many other questions about the different characters and the significance of some of their actions and interactions. The drama is artfully composed in a symphonic fashion, and it would take a full-scale study to do justice to the intricacy of meaning that is developed.

As the play ends, the question of the ultimate grounds for fidelity when spiritual values are severely menaced is brought to mind by Pascal.

The finale of the play involves a reprise of the question confronted by Professor Moreuil. This time, however, Pascal is ready to answer that for him, ultimately one's fidelity to France, honor, liberty, integrity, or a spirit of truth is founded in one's confidence in God's fidelity. One's fidelity draws on a trust that God will not abandon those who abandon themselves to his care, those who count on him as their ultimate recourse. As Marcel wrote in Creative Fidelity, the ultimate foundation of fidelity is faith in an Absolute Thou who is encountered as the ultimate recourse in one's dire distress.(5) Or, as Professor Moreuil phrased it, he had confidence that in his hour of distress, be it trial or torture, God would give him the strength to endure or would take his life before he succumbed to betrayal.(6)

It was apparently this confidence in Christ, who as a personal presence can assure one's fidelity, that founded Professor Moreuil's decision to stay in France. A similar trust in the personal presence of Christ is what inspires and enables Pascal's decision not to be coopted by a repressive regime.(7)

That is why Pascal can say to his radio audience in France that we live in a civilization where spiritual values are becoming more and more alien. Stay--stand firm, be faithful and true--and if you do not have the strength, be open to find your hope for fidelity secured in the faithfulness of a living God.

Abandoning pride, presumption, and stoic self-sufficiency, one can find God as an Absolute Thou present in a moment of dire distress. God comes then as our ultimate recourse.(8)

Perhaps our greatest strength comes when, in our weakness,

we draw on a strength that is other and more than our own.(9) Pascal´s decision and the message he broadcast, not to betray, is one that expresses the mysterious and intimate workings of freedom and grace.(10)

In the final moment of the play, and perhaps even of his life, Pascal´s decision becomes really his own, an act he owns and through which his life´s meaning is expressed.(11)

By using four dots Marcel often leaves phrases and perspectives of insight open-ended for the reader or spectator to inquire about and then fill in with his or her own light. The pointing is "and if you have not the strength...." Then there are the discrete stage directions. And then the stark confrontation with the radio, inviting each one of us to hear and consider the question ourselves.(12)

With dramatic power and discrete finesse, Marcel invites the spectator to reconstruct the play and to discern for himself or herself whether fidelity is possible and whether ways can be found to creatively incarnate it in our world today.

In the essay "The Real Issues in Rome Is No Longer In Rome," Marcel responds to some of the controversy stirred up by the play. He points out that techniques of "brainwashing," first recognized because of their prevalent use during the Korean War, changed the ground on which valor, honor, integrity, or faithfulness are viewed. Prior to the full-scale use of techniques of spiritual degradation or "brainwashing," the stoic options could suffice. The stoic attitude is based on a confidence or belief that the private regions of a person´s mind and will were regions that could not be violated, pressured, or altered. Patently mental and psychic states can be altered. That is why one would be well advised to write a declaration of one´s stand compos mentis and a renunciation or a retraction in advance of any statements conditioned by "brainwashing." Philosophically the question becomes: Is there anything more trustworthy than human strength of mind, virtue, or willpower when faced with forces of persecution whose techniques of spiritual degradation are dehumanizing indeed?(13)

The action of the play illustrates various options that Marcel evaluates concretely in the drama and examines philosophically in the essays on fidelity in Creative Fidelity and Homo Viator. (14)

Morality appears inadequate to transmit values; otherwise Marc André would surely have inherited the values of his mother, Esther. Abstractions such as "honor," "liberty,"

155

"mankind," or "patriotism," though powerful sounding in propaganda, are of themselves inadequate to ensure fidelity or to inspire creativity. Sterile arguments and abstract notions do not move hearts or nourish lives, though they can be used to feed emotions and to incite passions to promote fanaticism.

Fidelity is inspired by persons who communicate in love and in a spirit of truth, as do for instance, Pascal, Esther, and Marc André. The inspiration to fidelity is often through the person of someone present from beyond death. The presence of Marc André's father from beyond death certainly significantly influences Marc André, Esther, and also Pascal.(15)

Physical force and psychological blackmail can pressure behavior. Ideological propaganda can confuse thought and discourage feelings. Political and social power can dictate ideological propaganda and force behavioral compliance. Social control can be exercised by both totalitarian Marxist governments and reactionary regimes of clericalism, and very likely by other groups as well. Although these forces and power groups can dictate ideologies and manipulate behaviors, they are not enough to control a person of liberty, an individual who lives in a spirit of truth.

Then what enables a person to resist the insidious and powerful forces mentioned above; what can safeguard a person's fidelity?

Fidelity, in order to endure, like Pascal's, must be based on interpersonal presence lived in a spirit of truth and love. Pascal cares for his family, he cares with special concern for Marc André and Esther, and he also cares for others in his literary and radio audience who might try to live through this current crisis with integrity. Pascal, together with Marc André and Esther, through open, searching conversations tries to clarify what his responsibility is in living out fidelity to the spiritual heritage of France.

Pascal's fidelity is lived as an attempt to hear and respond to his particular vocation.(16) His response is a commitment to the values of life with honor. Pascal's fidelity is essentially animated and enlivened by interpersonal relations with Marc André and Esther. In the trial of persecution his fidelity is intensified. It deepens to the point that he experiences an intersubjective relationship with God. Pascal's fidelity and its moment of fullest saturation is founded finally in the intersubjective presence of Christ.

As Marcel wrote in his essay "The real issues in Rome Is No

Longer in Rome," the play certainly does not suggest that there is only one right way to preserve the honor of France. The play does not mean to state bluntly that Pascal should have remained in France, nor does it imply which is the right way to express faithfulness to the spiritual values of France´s heritage.(17)

Except for the case of Pascal, the play does not question whether people´s particular choices are expressive of their values. Each person´s choice is expressive of his or her values. Marc André wants to be able to live, hope, and love. Esther, his mother, wants the best for him, for Pascal, and later for Robert´s child as well. Renée, on a more practical and superficial level, wants a good life with all possible social advantages for herself and her children. Pascal, moved by the solidarity he senses with Marc André, feels responsible to provide the children a better opportunity for life than the political and social situation of France affords. Pascal judges his responsibility to be that of providing for his household a situation wherein life is possible. He hopes at the same time that he can also in some way remain faithful to France, his homeland and heritage. Robert chooses to remain in France and assure the reign of French communism when "the event" occurs.

People in the play do seem to question one another´s values. There is discussion for understanding. Pascal seems at times to deplore Renée´s expediency, but mostly he decries the way she demeans him, almost incapacitates him. Renée in turn disdains and eventually despises Robert´s ineffectiveness. Esther and Marc André seem to encourage Pascal´s effort to be faithful to his integrity and purpose. Only Robert and Pascal argue and condemn one another´s positions. Moreover, they try to undermine one another´s confidence in their values and in one another´s abilities to effectively incarnate their fidelity to those values.(18)

The conflict between Pascal and Robert not only shows the opposition between their value systems, it also serves to clarify concretely certain distinctions that are helpful toward developing a right understanding of the challenge to incarnate creative fidelity to spiritual values.

One´s effectiveness in responding to the challenge to incarnate one´s fidelity to spiritual values is not measured by one´s success in influencing socio-political trends. One´s effectiveness in preserving spiritual values and communicating them to others lies in one´s ability to awaken others´ awareness to the spiritual dimension of human dignity. This awareness is something that is communicated among individuals in a spirit of truth and love.

It seems that Robert's choice, which will help to assure "French" communism when "the event" occurs, has the most likelihood of being effective. His initiative is in line with socio-political forces. Robert will, it appears, serve to assure a postrevolutionary survival of a French form of communist government. But as Pascal foresees, Robert's initiative is not likely to prevail. Those who gave Robert a formal promise of French communism believe in dialectical truth that changes with the circumstances. So when Robert's tactics no longer serve to promote a changing goal, he is disposed of. It is unlikely that any individual's initiative will be effective in changing the direction of the socio-political history of Western civilization. An individual action rarely can control the force or the direction of socio-political trends. Neither Pascal's writing nor Robert's direct action can reverse a trend that has gained so much momentum. Social iniquity has gone too far.(19) Moreover, even if socio-political trends could be altered, something more would be still required to preserve and communicate values. Ideological propaganda and behavioral conditioning can promote doctrinal orthodoxy and behavioral social compliance. Force, physical or psychological, cannot communicate spiritual values. These can only be espoused in liberty and communicated in a spirit of truth that accompanies interpersonal love.

Pascal's decision and the sense of it that is revealed dramatically at the end of the play incarnate an authentic response to the challenge for creative fidelity to spiritual values.

As Gabriel Marcel wrote in his philosophical essays, it is not others or any critical public who can evaluate a person's fidelity.(20) It is oneself who is best suited to estimate the value of one's efforts. It is oneself who can recognize the extent to which one's creation corresponds to the original inspiration that gave rise to it. So it is Pascal who can best judge whether his actions in the final scene correspond to his deepest hope--not to betray but instead to preserve and transmit what is most valuable in the spiritual heritage of France.

Upon reflection it appears that Pascal in the final scene has posed an act of genuine creative fidelity. He has not betrayed. In his refusal to go along with a repressive clericalism, he has preserved his sense of honor and kept faith with what he esteems to be France's heritage of spiritual values. Moreover, in the final and crucial moment of his ordeal, the ultimate test of his fidelity, he has found that his strength to remain faithful resides neither in resources of sheer willpower nor in the lifeless ground of abstractions but in the lifegiving faithfulness of God present to him through the person of Jesus Christ.

Pascal's final decision has the characteristics of an act of creative fidelity. His act of fidelity not only preserves the values of his spiritual heritage for himself, but he also communicates them to others. Pascal's decision has an impact not only upon his life, but on the lives of others as well. The decision is life-affirming, especially for Marc André and for Esther. Marc André has begun to <u>live</u> in this new world. Esther too has grown. She has let go of Marc André and plans to return to France to care for her brother's child, a child whose survival depends on her caring.(21)

Pascal communicates not only his deeds but also what he lives by. He announces to people in France or wherever they are in exile that their strength not to betray will come from beyond themselves. Their faithfulness in time of trial in effect will be an expression of the unfailing faithfulness of God. Pascal also communicates what makes these deeds possible for him, namely that because he has experienced the presence of Christ, seen his face and heard his call through the faces and words of others, he is assured that his attempt to live out his act of fidelity will be assured by God's presence to him in his moment of distress. At the end Pascal can make his own the words of Professor Moreuil that Marc André had quoted to him earlier.

I don't know what that moment will make of me, perhaps a rag. I'm not presuming on my own strength alone. I'm counting on God, that he will not abandon me, that he will save me from a final disaster. Either he will take me to himself, or he will give me the strength to withstand the torture.(22)

Pascal has shared the meaning of his action in conversation with Marc André and Esther. They follow him with difficulty, and at a certain point they can go no further. But, with time, especially after his death, they will come to understand. Then his words will become their own, as Moreuil's have become his. For Pascal's words are a witness. They are not just words he says, they are words he supports with his very life and being.

A genuinely creative incarnation is one that is life-affirming and one that lets traditional values be present in a new way appropriate to altered circumstances. Certainly in this respect Pascal's action is creative. His creative gesture springs from resources of fidelity that are most deeply and intensely interpersonal.

The genuineness of any act of creative fidelity is also often indicated by the additional acts of creative fidelity it inspires in others´ lives. Whether or not this might be the case after Pascal´s plea is heard depends upon the openness of Pascal´s audience to hear his message and the willingness of this audience in turn to reflect....

Notes to Chapter IX. <u>Rome Is No Longer In Rome</u>: Challenge for Creative <u>Incarnations of Fidelity</u>

"Rome Is No Longer in Rome," has not yet been translated into English. Still, the title is underlined in the text of this essay to enable readers to easily recognize by the conventional sign that <u>Rome Is No Longer in Rome</u> is the title of the play analyzed in this chapter. This underlining is a departure from the system employed in Part Three of this book, wherein titles in English are not underlined in order to indicate that a work has not yet been translated and published in English.

1. <u>Rome Is No Longer in Rome</u>, a play in five acts, and "The Real Issues in <u>Rome Is No Longer in Rome</u>" to date have appeared only in French: <u>Rome n'est plus dans Rome</u>, pièce en cinq actes, et "Les vrais problèmes de <u>Rome n'est plus dans Rome</u>, pp. 1-148, 149-78 in <u>Rome n'est plus dans Rome</u>, Paris: La Table Ronde, 1951.

2. <u>Rome n'est plus dans Rome</u>, Act II, Scene I, p. 49.

3. Ibid., Act V, Scene V, pp. 142-43.

4. Ibid., Act V, Scene V, pp. 147-48.

5. <u>Creative Fidelity</u>, New York, Farrar, Straus and Co., 1964, pp. 167, 182.

6. <u>Rome n'est plus dans Rome</u>, Act II, Scene I, p. 49; cf. Act V, Scene V, pp. 145-48.

7. Ibid., Act V, Scene V, pp. 142-43.

8. Ibid., Act II, Scene I, p. 49; Act V, Scene V, pp. 145-48; "Les vrais problèmes de <u>Rome n'est plus dans Rome</u>," pp. 161-62; <u>Creative Fidelity</u>, pp. 164-73, 182-83.

9. <u>Rome n'est plus dans Rome</u>, Act V, Scene V, p. 145.

10. "Les vrais problèmes de <u>Rome n'est plus dans Rome</u>," p. 166.

11. Ibid., p. 165.

12. <u>Rome n'est plus dans Rome</u>, Act V, Scene V, p. 148; "Les vrais problèmes de <u>Rome n'est plus dans Rome</u>," p. 153.

13. "Les vrais problèmes de <u>Rome n´est plus dans Rome</u>," pp. 160-72, esp. 168-70.

14. <u>Creative Fidelity</u>, Ch. VIII, Ch. IX, pp. 147-74, 175-83; <u>Homo Viator, An Introduction to a Metaphysic of Hope</u>, Chicago, Ill., Henry Regnery Co., 1951; New York, Harper Bros., 1962, "Obedience and Fidelity," pp. 125-34.

15. <u>Rome n´est plus dans Rome</u>, Act II, Scene I, pp. 51, 80.

16. "Les vrais problèmes de <u>Rome n´est plus dans Rome</u>," pp. 164-66.

17. Ibid., pp. 152-59.

18. <u>Rome n´est plus dans Rome</u>, Act II, Scenes I and II, pp. 67-78.

19. Ibid., Act III, Scene I, p. 74.

20. <u>Homo Viator</u>, "Obedience and Fidelity," pp. 129-32.

21. <u>Rome n´est plus dans Rome</u>, Act V, Scene V, pp. 144.

22. Ibid., Act II, Scene I, p. 49.

Chapter X.   Conclusion: Sketch of the Essential Features
            Highlighted

     Reflection on eight Marcel plays and philosophic essays
commenting on the issues that the theater brings to light has
enabled us to highlight some of the essential features of
"creative fidelity."

     The Unfathomable lets us see that presence is central to a
life of creative fidelity.   Presence consists of a spiritual
exchange that can become a life of intersubjectivity, a veritable
co-esse.   Edith´s reflections in The Unfathomable and Marcel´s
philosophic clarification in Presence and Immortality enable us
to recognize the nature of presence.   Presence occurs as a
spiritual influx encountered by way of inwardness and depth.
These works also reveal presence as a witness of fidelity, a
co-authored communion, the benefit of whose renewals is always a
mysterious incitement to create.

     The two plays The Lantern and Dot the I reveal the essential
role of the light of truth in a life of creative fidelity. The
Lantern shows that the light of truth is an interpersonal
presence that enables one to discover in truth what one loves and
what it is that one hopes to live by. Dot the I shows that
existential witness discloses not merely ideas or the words one
says but also the very reality by which one lives.

     The Lantern brings to light several essential aspects of
creative fidelity.   Raymond´s life shows what essays of
philosophic reflection on creative fidelity confirm. Creative
initiatives issue from fidelity to the presence of loved ones in
one´s life. Genuine creativeness arises out of a faithfulness to
oneself.   It springs from keeping in touch with what is vital and
most deeply personal, what is ultimately revealed only to love.
Such faithfulness to oneself is most often discovered, however,
in conjunction with one´s attempts to remain faithful to one´s
family and loved ones. Creative fidelity involves coming to know
who one is in the sense of recognizing and freely deciding what
one wants to love and live for.   This self-discovery, a
precondition to any genuine creativity, occurs best in the
radiance of a light of truth that is experienced as a personal
presence.

     Dot the I reveals how existential witness is an essential
part of creative fidelity. This play shows how one can
communicate what one lives by. In Dot the I Aimée shows what
her experience cf forgiving and of feeling assured that she is
loved has been.   Through compassion, and love Aimée the child

becomes the mother of the woman. Aimée shares with Felicia not only the ideas she states but also the very reality by which she lives. Aimée's testimony enables Felicia to begin to experience within herself and in relation to her own life what it is that Aimée is talking about. Such communication of the interpersonal realities that are part of our lives can only occur through a communion of love.

The Rebellious Heart highlights, by its absence in the life of Daniel Meyrieux, what The Lantern portrays positively in the life of Raymond Chavière. Creativity is not distinguished by novelty, inventiveness, or spontaneity but rather by the fact that it is rooted in faithfulness. Any genuine creativity in the realm of art or of daily living requires as its basis faithfulness within a genuine communion of love. Creativity finds itself resourced in faithfulness to oneself, faithfulness to others, and ultimately in faithfulness to an absolute Other.

The Double Expertise leads us to recognize that creative fidelity, like the act of commitment initiating it, has as its condition of possibility availability, people's ability to invoke and provide actual renewals of interpersonal presence and their effective and consecrated resolve to do so.

The last three plays we considered, Colombyre or the Torch of Peace, The Sting, and Rome Is No Longer in Rome, all portray the contemporary situation wherein the survival of spiritual values is threatened. This situation of menace highlights the heroic attitudes that are necessary if human life is to survive.

Colombyre or the Torch of Peace shows the context that is necessary if creative fidelity is to endure. For values to be realized, both in the sense of being incarnately actualized and in the sense of being personally understood, they must be expressed among persons. A person-community whose atmosphere and one-to-one relations are characterized by a spirit of light and love from above is the necessary condition for the survival and growth of values. This context encourages individuals to get in touch with their own personal experience and heritage of values and to share this wealth with others. If spiritual values are to be communicated effectively to others, it will be when the spirit of light and love—the spirit that animates the one-to-one relations among persons in community and that is reflected in their use of the things that surround them—touches others by its radiance and by their existential witness.

The Sting reveals that in our times, when spiritual values are debunked and the very foundations of fidelity and trust are undermined, what is called for is not mediocrity but heroic attitudes. Creative fidelity requires the personal commitment and service of individuals who, like the artist and the believer who really prays, are consecrated in self-sacrificing love to quicken others´ sense of their spiritual dignity. Such persons will be protected by their heroic commitment. Yet, given the epidemic proportions of the malady of spiritual degradation that can destroy an individual from within, they will also need to draw on the self-sacrificing love of a martyr who lives on in them like a viaticum nourishing and sustaining fidelity among the living. Creative fidelity calls for heroic commitment. Creative fidelity also needs to draw on the support of an interpersonal bond of love that unites us with those who from beyond death assure the fidelity of the living.

Rome Is No Longer in Rome shows the situation wherein spiritual values are so alien to a culture that any attempt to promote them or live by them is almost sure to meet with violent persecution. In such a situation it becomes clear that no individual can assure by his or her strength alone that he or she will remain faithful through torture and brain-washing. Assurance can only come in relation to a ground of fidelity that can be experienced as one´s ultimate recourse in response to an appeal from one´s utter distress.

Rome Is No Longer in Rome shows that it is of the essence of creative fidelity to be resourced not merely in rational argumentation, stoic constancy, or unswerving loyalty to abstract ideals, but in the personal presence of God, whom we trust will not abandon and forsake, but who will rather be faithful and save his people.

This play also shows that genuine expressions of creative fidelity are not so much technical manoeuvers that influence a socio-political movement. Rather the concrete gestures that incarnate fidelity creatively are personal acts of witness and testimony that, like Pascal´s, share with others in a spirit of truth and love the living core of one´s spiritual heritage.

Signs of the authenticity of one´s acts of creative fidelity are that they seem to awaken a sense of life in others and that they seem to correspond to the original intent of their author.

Creative fidelity is centered in presence and is essentially a life rooted in a communion of love. Creative fidelity is rooted in an intersubjectivity of being that brings an uplifting of one´s being and an incitement to create whenever the conferral of presence is renewed. Creative fidelity involves a light of truth that is the personal presence of a loved one. The actual presence of a loved one, revealing what he or she loves and lives

165

for, brings a light of truth that illumines one´s own discovery of what it is one hopes to be. The communion of love that presence actualizes helps one not only to see, but also to decide in a light of truth what one hopes to love and live by.

Creativity, with its striving for generativity, be it artistic or human, is truly effective only when it finds its basis in a communion of love involving faithfulness to oneself, faithfulness to others, and ultimately faithfulness to an Other.

Faithfulness requires remaining in vital contact with what is alive in oneself, that deep personal spiritual center that is revealed only to love. Such faithfulness occurs and is often most readily recognized in terms of one´s response of faithfulness to another´s invitation and appeal for love.

A vow of creative fidelity is the voicing of a personal commitment to be with and for another in loving care. It is also the utterance of a hope and prayer that resources will be provided for us to remain faithful in our reciprocal commitment to love.

The bond of love that is lived out as creative fidelity develops through a dialogue of freedoms, an invitation or appeal, a free response and a reciprocal resolve to be with and for one another. The reciprocal self-gift of freedoms can progress from co-authoring an I-Thou encounter to constituting a co-esse or intersubjectivity of being that characterizes belonging and availability. This bonding and commitment to be with and for one another is what constitutes a communion of love. The pledge of its enduringness is what formalizes and enables the life-long commitment of creative fidelity.

Creative fidelity, like the act of commitment initiating it, has as its condition of possibility "availability," people´s ability to invoke and provide actual renewals of interpersonal presence and their consecrated and effective resolve to do so.

Family or person-community is the requisite context wherein creative fidelity, or a life of commitment and service to promote human values with and for others, can be lived out. In order for one´s sharing of values to be authentic, and not a farcical caricature, the interpersonal relations that characterize the community´s life must be animated by a spirit of light and love from above. This inspiration incarnate in the community´s one-to-one relations is also reflected in the atmosphere of the community´s dwelling place and in its dealings with others.

Spiritual values or a reverence for the existential

background of human dignity are not transmitted best when broadcast like sound waves from a transmitting set to be picked up by a receiving set. Communicating values is rather a question of awakening in others their sense of their worth as human individuals. Expressing toward others the act of adoration addressed to the particle of divine creation within them can awaken in others their sense of divine filiation. This communication is not so much a telling or even a giving of something as it is a quickening of another's appreciation of his or her situation in Being.

Creative fidelity may in fact simply designate an artful way of living out a loving and life-long personal relationship with oneself, others, and an Absolute Other.

There is a reciprocity in creative fidelity, one that is immediately sensed and one that can finally be discovered to be ontologically founded. It appears almost paradoxically. The creation of one's life as a personal response to an invitation to be with and for others and an Other is grounded in one's faithfulness to oneself, others, and an Other. This faithfulness, as revealed poignantly in time of test or trial, is in turn nourished by the faithfulness of others in their active communication of love and by the faithfulness of an Absolute Thou as the ultimate recourse and source of creative fidelity.

Sketching the main lines of the essence of creative fidelity risks portraying as a bare-bones skeleton what in reality has all the concrete richness of enfleshed individuals' lives.

Indeed, creative fidelity may be read as designating an individual's response to a continually renewed call to be. The response to that call is as creatively rich and varied as the individual's life situation and the particular invitations he or she received. In this perspective creative fidelity may be recognized as a descriptive clarification of the personal response and life story one writes as his or her answer to the question "Who am I?"

Gabriel Marcel's book Du Refus à l'Invocation, entitled in English Creative Fidelity, suggests that creative fidelity can denote a person's lifelong response to a continuous call to be. From this point of view it becomes evident that the meaning of the term "creative fidelity," reflective of the mystery it expresses, transcends in richness any particular expression or summary definition that might be given to it.

The purpose of this work is achieved if readers perceive a hint of the richness of Gabriel Marcel's thought on creative fidelity, and if they are at the same time attracted to explore his work and examine firsthand the concrete richness of thought on this and other themes that can be discovered there.

It is also my hope that this study has suggested, without betrayal through oversimplification, how Gabriel Marcel´s theater is a privileged gateway into areas of inquiry that his philosophic reflections serve to clarify.

The following section of this book offers information for those wanting to know more about Gabriel Marcel´s life and work.

There follow drawings by Stephen Healy that depict the commemorative medal commissioned by L'Hôtel des Monnaies (the National Mint of France) and created by Charlotte Engels. One side presents a likeness of Gabriel Marcel. The reverse side represents the myth of Orpheus and Eurydice and bears the words fidélité, fidelity; disponibilité, availability; and espérance, hope. Marcel remarked that if he were to choose mythological characters as a sign for his life he would choose Orpheus and Eurydice. Certainly this choice highlights the centrality of music in his life as well as his concern for loved ones who have passed beyond death.

COMMEMORATIVE MEDAL OF GABRIEL MARCEL

COMMISSIONED BY L'HÔTEL DES MONNAIES

Part Three: Resources for Research

I. GABRIEL MARCEL BIBLIO-BIOGRAPHY

1889   Born December 7 in Paris.

1893   November 15, death of his mother, born Laure Meyer, July
        30, 1866.

1898   His father, Henry Marcel, married Marguerite Meyer,
        sister of the first wife, before going to Stockholm as
        ambassador. They stayed in Sweden 1898-1899 until Henry
        Marcel returned to Paris to fill the post of Minister of
        Fine Arts.

1904   Submitted to Fernand Gregh a play in the style of Ibsen
        that was a childish presentiment of A Man of God.

1909   Friends at the Sorbonne with Jacques Rivière, Henri
        Franck and Jean Wahl. Degree conferred with the
        submission of "The metaphysical ideas of Coleridge and
        their connection with the philosophy of Schelling."
        Followed the lectures of Henri Bergson, who taught at the
        Collège de France.

1910   Agrégation de philosophie.

1911   Taught at Lycée de Vendôme.

1912-13 Taught in a small private school above Lake Geneva.

1914   Began writing his Metaphysical Journal. Published his
        first plays: Paris, Ed. Grasset, Le Seuil Invisible:
        Preface, La Grâce, Le Palais de Sable (The Invisible
        Threshold: Preface, Grace, The Sand Castle). During the
        war, he directed a Red Cross Center in Paris and an
        information service on those missing in action.

1915-18 Taught at Lycée Condorcêt in Paris.

1916-17 Metapsychical experiences.

1919   Married Jacqueline Boegner.

1919-23 Professor at Sens.

1921   Le Coeur des Autres (Rebellious Heart) published
        (Theatre: Ed. Grasset).

1922   Encounter with Charles Du Bos, whom he succeeded as
        editor of Plon´s Collection "Feux Croisés."

177

1923   Settled in Paris, 21 rue de Tournon. Worked with
        Nouvelle Revue Francaise, and became dramatic and then
        literary critic for L'Europe Nouvelle. L'Iconoclaste
        (The Iconoclast) published (Théâtre: Ed. Stock).

1925   Le Quatuor en fa dièse (Quartet in F#) published
        (Théâtre: Ed. Stock). Un Homme de Dieu (A Man of God
        published.

1926   March 6. Death of his father, Henry Marcel, who was born
        November 1854.

1927   Publication of Journal Métaphysique (Metaphysical
        Journal)(Ed. Gallimard).

1929   Religious experience and conversion. Baptised March 23
        with François Mauriac as sponsor.

1931   Published Trois pièces: Le Regard neuf, Le Mort de
        demain, La Chapelle ardente (Plon),(Three Plays: The New
        Look, Tomorrow's Dead, The Votive Candle).

1933   Le Monde cassé (The Broken World) published
        (Théâtre: Ed. Desclée de Brouwer), followed by the
        essay "Position et approches concrète du mystère
        ontologique" ("On the Ontological Mystery").

1935   Etre et avoir (Being and Having) published (Aubier).

1936   Le Chemin de crête, Ariadne published (Théâtre:
        Ed. Grasset). Le Dard (The Sting) published (Théâtre:
        Ed. Plon).

1938   La Soif (Thirst)(Théâtre: Ed. Desclée de Brouwer)
        reedited under the title Les Coeurs avides (Eager Hearts)
        (La Table Ronde, 1952).

1939-40 Taught at Lycée Louis-le-Grand.

1940   Death of Henry Marcel's second wife Marguerite, who
        raised Gabriel Marcel. Published Du Refus à
        l'invocation (Creative Fidelity) (Gallimard). Acquired
        the Chateau de Peuch in Corrèze, where the family lived
        from 1941-1943.

1941   Taught several months at Lycée de Montpellier.

1944   Became drama critic for Nouvelles Littéraires. Before
        the war he worked for several reviews, L'Europe Nouvelle,
        La Nouvelle Revue Francaise, Sept, Temps présent, La
        Vie intellectuelle, etc.

1945   L'Horizon (The Horizon) published (Théâtre; Edition
        des Etudiants de France). Homo Viator (Homo Viator)
        published (Aubier). La Métaphysique de Royce (Royce's
        Metaphysics) published (Aubier). For the years 1945
        through 1947 music was at the center of creative
        activities.

1947   Death of his wife. Apercus phénoménologiques sur
        l'être en situation (Phenomenological notes on being in
        a situation) (Boivin). Théâtre Comique: Colombyre,
        ou le Brasier de la Paix; La Double Expertise; Les
        Points sur les I; Le Divertissement posthume. (Comic
        Theater: Colombyre, or the Torch of Peace, The Double
        Expertise, Dot the I, The Posthumous Joke.) (Albin
        Michel). Existentialisme Chrétien (Christian
        Existentialism) (Plon, collection "Présences" in
        collaboration with Etienne Gilson, Jeanne Delhomme, Roger
        Troisfontaines, Pierre Colin, J.-P. Dubois-Dumée).

1948   Directed a UNESCO conference at Beyrouth.

1949   Received the Grand Prize for Literature from the French
        Academy. Published Vers un autre Royaume: L'Emissaire; Le
        Signe de la Croix, (Toward another World: The Emissary,
        The Sign of the Cross). (Théâtre: Ed. Plon).
        Delivered the Gifford Lectures at University of Aberdeen,
        Scotland, The Mystery of Being, I. Reflection and
        Mystery, II. Faith and Reality.

1950   La Fin des temps (The End of Time) Théâtre:
        Réalités.

1951   Le Mystère de l'être, (The Mystery of Being,) 2
        vols. (Aubier). Rome n'est plus dans Rome (Rome Is No
        Longer in Rome) (Théâtre: Ed. de La Table Ronde).
        Les Hommes contre l'humain (Man Against Mass Society) (La
        Colombe). Travel in North Africa, then in South America.

1952   Elected a Member of the Institute of France, Academy of
        Political and Moral Sciences.

1953   Le Declin de la sagesse (The Decline of Wisdom) (Plon).

1954   L'Homme problématique (Problematic Man) (Aubier).

1955   Mon temps n´est pas le vôtre (My Time is not Your
        Time) (Théâtre: Ed. Plon). Croissez et multipliez
        (Increase and multiply) (Théâtre: Ed. Plon).

1956   Received the Goethe Prize from the town of Hamburg,
        conferred in Germany for one who fosters a supranational
        spirit and work in favor of humanity.

1956-66 Numerous trips in the United States and Canada and to
        Japan where he was received by the emperor.

1958   Received the National Grand Prize for Literature. La
        Dimension Florestan, "Le Crepuscule du sens commun,"
        (The Florestan Dimension,)("The Twilight of Common Sense")
        (Plon).

1959   Présence et immortalité, (Presence and Immortality.)
        (Flammarion) L´Heure théâtrale (The Theater Hour)
        (Plon).

1960   La Prune et la prunelle, (L´Avant scene). (The Plum and
        the Apple of My Eye).

1961   Delivered the William James Lectures at Harvard
        University. The Existential Background of Human Dignity.

1963   Received the Osiris Prize. The Existential Background of
        Human Dignity, Harvard University Press.

1964   Received the Frankfurt Peace Prize, conferred by German
        editors, publishers, and book dealers. Auf der Suche
        nach Wahrheit und Gerechtigkeit, (Searchings) ed.
        Wolfgang Ruf, Freiburg im Bresgau, Verlag Knecht.
        Regards sur le theatre de Claudel , (Reviews of Paul
        Claudel´s Theater), (Beauchesne).

1965   Delivered the opening discourse at the Salzburg Music
        Festival. Paix sur la terre (Peace on Earth) (Aubier).
        Lectures in the United States.

1967   Le Secret est dans les îles (The Secret is in the
        Isles) (Plon).

1968   Entretiens Paul Ricoeur, Gabriel Marcel (Conversations
        between Paul Ricoeur and Gabriel Marcel) (Aubier).

1969   Received the Erasmus Prize. "An Autobiographical Essay"
        (1969) in The Philosophy of Gabriel Marcel, La Salle,
        Open Court, 1984. Visited Dresden and Prague.

180

1971   Le Siècle à venir, (The Century to Come) Fondation
        Roland de Jouvenel. Pour une sagesse tragique et son
        au-delà, (Tragic Wisdom and Beyond) (Plon). En
        chemin, vers quel eveil? (En Route Toward What an
        Awakening?) (Gallimard). Coleridge et Schelling
        (Coleridge and Schelling) (Aubier).

1972   Received the Dignity of the Grand Cross of the National
        Order of Merit of the Legion of Honor, of which he was
        already an Officer and a Commander.

1973   Percées vers un ailleurs (Breakthrough Toward a
        Beyond) (Fayard). Cinq Pièces Majeures (Five Major
        Plays) (Plon). Colloquium at Cerisy la Salle,
        International Cultural Center, Aug. 24-31, 1973,
        discussing his theater and philosophy.

1973   October 8. Died in Paris.

1975   Foundation of an international association, Présence de
        Gabriel Marcel, which groups his family, friends, and
        associates and continues the study of his work.   Social
        Center: 85 boulevard de Port-Royal, Paris, 75013.
        Secrétariat: 9 avenue Franklin-Roosevelt, Paris 75008.

1976   Entretiens autour de Gabriel Marcel (Conversations Around
        Gabriel Marcel) (Neuchâtel, à la Baconnière).
        Proceedings of 1973 international colloquium on the
        Theater and Philosophy of Gabriel Marcel, published with
        the sponsorship of the European Cultural Foundation, 9
        avenue Franklin-Roosevelt, Paris 75008, France.

1977   Gabriel Marcel interrogé par Pierre Boutang, (Gabriel
        Marcel interviewed by Pierre Boutang) (Archives du XXe
        Siècle) Editions J.-M. Place, 1978. Followed by a
        reedition of "Position et approches concrètes du
        mystère ontologique," ("On the Ontological Mystery").

Sources for Biographic and biblio-biographic information:

        Louis Chaigne, Vie et oeuvres d'écrivains, (Life and
        Works of Writers), Vol. 4, F. Lanore, 1954, pp. 183-201.

        Jeanne Parain-Vial, Gabriel Marcel et les niveaux de
        l'expérience, (Gabriel Marcel and the levels of
        experience)Seghers, 1966, Biblio-biographie, pp. 99-107.

        Gabriel Marcel interrogé par Pierre Boutang, (Gabriel
        Marcel Interviewed by Pierre Boutang) J.-M. Place Ed.,
        1978, p. 116.

Biblio-biography of Gabriel Marcel's Entrance into the
English-Speaking World.

1949   The Philosophy of Existence, London, Harvill Press,
        1949; New York, The Philosophical Library, 1949;
        Freeport, New York, Books for Libraries Press, 1969
        reprint of 1949 edition. English version of "Positions
        et approches concrètes du mystère ontologique."

        Being and Having, Westminister, Dacre Press, 1949; New
        York, Harper and Row, 1965.

1949-50 Gifford Lectures at Aberdeen University, Scotland.

1950   The Mystery of Being. Vol. I. Reflection and Mystery.
        Vol. II. Faith and Reality. London, Harvill Press,
        1950-51; Chicago, Regnery/Gateway, 1960; Lanham,
        Maryland, University Press of America, 1984.

1951   Homo Viator, London, V. Gollanoz, 1951; Chicago, H.
        Regnery Co., 1951; New York, Harper and Row, 1962;
        Peter Smith, Magnolia, Mass. 1978.

1952   Three Plays by Gabriel Marcel, A Man of God, Ariadne,
        and The Votive Candle (The Funeral Pyre), London,
        Secker and Warburg, 1952; New York, Hill and Wang,
        1965. Includes preface "The Drama of the Soul in
        Exile" (A lecture given in July 1950 by Gabriel Marcel
        at L'Institut Français in London).

        Metaphysical Journal, Chicago, H. Regnery Co., 1952;
        London, Rockliff Press, 1952, with essay "Existence and
        Objectivity" in appendix.

        Man Against Mass Society, London, Harvill Press, 1952;
        Chicago, H. Regnery, 1952; Gateway edition, 1962.

1954   The Decline of Wisdom, London, Harvill Press, 1954; New
        York, The Philosophical Library, 1955; and Chicago, H.
        Regnery, 1955.

1956   The Philosophy of Existentialism, New York, The
        Philosophical Library, The Citadel Press Inc., 1956;
        1961.

        Royce's Metaphysics, Chicago, H. Regnery Co., 1956;
        1975.

1958   The Lantern in Cross Currents, West Nyack, New York,
        1958.

182

1961   The William James Lectures delivered at Harvard
         University.

1963   The Existential Background of Human Dignity, Cambridge,
         Mass., Harvard University Press, 1963.

1964   Creative Fidelity, New York, Farrar, Straus, and Co.,
         1964.

1964-65 Lectures and travel throughout the United States and
         Canada.

1965   Philosophical Fragments (1904-1914) and The Philosopher
         and Peace, Notre Dame, Indiana, Notre Dame University
         Press, 1965.

1967   Problematic Man, New York, Herder and Herder, 1967.

         Presence and Immortality, Pittsburgh, Pa., Duquesne
         University Press, 1967. Includes The Unfathomable, the
         first act of an unfinished play. (1919).

         Searchings, New York, Paulist-Newman Press, 1967.
         Includes "My Dramatic Works as Viewed by the
         Philosopher" (1959).

1973   Conversations between Paul Ricoeur and Gabriel Marcel
         included in Tragic Wisdom and Beyond, Evanston,
         Illinois, Northwestern University Press, 1973.

1974   The Existentialist Drama of Gabriel Marcel: The Broken
         World, The Rebellious Heart and an Introduction by
         Gabriel Marcel, ed. F. J. Lescoe, West Hartford, Conn.,
         McAuley Institute, St. Joseph College, 1974.

1984   "An Autobiographical Essay" in The Philosophy of
         Gabriel Marcel, (The Library of Living Philosophers,
         Vol. XVII), ed. P. A. Schilpp and L. E. Hahn, LaSalle,
         Illinois, Open Court, 1984.

1986   Two One Act Plays by Gabriel Marcel: Dot the I, and The
         Double Expertise. Introduction by Jean-Marie and Anne
         Marcel, Lanham, Maryland, University Press of America,
         1986.

183

GABRIEL MARCEL (1889-1973)

Dramaturge

La Lumière sur la montagne   (1905) inédit
Le Seuil invisible   (1914)
    La Grâce   (1911)
    Le Palais de sable   (1913)
Le Quatuor en fa dièse   (1916-17)
Un Juste   (1918)
L'Insondable   (1919)
Le Petit Garçon   (1919) inédit
Trois Pièces (1931)
    Le Regard neuf   (1919)
    La Mort de demain   (1919)
    La Chapelle ardente   (1925) (plusieurs versions 1920-25)
L'Iconoclaste   (1920)
Le Coeur des autres   (1920)
Un Homme de Dieu   (1922)
L'Attelage ou le Noeud coulant   (1926) inédit
L'Horizon   (1928)
Le Monde cassé   (1932)
Le Fanal   (1935)
Le Chemin de Crête   (1935)
Le Dard   (1936)
Théâtre comique   (1947)
    Les Points sur les I   (1936)
    Le Divertissement posthume   (1923)
    Colombyre ou le Brasier de la Paix   (1937)
    La Double Expertise   (1937)
La Soif   (1937)
Vers un autre Royaume   (1949)
    L'Emissaire   (1945)
    Le Signe de la Croix   (1938-48)
La Fin des Temps   (1948)
Rome n'est plus dans Rome   (1951)
Mon Temps n'est plus le votre   (1955)
Croissiez et multipliez   (1955)
La Dimension Florestan   (1958)
La Prune et la prunelle   (1960)

GABRIEL MARCEL (1889-1973)

Dramatist

The Light on the Mountain   (1905) unpublished
The Invisible Threshold   (1914)
   Grace   (1911)
   The Sand Castle   (1913)
Quartet in F#   (1916-17)
A Just One   (1918)
The Unfathomable   (1919)
The Little Boy   (1919) unpublished
Three Plays (1931)
   The New Look   (1919)
   Tomorrow's Dead   (1919)
   The Votive Candle   (1925) (several versions 1920-25)
Rebellious Heart   (1920)
The Iconoclast   (1920)
A Man of God   (1922)
The Yoke or the Noose   (1926) unpublished
The Horizon   (1928)
The Broken World   (1932)
The Lantern   (1935)
Ariadne   (1935)
The Sting   (1936)
Comic Theater   (1947)
   Dot the I   (1936, 6-9 Nov.)
   Posthumous Joke   (1923)
   Colombyre or the Torch of Peace   (1937)
   The Double Expertise   (1937)
Thirst   (1938) reedited as Eager Hearts   (1952)
Toward another World (1949)
   The Emissary   (1945)
   The Sign of the Cross   (1938-48) Epilogue   (1953)
Out of Time   (1950)
Rome is no longer in Rome   (1951)
My time is not your time   (1955)
Increase and Multiply   (1955)
The Florestan Dimension   (1958)
The Plum and the Apple of my Eye   (1960)

*Titles not underlined have not yet been published in English.

185

Coleridge et Schelling (1909), Paris, Aubier, 1971.
Fragments philosophiques (1909-1914), Louvain and Paris,
Nauwelaerts, 1961.
La Métaphysique de Royce (1917-1918), Paris, Aubier, 1945.

Journal métaphysique (1914-1923), Paris, Gallimard, 1927.

Position et approches concrètes du mystère ontologique
(1933), Paris, Desclée de Brouwer 1933, Nauwelaerts, 1949,
J.-M. Place, 1977.
Etre et avoir (1928-1933), Paris, Aubier, 1935.

De Refus à l'invocation, Paris, Gallimard, 1940.

Homo Viator (1941-1943), Paris, Aubier, 1945.

Le Mystère de l'être, 2 volumes, (1949-1950), Paris, Aubier,
1951.

Les Hommes contre l'humain, Paris, La Colombe, 1951.

Le Declin de la sagesse, Paris, Plon, 1954.

L'Homme problématique, Paris, Aubier, 1955.

Présence et immortalité (1919-1951), Paris, Flammarion,
1959.

Auf der Suche nach Wahrheit und Gerechtigkeit (1959-1963),
Freiburg im Bresgau, Verlag Knecht, 1964.

La dignité humaine et ses assises existentielles (1961),
Paris, Aubier, 1965.
Paix sur la terre (1964), Paris, Aubier, 1965.

Entretiens Paul Ricoeur-Gabriel Marcel, Paris, Aubier, 1968.
Pour une sagesse tragique et son au-delà, Paris, Plon, 1969.

En chemin, vers quel éveil? Paris, Gallimard, 1971.
Entretiens autour de Gabriel Marcel (1973), Neuchâtel, à la
Baconnière, 1976.

186

Philosopher

Coleridge and Schelling (1909) (Preface 1967) Aubier, 1971.
Philosophical Fragments (1909-1914) Nauwelaerts, 1961;
University of Notre Dame Press, 1965.
Royce's Metaphysics (1917-1918) Montaigne, 1945; Regnery, 1956,
1975.
Metaphysical Journal (1914-1923) Gallimard, 1927; Chicago, H.
Regnery, 1952.
On the Ontological Mystery (1932) Desclee de Brouwer, 1933;
Nauwelaerts 1949; J.-M. Place, 1977; pp. 9-46 in The Philosophy
of Existentialism: Secaucus,N.J., The Citadel Press, 1956.
Being and Having (1928-1953) Aubier, 1935; New York, Harper and
Row, 1965; New York, Crossroad Press, 1982.
Creative Fidelity, Gallimard, 1940; New York, Farrar, Straus and
Co., 1964.
Homo Viator (1941-1944), Aubier, 1945; Homo Viator, New York,
Harper and Bros., 1962; available Peter Smith, 6 Lexington Ave.,
Magnolia, MA 01930, 1978.
The Mystery of Being, 2 vols. (1949-50), Aubier, 1951; Chicago,
H. Regnery, 1962, Lanham, Maryland, University Press of America,
1984.
Man Against Mass Society, La Colombe, 1951; Fayard, 1968;
Chicago, H. Regnery, 1962.
The Decline of Wisdom, Plon, 1954; London, Harvill Press, 1954;
New York, Philosophical Library, 1955.
Problematic Man, Aubier, 1955; New York, Herder and Herder,
1967.
Presence and Immortality (1919-1951) Flammarion, 1959;
Pittsburgh, Pa., Duquesne University Press, 1967; Louvain, Ed.
Nauwelaerts, 1967.
Searchings (1959-1965), Freiburg im Bresgau, Verlag Knecht,
1964; New York, Paulist Newman Press, 1967.

The Existential Background of Human Dignity, (1961), Cambridge,
Mass., Harvard University Press, 1963; Paris, Aubier, 1965.
"The Philosopher and Peace" (1964), in Philosophical Fragments
and The Philosopher and Peace, Notre Dame, Indiana, University
of Notre Dame Press, 1965.
Conversations between Paul Ricoeur and Gabriel Marcel, Aubier,
1968, included in Tragic Wisdom and Beyond, Plon, 1969;
Northwestern University Press, 1973.
"An Autobiographical Essay" (Spring 1969) in The Philosophy of
Gabriel Marcel, (The Library of Living Philosophers, Vol. XVII)
ed. P. A. Schilpp and L. E. Hahn, LaSalle, Illinois, Open Court,
1984.
En route, Toward What an Awakening?, Gallimard 1971.
Conversations around Gabriel Marcel, (1973), Neuchatel, a la
Baconniere, 1976.

* Dates in parentheses are dates of composition. Dates not in
parentheses are dates of publication.

187

The Light on the Mountain   (1905) unpublished
The Invisible Threshold   (1914)
    Grace   (1911)
    The Sand Castle   (1913)
Quartet in F#   (1916-17)
A Just One   (1918)
The Unfathomable   (1919)
The Little Boy   (1919) unpublished
Three Plays (1931)
    The New Look   (1919)
    Tomorrow's Dead   (1919)
    The Votive Candle   (1925) (several versions 1920-25)
Rebellious Heart   (1920)
The Iconoclast   (1920)
A Man of God   (1922)
The Yoke or the Noose   (1926) unpublished
The Horizon   (1928)
The Broken World   (1932)
The Lantern   (1935)
Ariadne   (1935)
The Sting   (1936)
Comic Theater   (1947)
    Dot the I   (1936, 6-9 Nov.)
    Posthumous Joke   (1923)
    Colombyre or the Torch of Peace   (1937)
    The Double Expertise   (1937)
Thirst   (1938) reedited as Eager Hearts   (1952)
Toward another World   (1949)
    The Emissary   (1945)
    The Sign of the Cross   (1938-48) Epilogue   (1953)
Out of Time   (1950)
Rome is no longer in Rome   (1951)
My time is not your time   (1955)
Increase and Multiply   (1955)
The Florestan Dimension   (1958)
The Plum and the Apple of my Eye   (1960)

*Titles not underlined have not yet been published in English.

To Philosophy

Coleridge and Schelling (1909) (Preface 1967) Aubier, 1971.
Philosophical Fragments (1909-1914) Nauwelaerts, 1961;
University of Notre Dame Press, 1965.
Royce's Metaphysics (1917-1918) Montaigne, 1945; Regnery, 1956,
1975.
Metaphysical Journal (1914-1923) Gallimard, 1927; Chicago, H.
Regnery, 1952.
On the Ontological Mystery (1932) Desclee de Brouwer, 1933;
Nauwelaerts 1949; J.-M. Place, 1977; pp. 9-46 in The Philosophy
of Existentialism: Secaucus,N.J., The Citadel Press, 1956.
Being and Having (1928-1953) Aubier, 1935; New York, Harper and
Row, 1965; New York, Crossroad Press, 1982.
Creative Fidelity, Gallimard, 1940; New York, Farrar, Straus and
Co., 1964.
Homo Viator (1941-1944), Aubier, 1945; Homo Viator, New York,
Harper and Bros., 1962; available Peter Smith, 6 Lexington Ave.,
Magnolia, MA 01930, 1978.
The Mystery of Being, 2 vols. (1949-50), Aubier, 1951; Chicago,
H. Regnery, 1962, Lanham, Maryland, University Press of America,
1984.
Man Against Mass Society, La Colombe, 1951; Fayard, 1968;
Chicago, H. Regnery, 1962.
The Decline of Wisdom, Plon, 1954; London, Harvill Press, 1954;
New York, Philosophical Library, 1955.
Problematic Man, Aubier, 1955; New York, Herder and Herder,
1967.
Presence and Immortality (1919-1951) Flammarion, 1959;
Pittsburgh, Pa., Duquesne University Press, 1967; Louvain, Ed.
Nauwelaerts, 1967.
Searchings (1959-1965), Freiburg im Bresgau, Verlag Knecht,
1964; New York, Paulist Newman Press, 1967.

The Existential Background of Human Dignity, (1961), Cambridge,
Mass., Harvard University Press, 1963; Paris, Aubier, 1965.
"The Philosopher and Peace" (1964), in Philosophical Fragments
and The Philosopher and Peace, Notre Dame, Indiana, University
of Notre Dame Press, 1965.
Conversations between Paul Ricoeur and Gabriel Marcel, Aubier,
1968, included in Tragic Wisdom and Beyond, Plon, 1969;
Northwestern University Press, 1973.
"An Autobiographical Essay" (Spring 1969) in The Philosophy of
Gabriel Marcel, (The Library of Living Philosophers, Vol. XVII)
ed. P. A. Schilpp and L. E. Hahn, LaSalle, Illinois, Open Court,
1984.
En route, Toward What an Awakening?, Gallimard 1971.
Conversations around Gabriel Marcel, (1973), Neuchatel, a la
Baconniere, 1976.

* Dates in parentheses are dates of composition. Dates not in
parentheses are dates of publication.

189

III. Works by Gabriel Marcel in Chronological Order of
Composition with Publisher References

III. A.   Philosophical Works
(in chronological order of composition)

Les idées métaphysique de Coleridge dans leurs Rapports avec
la Philosophie de Schelling (1910) Coleridge et Schelling,
(Présence et Pensée) Paris, Aubier Montaigne, 1971, 271 pp.

Fragments philosophiques, 1909-1914, Louvain, Editions
Nauwelaerts, 1961. Philosophical Fragments, 1909-1914, Notre
Dame, Indiana, University of Notre Dame Press, 1965, 127 pp.
English version includes Editor´s Note, The Philosopher and
Peace by Gabriel Marcel, Foreword by Gabriel Marcel,
Introduction by Lionel Blain, Philosophical Fragments 1909-1914,
and Epilogue by Gabriel Marcel.

Journal métaphysique (1914-1923), Paris, Gallimard, 1927, Vol.
XI, 341 pp. Metaphysical Journal, translated by Bernard Wall,
Chicago, Henry Regnery Company, 1952, Vol. XIII, 344 pp.
English version adds translator´s note, p. v, and author´s
preface to the English edition, p. VII-XIII, 1950.

La Métaphysique de Royce, Paris, Aubier, 1945, 225 pp. Royce´s
Metaphysics, translated by Virginia and Gordon Ringer, Chicago,
Henry Regnery Co., 1956, Vol. XVIII, 180 pp. English version
includes Preface by William Ernest Hocking, August 1956,
p. V-VIII, Author´s Foreword to the English edition of Royce´s
Metaphysics, July 1956, p. IX-XII. Reprinted 1975 by Greenwood
Press, a division of Williamhouse-Regency Inc.

"Position et approches concrètes du mystère ontologique"
(1932) is the text of a lecture delivered to the Marseille
philosophic society, January 23, 1933. The essay was published
in a volume with the play entitled The Broken World, published
by Desclée de Brouwer, Paris, 1933. The essay was later
reprinted with an introduction by Marcel de Corte and published
by Louvain, Nauwelaerts, and Paris, Vrin, 1949. The essay was
again reprinted in the book Gabriel Marcel interrogé par
Pierre Boutang, Paris, J. M. Place, 1977, pp. 121-41, cf.
p. 143. The essay appeared in English translation by Manya
Harari "On the Ontological Mystery" in The Philosophy of
Existentialism, Secaucas, NJ, Citadel Press, pp. 9-46.
Copyright 1956 The Philosophical Library. (Etienne Gilson
considers these pages as important to an understanding of
Gabriel Marcel´s thought as is the Introduction to Metaphysics
to the understanding of Henri Bergson´s thought.)

Être et Avoir (1928-1933) Paris, Aubier, 1935, 357 pp. Being
and Having, Westminster, Dacre Press, 1949. Reprinted: New
York, Harper and Row, 1965, Vol. XVII, 236 pp., with An
Introduction to the Torchbook Edition by James Collins,
pp. VI-XVII.

Du Refus à l'invocation, Paris, Gallimard, 1940, 326 pp.
Creative Fidelity, translated with introduction by Robert
Rosthal, New York, Farrar, Straus, and Company, 1964, Vol. XXVI,
261 pp.; New York, Crossroad Press, 1982.

Homo Viator, Paris, Aubier, 1945, 358 pp. Homo Viator,
Introduction to a Metaphysic of Hope, translated by Emma
Craufurd; originally published in English by Victor Gollancz,
Ltd., London, and Henry Regnery Company, Chicago, in 1951 and
reprinted through arrangement with Editions Montaigne, New York,
Harper and Brothers, 1962, 270 pp.

"Regard en arrière" in Existentialisme chrétien: Gabriel
Marcel, Présentation de Etienne Gilson, Paris, (Présences),
Plon, 1947, p. 291-319. "An Essay in Autobiography," translated
by Manya Harari, Secaucus, NJ, Citadel Press, copyright 1956 by
Philosophical Library, p. 104-28, in The Philosophy of
Existentialism.

Le Mystère de l'être, I. Réflexion et mystère, II. Foi
et Réalité, Paris, Aubier, 1951, 235, 188 pp. The Mystery of
Being, I. Reflection and Mystery, II. Faith and Reality, I
translated by G. S. Fraser, II translated by René Hague,
London, Harvill Press, 1951. Gateway Edition, Henry Regnery,
Chicago, IL, 1960. The Gifford Lectures, delivered at the
University of Aberdeen, Scotland, 1949. Reprinted Lanham, MD,
University of America Press, 1984.

Les Hommes contre l'humain, Paris, La Colombe, 1951, 206 pp.
Man Against Mass Society, translated by G. S. Fraser, Foreword
by D. M. Mackinnon, first published in Great Britain; A Gateway
Edition, Chicago, IL, Henry Regnery Company, 1962, 273 pp.

Le Declin de la Sagesse, Paris, Plon, 1954, 117 pp. The Decline
of Wisdom, translated by Manya Harari, London, Harvill Press,
1954, 56 pp., New York Philosophical Library, 1955.

L'Homme problématique, Paris, Aubier, 1955. Problematic Man,
translated by Brian Thompson, introduction by Leslie Dewart, New
York, Herder and Herder, 1967, 144 pp.

"Le Crépuscule du sens commun," in one volume with La
Dimension Florestan, Paris, Plon, 1958, 212 pp., pp. 170-212.

Présence et immortalité, Paris, Flammarion, 1959. Presence
and Immortality, Pittsburgh, PA., Duquesne University Press;
Louvain, Editions Nauwelaerts, 1967, 284 pp.

Auf des Suche nach Wahrheit und Gerichtigkeit, (1959-1963), ed. Wolfgang Ruf, Freiburg, im Bresgau, Verlag Knecht, 1964. Searchings, New York, Newman Press, 1967, 118 pp.

La Dignité humaine et ses assises existentielles, Paris, Aubier, 1964. The Existential Background of Human Dignity, The William James Lectures Delivered at Harvard University, 1961-62, Cambridge, MA., Harvard University Press, 1963.

"Le Philosophe devant la Paix," (1964), in Paix sur la Terre, deux discours et une tragédie, Paris, Aubier, 1965, 177 pp., pp. 41-60. "The Philosopher and Peace" in Philosophical Fragments, (1909-1914) and The Philosopher and Peace, translated by Viola Herms Drath, p. 6-19, Notre Dame, IN., University of Notre Dame Press, 1965, 127 pp.

Entretiens Paul Ricoeur-Gabriel Marcel, Paris, Aubier, 1968. Pour une sagesse tragique et son au-delà, Paris, Plon, 1971. Tragic Wisdom and Beyond, including Conversations between Paul Ricoeur and Gabriel Marcel, translated by Stephen Jolin and Peter McCormick, Evanston, IL., Northwestern University Press, 1973, XXXV-p. 256. Includes translators´ introductions and author´s prefaces for English versions.

"An Autobiographical Essay" (Spring 1969), in The Philosophy of Gabriel Marcel, Library of Living Philosophers, Ed. P. A. Schilpp and L. E. Hahn, La Salle, Il, Open Court, 1984, XVIII, 624 pp., pp.3-68.

En Chemin, vers quel eveil? Paris, Gallimard, 1971, 301 pp.

"De l´Audace en métaphysique," in Percées vers un ailleurs, Paris, Fayard, 1973, pp. 405-21.

Entretiens autours de Gabriel Marcel, "De la recherche philosophique" in Neuchâtel: Editions de la Baconnière; Paris, Diffusion Payot, 1976, 287 pp., pp. 9-19.

Gabriel Marcel interrogé par Pierre Boutang, Followed by Position et approches concrètes du mystère ontologique, (Archives du XXe Siècle, no. 1), Paris, J. M. Place, 1977, 143 pp.

Présence de Gabriel Marcel, Cahier 4, Gabriel Marcel et les injustices de ce temps, La responsabilité du philosophe. Cahier publié avec le concours de la Fondation Européene de la Culture, Membership subscription received at Secrétariat de la Présence de Gabriel Marcel, 9 avenue Franklin-Roosevelt, 75008, Paris, France.

III. B.   Gabriel Marcel's Plays
(In chronological order of composition)

La Lumière sur la montagne (1905). Unpublished.

Le Seuil invisible. Paris: Grasset, 1914. Contains two plays:
La Grâce (composed March-April 1911) and Le Palais de sable
(composed August-September 1913).

Le Quatuor en fa diése. Paris:Plon, 1925. Written in
1916-1917.

Un Juste. First act of an unfinished play written in early 1918
published in Paix sur la terre, deux discours et une
tragédie, Paris:Aubier, 1965, pp. 61-176.

L'Insondable. First act of an unfinished play written March
1919, published in Présence et immortalité, Paris:
Flammarion, 1959, pp. 195-234.

Le Petit Gaçon. An unpublished play in four acts written
December 18-20, 1919.

Trois Pièces. Postwar 1919-1920, Paris: Plon, 1931. Contains
three plays: Le Regard neuf, La Mort de demain, December
6-12, 1919; and La Chapelle ardente. (Several versions; 1949
edition contains revision and first version entitled Le Sol
detruit.)

L'Iconoclaste. Paris: Stock, 1923. Original idea, 1914, first
draft, 1916 entitled Le Porte-glaive: written 1919-1920.

Le Coeur des autres. Paris: Grasset, 1921 (Cahiers verts).
Written 1920.

Un Homme de Dieu. Paris: Grasset, 1925 (Cahiers verts). Written
1922; New edition: La Table Ronde, 1950.

L'Attelage ou le Noeud coulant. An unpublished play in four
acts. Written 1926.

L'Horizon. Paris: Aux Étudiants de France, 1945. Written
1928.

Le Monde cassé, followed by a philosophic meditation entitled
Position et approches concrètes du mystère ontologique.
Paris: Desclée De Brouwer, 1933. Written 1932.

Le Fanal. Paris: La Vie Intellectuelle (Supplément, 1936);
Paris: Stock, 1936. Written December 26-28, 1935.

Le Chemin de Crête. Paris: Grasset, 1936.

Le Dard. Paris: Plon, 1936.

Théâtre comique. Paris: Albin Michel, 1947. Contains four plays: Les Points sur les I. Written November 6-9, 1936. First published, Paris: Fayard, 1938 in Les oeuvres libres No. 208, October, 1938. Le Divertissement posthume. Written 1923. Colombyre ou le Brasier de la Paix. Written 1937. La Double Expertise. Written 1936.

La Soif. Paris: Desclée De Brouwer, 1938. Re-edition entitled Les Coeurs avides, Paris: La Table Ronde, 1952.

Vers un autre royaume. Paris: Plon, 1949. Contains L'Émissaire, 1945 and Le Signe de la Croix, 1949.

La Fin des Temps. Paris: Réalités, 1950.

Rome n'est plus dans Rome. Paris: La Table Ronde, 1951.

Mon Temps n'est plus le votre. Paris: Plon, 1955.

Croissiez et multipliez. Paris: Plon, 1955.

La Dimension Florestan. Paris: Plon, 1958.

La Prune et la prunelle. Paris: L'Avant-Scène, 1960.

Published English Translations of Gabriel Marcel's Plays
(In chronological order of composition)

The Unfathomable. March, 1919. First act of an unfinished play, L'Insondable. Trans. Michael A. Machado, Rev. Henry J. Koren, published Pittsburgh: Duquesne University Press, 1967, Presence and Immortality.

The Funeral Pyre. Original title of Rosalind Heywood's translation of La Chapelle ardente (c. 1920) published London: Secker & Warburg, 1952; paperback edition, New York: Hill and Wang, 1965: Three Plays has the translation of La Chapelle ardente entitled The Votive Candle, pp. 225-82.

The Votive Candle. Revised title given to trans. of La Chapelle ardente originally entitled The Funeral Pyre Supra.

The Rebellious Heart. trans. by Francis C. O'Hara, M.Ss.A, of Le Coeur des autres, a play in three acts (written 1920) in

The Existential Drama of Gabriel Marcel, F. J. Lescoe (ed.) West
Hartford, Conn.: St. Joseph College McAuley Institute Press,
1974, pp. 145-215.

A Man of God. Trans. by Marjorie Gabain of Un Homme de Dieu, a
play in four acts (written 1922), published in Three Plays,
London: Secker and Warburg, 1952; New York: Hill and Wang, 1965,
pp. 35-144.

Broken World. Trans. by J. M. P. Colla, R.S.M., of Le Monde
cassé, a play in four acts (written 1932) published in
Existential Drama of Gabriel Marcel, 1974, pp. 19-144.

The Lantern. Trans. by J. Cunneen & E. Stambler of Le Fanal, a
one act play (written December 26-28, 1935), Cross Currents,
VIII, 2 (Spring 1958), pp. 129-43.

Ariadne, translation by Rosalind Heywood of Le Chemin de Crête
(written 1935) a play in four acts published in Three Plays, New
York: Hill and Wang, 1965, pp. 115-224.

Dot the I. Trans. by Katharine Rose Hanley (written 1936) in Two
One Act Plays by Gabriel Marcel, Introduction by Jean-Marie and
Anne Marcel, Lanham, Maryland: University Press of America,
1986, pp. 1-21.

The Double Expertise. Trans. by Katharine Rose Hanley (written
1937) in Two One Act Plays by Gabriel Marcel, Introduction by
Jean-Marie and Anne Marcel, Lanham, Maryland: University Press
of America, 1986, pp. 23-38.

III. C. Drama Criticism

Gabriel Marcel's Essays in English on Drama and Relations of Theater and Philosophy in his Work:

"The Drama of the Soul in Exile," Preface, pp. 13-34 in Three Plays. (A lecture given in July 1950 at l'Institut Français in London.)

"My Dramatic Works as Viewed by the Philosopher" (1959), pp. 93-118 in Searchings, New York: Newman Press, 1967.

The Existential Background of Human Dignity (The William James Lecture Series 1961-62). Cambridge, MA: Harvard University Press, 1963. 178 pp.

Introduction to The Existential Drama of Gabriel Marcel, ed. F. J. Lescoe, pp. 9-18. West Hartford, CT: McAuley Inst. Press, St. Joseph's College, 1974.

"An Autobiographical Essay" (1969) in The Philosophy of Gabriel Marcel, Library of Living Philosophers Vol. XVII, ed. P. A. Schilpp & L. E. Hahn. La Salle, Illinois: Open Court, 1984, pp. 1-68.

Gabriel Marcel's Books of Drama Criticism in French

Théâtre et Religion, Paris: Vitte, 1958, 107 pp.

L'Heure Théâtrale De Giraudoux à Jean Paul Sartre, Paris: Plon, 1959, 230 pp.

Regards sur le théâtre de Claudel, Paris: Beauchesne, 1964, 175 pp.

For additional essays published in French cf. Chronological Bibliography of Works by Gabriel Marcel about his Theater, pp. 39-42.

Drama reviews in periodicals are listed in Roger Troisfontaines, De l'existence à l'être. La philosophie de Gabriel Marcel, pp. 385-464, (1953; 2nd ed. 1968), Louvain, Nauwelaerts, Paris: Vrin.

Cf. François H. and Claire C. Lapointe: Gabriel Marcel and His Critics, An International Bibliography, (1928-1976). New York and London: Garland Press, 1977.

Also F. Lapointe, "A Bibliography of the Writings of Gabriel Marcel" in The Philosophy of Gabriel Marcel. The Library of Living Philosophers, Vol. XVII, pp. 583-609 (1984).

III. D.   Musical Compositions

Hommage à la Vie. (In Praise of Life), pp. 201-208.

Mes Manes à Clytie Music composed by gabriel Marcel for a poem
by André Chenier. Appended in Marie-Madeleine Davy, Un
Philosophe Itinérant, Gabriel Marcel, (Homo Sapiens), Paris:
Flammarion, 1959, p. 347.

Mélodie. Le Double. Music composed by Gabriel Marcel for a poem
by Jules Supervielle, pp. 321-24 in Existentialisme chrétien:
Gabriel Marcel, presentation by Etienne Gilson, (Présences),
Paris: Plon, 1947, p. 325.

Essays on Music Cahier 2-3, Présence de Gabriel Marcel

L'Esthétique musicale de Gabriel Marcel, par Jeanne Parain-Vial
ARTICLES GENERAUX
Introduction: Gabriel Marcel et la critique musicale.
         Réflexions sur la nature des idées musicales.
L'idée chez César Franck.
         Bergsonisme et musique.
         Musique comprise et Musique vécue.
         La Musique et le règne de l'esprit.
         La Musique selon St. Augustin.
         Réponse à l'enquête de "Image Musicale."
         Irruption de la Mélodie.
         La Musique et le merveilleux.
         Méditation sur la musique.
         Humanisme et musique.
         La musique dans ma vie et mon oeuvre.
GABRIEL MARCEL ET L'AUTRICHE
         Les mélodies espagnoles et italiennes d'Hugo Wolf.
         Discours d'ouverture du Festival de Salzburg 1965.
L'ECOLE FRANÇAISE
         Un intimiste: Ernest Chausson.
         Le lyrisme Debussiste.
         Paul Dukas.
         Henri Duparc.
         Gabriel Fauré.
         César Franck.
         Vincent d'Indy.
         Albéric Magnard.
         Maurice Ravel.
         Albert Roussel.

DIVERS
REFERENCES
    Métaphores et exemples musicaux dans l'oeuvre de
Gabriel Marcel.
TEMOIGNAGE
    Gabriel Marcel et le disque.
INDEX DES COMPOSITEURS CITES
INFORMATIONS
Cahier publié avec le concours de la FONDATION EUROPEENNE DE LA
CULTURE
Subscriptions: Secretariat, Présence de Gabriel Marcel
                9, avenue Franklin-Roosevelt, 75008 Paris, France

Cf. L. Chaigne, Vie et oeuvres d'Écrivains, Vol. 4, Paris:
Lanore, 1954, pp. 252-53.

Hommage à la Vie. (In Praise of Life) is a copy of the piano
composition Gabriel Marcel improvised to bring J. Supervielle's
poem to its full expression as song. Gabriel Marcel improvised
musical compositions at the piano. His wife Jacqueline Boegner
Marcel noted the musical score for these piano compositions.
This activity was frequent and especially significant 1945-47.
The sheet music for Hommage à la Vie is reprinted here by kind
permission of the family of Gabriel Marcel.

Hommage à la Vie

J. Supervielle

203

205

De l'avoir enfermé - e Dans cette poé. sie .

à Paris .
le 2 sept. 1946

Hommage à la Vie

Paroles de JULES SUPERVIELLE
Musique de GABRIEL MARCEL

C´est beau d´avoir élu
Domicile vivant
Et de loger le temps
Dans un coeur continu,

Et d´avoir vu ses mains
Se poser sur le monde
Comme sur une pomme
Dans un petit jardin,

D´avoir aimé la terre,
la lune et le soleil,
Comme des familiers
Qui n´ont que leur pareils,

Et d´avoir confié
Le monde à sa mémoire
Comme un clair cavalier
À sa monture noire,

D´avoir donné visage
À ces mots: femme, enfants,
Et servi de rivage
A d´errants sentiments,

Et d´avoir atteint l´âme
A petits coups de rame
Pour ne l´effaroucher
D´une brusque approchée.

O´est beau d´avoir connu
L´ombre sous le fEuillage
Et d´avoir senti l´âge
Ramper sur le corps nu,

Accompagné la peine
Du sang noir dans nos veines
Et doré son silence
De l´étoile Patience,

Et d´avoir tous ces mots
Qui bougent dans la tête,
De choisir les moins beaux
Pour leur faire une en fête,

D´avoir senti la vie
Hâtive et mal aimée,
De l´avoir enfermée
Dans cette poésie.

208

Homage to Life

Words by JULES SUPERVIELLE
Music by GABRIEL MARECL

It is nice to have chosen
A living residence
And to house time
In a continuous heart,

And to have seen one´s hands
Placed on the world
As on an apple
In a little garden,

To have loved the earth,
The moon and the sun,
As intimates
Which have no equals,

And to have entrusted
The world to one´s memory
As a pale cavalier
On his black mount,

To have been friendly
To these concepts: wife, children,
And served as a shore
To wandering feelings,

And to have reached the soul
By small oar-strokes
Not to frighten it
By an abrupt approach.

It´s nice to have known
The shade under the foliage
And to have felt age
Creep over one´s nude body,

To have accompanied the pain
Of black blood in our viens
And gilded its silence
With the star Patience,

And to have all these words
Moving around in one´s head,
To choose the least loving
And celebrate it,

To have felt life
Premature and badly loved,
To have captured it
Into this poetry.

Translated by
Janet Kawa and Judith Woodard

209

III.   E. Combination Works by Gabriel Marcel
Books containing Works of both Theater and Philosophy
(in chronological order of composition)

Broken World and "On the Ontological Mystery" published together
in 1933 in Le Monde Cassé, Paris: Desclée de Brouwer & Cie.,
1933 (Collection "les Iles") followed by "Position et approches
concrètes du mystere ontologique."

Le Dard et L'Universel contre les masses. Plon, 1936.
Flammarion, 1951. (The Sting) and Man against Mass Society,
Chicago: H. Regnery, 1952, 1962.

La Soif, followed by Gaston Fessard's essay "Théâtre et
Mystère," Paris: Desclée de Brouwer, 1938.

Rome n'est plus dans Rome et "Les vrais problèmes de Rome n'est
plus dans Rome," Paris: La Table Ronde, 1951. (Rome is no longer
in Rome) and "The real issues of Rome is no longer in Rome,"
extract of an article to appear in Hommes et Monde, presented by
Gabriel Marcel as an address May 18, 1951, at the Hébertot
Theater.

La Dimension Florestan, Postface, "Le Crepuscule de Sens Commun"
1953-1954. (The Florestan Dimension) and ("The Twilight of Common
Sense") and a Postface.

Presence et Immortalité, Paris: Flammarion, 1959, contains
Metaphysical Journal 1938-43; essay, My Fundamental Purpose
(1937); essay Presence and Immortality (1951), originally
entitled, "On the Existential Premises of Survival," and The
Unfathomable (1919), the first act of an unfinished play.

Paix sur la terre, containing Un Juste (first act of an
unfinished play) and "Le philosophe devant la paix" (The
Philosopher and Peace, discourse pronounced upon the awarding of
the Frankfurt Peace Prize, Germany, 1964). Paris: Aubier, 1965,
177 pp.

Le Secret est dans les Iles, Paris: Plon, 1967, contains essay
"Le Secret est dans les Iles," Le Dard, L'Emissaire, La Fin des
Temps. (The Secret is in the Islands), contains a Preface by that
title, the plays (The Sting), (The Emissary), and (The End of
Time).

Percées vers un Ailleurs, Paris: Fayard, 1973, contains
Preface, L'Iconoclaste, Commentaire de l'abbé Belay, L'Horizon,
Postface de l'Horizon, Commentaire de l'abbé Belay, essai "De
L'Audace en Metaphysique." (Breakthrough Toward a Beyond)

Contains two plays, (The Iconoclast) and (The Horizon), a preface to one and a postface to the other, two commentaries by Marcel Belay, and an essay by Gabriel Marcel, "Daring in Metaphysics."

10. Cinq Pièces Majeures. Un Homme de Dieu, Le Monde cassé, Le Chemin de crête, La Soif, Le Signe de la croix. (Five Major Plays:) A Man of God, The Broken World, Ariadne, (The Thirst) and (The Sign of the Cross) Paris: Plon, 1973. At the end of this book, Marcel noted that he planned to reedit L'Emissaire, "The Emissary," and to publish with it an essay "La Philosophie de l'Epuration" (1945) which until that date (1973) had only appeared in a Canadian review. The essay "La Philosophie de l'Epuration" appeared in Presence de Gabriel Marcel, Cahier 4, Gabriel Marcel et les injustices de ce temps. La responsabilité du philosophe, published with the sponsorship of the European Cultural Foundation, Paris: Aubier, 1983, pp. 77-103. Subscriptions: Secrétariat. Présence de Gabriel Marcel, 9 Avenue Franklin Roosevelt, 75008 Paris.

IV. Bibliographies

Lapointe, François H., "A Bibliography of the Writings of Gabriel Marcel," pp. 583-609, in The Philosophy of Gabriel Marcel, (The Library of Living Philosophers, Vol. XVII), ed. P. A. Schilpp and L. E. Hahn, LaSalle, IL: Open Court, 1984.

Lapointe, François H., "Bibliography on Gabriel Marcel," The Modern Schoolman, Vol. 49, (November 1971), pp. 23-49.

Lapointe, François H. and Claire C. Lapointe, Gabriel Marcel and His Critics, An International Bibliography, (1928-76), New York and London: Garland Publishing, Inc., 1977.

Troisfontaines, Roger, S. J., De l'existence à l'être, La Philosophie de Gabriel Marcel, Louvain, Nauwelaerts, Paris: Vrin, 1952 and 1968. Bibliography through 1964, Vol. 2, pp. 381-464.

Wenning, Gerald G., "Works By and About Gabriel Marcel," The Southern Journal of Philosophy, Vol. 4, No. 2, (Summer 1966), pp. 82-96.

V. Partial List of Plays Produced

Information to update and add to this partial listing will be gratefully received by the author, c/o Gabriel Marcel Institute of Existential Drama, Le Moyne College, Syracuse, NY 13214

La Grâce
Grace
    At the Théâtre Mathurins, by the Grimace Company, Paris, 1921

Le Coeur des autres
The Rebellious Heart
    At the Théâtre Grévin, by the Canard Sauvage Group, Paris, 1921. In English at Le Moyne College, Gabriel Marcel Institute for Existential Drama, November 10-12, 1975.

Le Regard neuf
The New Look
    At the Ambigu, under the patronage of the Escholiers, Paris, 1922.

La Mort de demain
Tomorrow's Dead
    At the Théâtre des Arts, then by the Deux-Masques, Paris, 1937.

La Chapelle Ardente
The Votive Candle
The Funeral Pyre
    At the Théâtre des Jeunes Auteurs au Vieux Colombier, Paris, 1925.

    In English The Funeral Pyre at Newton College of the Sacred Heart, Newton, MA., 1961.

Un Homme de Dieu
A Man of God
    Presented by the Comédie de l'Est at the Théâtre Montparnasse, June, 1949, and extended to the Théâtre de l'Oeuvre where it was performed for several months, 1949-50. It was performed at Cobourg in Germany, and in German at Munster, Westphalia. It was also performed in England.

215

In English, Readers´ Theater versions
were performed at De Paul University,
Drama Program, February 1974, and at Le
Moyne College, Gabriel Marcel Institute
for Existential Drama, April 1978.

L´Horizon
The Horizon   Readers´ Theater, Paris, 1957.

Le Monde cassé
The Broken World   In German at Munster and at Karlsruhe.
                              In Dublin, Ireland, 1959.
                              In English version at St. Joseph´s
                              College, West Hartford, CT., 1974.
                              Readers´ Theater version, Le Moyne
                              College, Gabriel Marcel Institute for
                              Existential Drama, December, 1979.

Le Fanal
The Lantern   At the Comédie-Française, Paris, 1938.
                              In English at Le Moyne College, Gabriel
                              Marcel Institute for Existential Drama,
                              television April, 12-14, 1976.

La Double Expertise
The Double Expertise   Presented at Le Moyne College, Gabriel
                              Marcel Institute for Existential Drama,
                              October 27-29, 1977. Guest Artist
                              Series, City Theater Festival, New
                              Theater, New York City, May 1986.

Les Points sur les i
Dot the I   Presented at Le Moyne College, Gabriel
                              Marcel Institute for Existential Drama,
                              October 13-14, 1978. Guest Artist
                              Series, City Theater Festival, New
                              Theater, New York City, May 1986.

Le Chemin de crête
Ariadne   Created at the Théâtre du Parc,
                              Brussels, 1950.
                              Presented at the Vieux-Colombier, Paris,
                              1953.
                              Presented in London, August, 1958.

Le Dard
The Sting   Presented at the Théâtre des Arts,
                              the future Théâtre Hebertot; extended
                              at the Théâtre des Deux Masques.

Le Signe de la Croix
The Sign of the Cross Presented by La Baraque Company at
Nantes, 1954.

Colombyre ou le brasier de la paix
Colombyre or the Torch of Peace

Created at Antwerp by the Theater Club of
Louvain, 1957.
Presented in English at Fordham
University, New York, 1951.

La Soif
Thirst Presented at the Théâtre du Parc,
Brussels, 1952.
Also presented by amateur theater groups
in Marseilles and in Paris.

L'Emissaire
The Emissary Presented only in German, at Essen under
the title Der Gesandte and at
Bielefeld-Wupperthal, 1950-51, under the
title Der Bote.

La Fin des Temps
The End of Time Presented for radio, Third Programme of
the British Broadcasting Company.

Rome n'est plus dans Rome
Rome is no longer in Rome

Presented at the Théâtre Hébertot,
Paris, 1951 for three months
performances, then on tour in France,
Belgium, and Holland.

Mon Temps n'est plus le votre
My Time is not Your Time
At Sarrebruck on stage, 1956
In France only on the radio, presented by
French actors. Broadcast January 26,
1969.

Croissez et multipliez
Increase and Multiply At Vienna, 1955, in German.

La Dimension Florestan
Die Wacht am Sein
The Florestan Dimension

Readers' Theater in France 1953, at the Institut international d'études humanistes.
Readers' Theater Performance at Oberhausen in the Ruhr, April 1957, and performed at a theater in Innsbruck, 1967.

La Prune et la prunelle
The Plum and the Apple of My Eye

Presented at the Salons of Plon Publishers, 1960. Directed by Suzanne Nivette of the Comédie Française, set and staging by Marie-Ange Rivain

Persons who wish to receive a list of references to synopses and commentaries for Gabriel Marcel's plays may request this of the author, K.R. Hanley, Department of Philosophy, LeMoyne College, Syracuse, New York 13214.

VI. Centers of Research

Présence de Gabriel Marcel

    Siège social:
        85 boulevard de Port-Royal, 75013 Paris,
        France

    Secrétariat:
        9 avenue Franklin-Roosevelt, 75008 Paris,
        France

    Publication:
        Présence de Gabriel Marcel, Cahier
        address as above.

Cercle Gabriel-Marcel

    Siège social:
        Case Postale 67
        Cap-de-la Madeleine, Québec
        Canada G8T 7W1

    Publication:
        Bulletin du Cercle Gabriel-Marcel
        Revue philosophique et littéraire.
        Published six times a year since 1979.
        address as above.

Gabriel Marcel Institute for Existential Drama
Le Moyne College, Syracuse, New York 13214

English-Speaking Gabriel Marcel Society
        Department of Philosophy
        Marquette University
        Milwaukee, Wisconsin 53208

About the Author

Katharine Rose Hanley holds a Ph.D. degree from the Higher Institute of Philosophy, Louvain University, Belgium, where she first met Gabriel Marcel in 1955. She is a Professor of Philosophy at Le Moyne College, Syracuse, New York, where she has taught since 1961. Since 1975 she has been Director of the Gabriel Marcel Institute of Existential Drama at Le Moyne.

Professor Hanley has authored books and numerous articles on metaphysical topics and on aspects of Gabriel Marcel's thought. She has lectured to national and international audiences. Recently she addressed the International Gabriel Marcel Society in Paris as well as the Société francaise de Philosophie at the Sorbonne.

The author has for several years been involved in translating and editing some of Gabriel Marcel's 30 plays for English-speaking audiences and in producing some of these plays for stage and television.

By VARDE

SUMMARY

Dramatic Approaches to Creative Fidelity, A Study in the
Theater and Philosophy of Gabriel Marcel is a unique study of the
work of Gabriel Marcel, a twentieth-century philosopher of
international renown. This book brings a fresh perspective to
the examination of Marcel´s thought, highlighting facets that are
sure to interest many different audiences.

Dramatic Approaches to Creative Fidelity presents a clear
exposition of the nature of creative fidelity, a central theme in
Marcel´s life and work. The distinctive contribution of this
book, however, is its illustration of how theater and philosophy
are complementary in Marcel´s investigation and reflective
clarification of life´s existential questions. Each chapter of
the book studies a play and a complementary philosophic essay and
examines how they relate to clarify a particular aspect of
creative fidelity. Thus, this work communicates Marcel´s
understanding of the nature of creative fidelity, illustrates the
relationship that links theater and philosophy, and demonstrates
the important role theater plays in providing a privileged way
into personal philosophizing.

The principal aim of this book is to introduce
English-speaking audiences to Gabriel Marcel´s theater. The book
also intends to suggest to students, teachers, scholars, and
theatrical personnel the heuristic as well as the pedagogical
advantages offered by an integrated approach that sees Marcel´s
theater and philosophy as essentially complementary.